"WHO KILLA da CHIEF?"

by J. C. Berkery

RISM

"covering the spectrum of publishing"

PRISM PRESS SYNDICATE

PHILADELPHIA

Library of Congress Cataloging in Publication Data:
Berkery, John Carlyle (1934-   ) 'Who Killa da Chief?"
ISBN: 9798482615980
Library of Congress Catalog Number:2016939730
1.   Mafia – Louisiana – New Orleans Metropolitan Area – Case Studies
2.   Matranga, Charles (1846-1943) 3.–Social Conditions. 4. Gangs &
Gangsters – Louisiana – New Orleans. 5. Lynchings – Nineteenth Century

Books by J.C. Berkery:

- **THE REAL IRISHMAN: THE YOUNG MANHOOD OF JOHNNY BURKE:** Muggs, Molls, Mobsters & Murder in the City of Brotherly Love
- **KILLING IRELAND: The Great Hunger (An Gorta Mor) (18451850):** The Irish Potato Famine & Its Effects on the MacDiabheid Family
- **HARRY'S GAMBLE**

The events in this book are factually accurate. However, some names have been altered and events compressed in the interests of space limitations, privacy, continuity, and dramatic effect. The main characters such as Charlie Matranga, Joe Provenzano, Chief David Hennessy, Joseph Shakspeare, Giuseppe Esposito, Abbie Reed, Kate Townsend, Bill Parkerson, the lynching victims, and all the townspeople, including the vigilantes, were real people, as were their families, deeds, and misdeeds. Charlie Matranga's early life, both in Sicily and New Orleans, has been hypothesized and dramatized from the best available information, as have the events leading up to Il Leone's kidnapping of John Forrester Rose in Sicily (although the kidnapping, mutilation, etc. took place as described). Esposito's life after his extradition has been hypothesized (except for his death at San Stephano prison at 37), as have many of the conversations between the characters in this story. The character Clive Clifford is fictional. Historical characters such as Paddy Ryan, Sullivan, Garibaldi, Crespi, Mazzini, Miceli, Farragut, Gen.

Benjamin "Spoons" Butler, Garfield, Harrison, Blaine, Platt, Quay, Gould, Baron Fava, Marquis di Rudini, Consul Corte, and PM Disraeli, not only existed, but pretty much did the things attributed to them. "Red Rock" Farrell, and the brothers "Slops" and "Baboon" Connelly, as well as Paul Kelly (Paolo Vacarelli), and their gang, the Whyos, were a New York City institution at the time described, but were brought into this story only for continuity. Alderman Cornelius McGillicuddy is fictional. The character Buford Alley is fictional.   *J. C. Berkery*

WHO KILLA DA CHIEF?

PROLOGUE

The ancient isle of Sicily had been occupied and often ravaged by Phoenician, Greek, Roman, Carthaginian, Vandal, Ostrogoth, Byzantine, Arab, Norman, French, Spanish, and Austrian invaders. Most recently to the events in this book, the Bourbon Spanish rule which began in 1734, and which even included a British occupation from 1809-1815, and had continued the so-called Kingdom of the Two Sicilies, Naples and Sicily.

Started by the Normans under Roger II in 1730, the Kingdom of the Two Sicilys was re-consolidated by the Spanish in 1759 when Charles ascended to the Spanish throne and installed his son as King Ferdinand IV of Naples and Ferdinand III of Sicily. Ferdinand ruled for sixty-six years and in 1815 moved to the Italian mainland to rule from Naples, dissolving the Sicilian Parliament, doing away with the Sicilian flag, and declaring himself Ferdinand I of the Kingdom of the Two Sicilies.

Naples had long enjoyed hegemony over Sicily under Spanish rule, but now the gap widened with the Napoleonic Code exported to Sicily. Within five years, in 1820, Palermo had a short-lived rebellion, put down by the Neapolitan Parliament. Slowly, a movement gained popularity to join a federated Italy. A more successful rising took place in 1848-49 when bravos such as Salvatore Miceli, from Monreale, took his Stoppaglieri squads into the streets of Palermo in early1849. The revolt ended. But the seeds of discontent were sown.

Miceli was pardoned and made a Captain at Arms by the Spanish, only to join Garibaldi in 1860 (and was later killed fighting the Piedmontese in 1866). A Captain at Arms was a Bourbon invention set up to protect a certain district from pillaging by bandits. If the Captain at Arms was popular and powerful, as Miceli was, he might make sure the local bandits didn't operate in his district, but might give refuge to these same bandits in return for allegiance or tribute.

During this same period, the Genovese adventurer, Giuseppe Mazzini, played an important role. After a brief imprisonment by the French in Naples as an insurrectionist, Mazzini, an educated young man who held a law degree, started the Young Italy Society, which preached revolution and also death to informers.

Mazzini spent 1859 in London and was a favorite of leading literary and arts figures such as Swinburne, Rossetti, and the Brownings. In April, 1860, in coordination with Garibaldi's and Mazzini's agents in Sicily – the bourgeoisie lawyer, Francisco Crespi, and the young nobleman, Rosalino Pino—Mazzini's groups in Palermo overthrew the Bourbons there and Mazzini arrived to lead them.

Garibaldi set out from Genoa in two steamers on May 5, 1860, and landed at Marsala, Sicily on May 11th with 1,000 Red Shirts. In the face of a large Bourbon force of infantry, cavalry, and artillery, Garibaldi claimed Sicily in the name of Victor Emanuel of Piedmont at Salemi. Crespi was named Secretary of State. Garibaldi abolished the hated ancient Spanish grain tax, the macinato.

Garibaldi defeated a 3,000 man Bourbon force under General Landi at Calatafimi. He then made a forced march on Palermo through Misilmeri, avoiding Monreale where General Collonna had laid in wait for him with a large force. In Palermo, with the assistance of the squads like those of Miceli, he defeated General Lanza, who subsequently left the island with 5,000 Bourbon troops, leaving the Garibaldi forces masters of Sicily.

Garibaldi stayed five months, then left to finish his conquest of the mainland and with it, the ousting of Francis I from Naples. He left Sicily with the people's unanimous consent to join a federated Italy. When Garibaldi left, Mazzini, an unashamed anti-Monarchy Republican, stayed behind with his piccioti and kept Palermo in arms.

Squad leaders took advantage of the general upheaval to ingratiate themselves to the gabellotti by murdering police officials. It is believed, due to Mazzini's close ties to the Neapolitan Camorra and his familiarity with its structure, that he imported some Camorristas into Palermo and that this is when the agrarian societies, such as the Fratuzzi of Bagheria, the Blessed Pauls (Beati Paoli), and the Stoppaglieri of Monreale, became sects of an organized criminal society based in Palermo, called Mafia, a name that had been previously limited to an adjective denoting bravery and manliness.

The unification of Sicily held from that day forward. However, Sicilians soon found that the self-government that had been promised, or at least implied to them, wasn't to be. Rule was to be by Piedmontese bureaucrats sent in by Count Cavour, heavy-handed administrators from Turin, who cared little for the traditional Sicilian idiosyncrasies and problems.

Conscription was instituted, anathema in a farming country where manpower was at a premium. Many potential *conscriptees,* watching wealthier young men simply legally buy their way out, fled the towns and joined the hill bandits who in turn found plenty of enforcement work for the *gabellotti* at the sulfur mines and on the *latifondia.* In fact, there was so much strong-arm work that the sects which, united, had helped Garibaldi win the island, now often found themselves on opposite sides, one perhaps in the employ of a landlord *latifondista* and one working for an up-and-coming *gabellotto.* Such was the Sicilian socio/political landscape in 1862.

CHAPTER ONE
CHARLIE, KATE, & JOE

NEW ORLEANS, LOUISIANA
THURSDAY, OCTOBER 28, 1943

Buford Alley navigated his beat-up '39 Plymouth business coupe up Bourbon Street at a crawl, shirtsleeved arm out the driver's window, an Old Gold between his fingers. Bewf was a general assignment reporter for the Atlanta Constitution; he also had a popular bi-weekly column, "Back Alley," always on the last page, which covered anything that caught his fancy.

It recently had become syndicated to the major Southern newspapers, including the New Orleans Times-Picayune. Today was a bright sunny day and all seemed to be improving with the world. The tide was turning with the War; the Allies had just captured Naples. And the NY Yankees had recently beat the Cards 4 games to 1 to win the 40th World Series.

Today, though, Bewf was chasing down what might prove to be an interesting piece of Southern history, the death, and mainly the life, of 97year-old Charles Matranga, principal of the giant United Fruit Company, whose stock had closed the previous day at $74 on the New York Stock Exchange. But according to Bewf's source, there was a lot more than that to the old man's story, going back before Bewf was born. Bewf had driven straight through from Georgia and was dying to dig into the Picayune's morgue for all the dirt, but he didn't want to miss the funeral. So everything else would have to wait. If true, though, what a column it would make! A serial, probably.

The Plymouth's grey primer paint, considered patriotic during the war, was in marked contrast to the shiny LaSalles, Packards, and Cadillacs which lined both sides of the street for a block in either direction from the funeral home.

Bewf's aquiline features by rote checked the gasoline ration stickers on the fancy cars' windshields. He had done a good exposé on counterfeits the year before for his column. This time he caught himself and smiled sardonically. "Not these guys," he thought as he parked between a '38

Fleetwood and a '41 Continental, "they can just call Washington and get all the stickers they want, legit."

Bewf walked toward the manicured lawn of the funeral home. The receiving line was out the door three hundred feet. Many well-dressed men with a few women. Also, a goodly number of humble immigrant types, embarrassed to be in such august company. The line shuffled slowly forward. By the inner door was a sign that read, MATRANGA. Bewf was nearing the casket now and the multiplicity of elaborate sprays of flowers surrounding it.

In addition to United Fruit, it was said, Mr. Matranga also had been known to control a large share of the Poydras (French) Market, and maintained an office across from the market until the time of his death. Mr. Matranga also had interests in the local stevedore's unions, and it was rumored that Mr. Matranga had income from myriad other enterprises.

When it came Bewf's turn to view the corpse, he stepped before the coffin, and was amazed at the frail, little figure lying there, dressed in a dark blue vested suit. A little wisp of white hair on the bony head, prominent nose, small, white moustache, two ivory hands clutching rosary beads, crossed over a heavy gold watch fob. For all intents an unimposing man. Of course, Bewf had no way of seeing the piercing grey eyes under whose gaze many strong men had wilted.

Further on, Bewf could see the Matranga offspring, which now consisted of four children and their spouses, ten grandchildren and their spouses, and seven great-grandchildren. The four immediate family members stood just past the coffin, accepting condolences, and Bewf correctly deduced that the tall, courtly-looking gentleman in his late sixties must be Matranga's eldest son, Dr. Charles Matranga, Jr..

Bewf crossed himself and moved his lips; he hadn't said a real prayer in 35 years. He moved on to the receiving line, grasping the tall man's hand, "Dr. Matranga?" he whispered, "sorry about your father…Please excuse me, sir, but I've traveled all the way from Atlanta and I wonder could you spare me a minute in private?"

Dr. Matranga hid his annoyance. "Certainly. My sisters and brother can take care of the line. There's a room on the side there." They entered the side room and Bewf introduced himself. "I'm with the Atlanta Constitution and we're planning to do a story on your father." The doctor spread his arms. "But I've already given a full obituary release," he said deprecatingly. "No," Bewf replied, "I mean a story…an in-depth story. About the, ah, highlights of your father's career. It would be much better and, I'm sure, more fair to your family if I did it with the family's help." The doctor stifled a frown. "Let me think about it. Where can I reach you? I'll call you after the funeral tomorrow. This is not the place…" Bewf faced both palms toward the doctor. "I know. I know. And I appreciate your courtesy, sir. I'll be staying at the Roosevelt and I'll await your call."

The following morning, during the funeral, Bewf rifled through boxes of old records and clippings at the Picayune, making copious notes. By one o'clock, he was back at his hotel. The desk clerk handed him a note. "12:05 P.M., Dr. Matranga called. Will be at the Elks club, 121 S. Basin Street, at 5 p.m. if you care to meet him." Bewf smiled, folded the note, and got on the elevator.

ELKS CLUB
121 S. BASIN STREET (formerly 40 Basin Street)
NEW ORLEANS
FRIDAY, OCTOBER 29, 1943 5:00
P.M.

Buford Alley ascended the steps of the stately mansion and pulled the brass doorbell. "Fanciest goddamned Elks Club I ever saw," he mumbled to himself. He looked down at his well-worn tweed jacket and scuffed shoes and shuffled a bit uncomfortably as a liveried porter swung open the huge oak door. "Are you here to see a member, sir?" "Yes. Dr. Matranga." "He's expecting you, Suh. Follow me."

Bewf was led to a lounge with a small oak bar. The ornately carved white marble fireplace surrounded a blazing hearth; its flickering flame reflected from the gleaming black oak floor. Near the fire were two wellused red leather club chairs with a marble-topped table between them.

Dr. Carlo Matranga arose from one of the chairs and extended his hand, the fire's glow highlighting his long, angular, handsome face. Bewf noticed, for the first time, the piercing grey eyes. "Sit down, sir", said the doctor, "we'll have brandy and cigars and talk."

When they had settled, Bewf broke the ice. "Your father was a great man, doctor; I've been reading about him all morning. I'd like to know how he became a man of such respect in the community; how he came to America, if you know. And the details," he looked at the doctor intently, "…of the lynching." The doctor gazed into the fireplace a moment before responding. It was what he expected, and part of him objected to the intrusion on his family's privacy. But for a long time he had felt that his father's story needed to be re-told. This time, truthfully. Some of the prominent families the doctor now associated with on almost equal footing wouldn't like it. Like the Flowers, the Walmsleys, the Houstons. All the more reason. Let them remember what they had done a half century prior." He faced Bewf candidly. "Well, you are in luck, sir. I am thoroughly conversant with my family's history. It's a tradition. You see, both my mother's and father's families, and our whole village, Piana dei Greci, for that matter, were originally Albanian refuges from the Turkish conquest of the Balkans. We immigrated o Sicily around 1600 and have always maintained our own traditions and folk dress. I have been to Sicily many times and know all the locations intimately.

"My father's story begins around the time of Garibaldi's invasion of Sicily in 1860. My father was only 14 then. His father, my grandfather, was a doctor as many of our male line had been and he had planned for my father to be a doctor as well." They lit Cuban cigars, and the doctor continued. "But my father, with the fervor of youth, wanted to oust the oppressive Bourbon Spanish rule which had been in effect for a hundred years at the time.

"My father fell in with a subordinate of Giuseppe Mazzini, a very interesting adventurer in his own right. Mazzini had been instrumental in drumming up support for Garibaldi in the villages, to unite Sicily and Italy under Mazzini's "Young Italy" banner.

In 1862, two years after Garibaldi's landing, my father and two other young men, Frank Romero and Giuseppe Esposito, were called upon by Miceli, to execute a scoundrel who had dishonored the wife of a friend of Fernando Crespi. Crespi was a lawyer and Mazzini's chief lieutenant in Sicily. The intended target's name was Giuseppe Provenzano. He was from a different sect, the Fratuzzi of Bagheria. The sect of my father and Miceli was the Stoppaglieri, based in Monreale."

Bewf had been writing furiously, and the doctor smiled indulgently. "Let's take a break and have a little brandy," he said. "Good idea," Bewf said, "but let me ask you a question while it's fresh in my mind. When you say sects, Doctor, are you saying these sects are divisions of the Mafia?" The doctor motioned to the brandy, which they each sipped. He gave Bewf a patient smile.

"This is a concept that's not easy to explain to an Anglo-Saxon…" Bewf raised his hand, palm up. "Hold it right there, doctor. My mother's Irish". The doctor nodded in mock apology. "Then you might understand a little better, Ireland and Sicily both being islands who have historically had to contend with invaders and have had agrarian economies. Our villages, like those of Ireland, have had secret agrarian societies with their own blood oaths and rituals. We refer to these societies as sects. These sects would cooperate with each other when it suited their purpose, or fight each other. The word mafia was just a Sicilian adjective denoting one's bravery or manliness. Members of these various sects who were thought to perform brave deeds as a group eventually acquired the name Mafiusi, after Garibaldi's time.

"To bring it closer to home, it would be like the difference between a caballero and the cavalry." The doctor eyed Bewf candidly. "I don't know if that's a good metaphor so I'll answer your question more directly. There is no such thing as a Sicilian organization known as the Mafia. It's a label placed on unwanted immigrants by bigots." In the steady gaze of those unblinking grey eyes, Buford Alley knew the subject was closed and didn't broach it again during the interview.

The doctor continued. "Getting back to Provenzano, he escaped the attempt on his life by the three young men and ironically fled here to New Orleans. However, a woman was accidentally killed in the attempt and my father and Romero had to become fugitives. Esposito was only a kid of 10 or 12 then and had only served as a lookout. He wasn't wanted although he, too, came here in 1878. My grandfather arranged with some Corsicans he knew for passage to America for my father, his brother who was my uncle Tony, and Romero. My grandfather later told me he did this because politicians like Crespi were evil men and my grandfather feared they would kill my father before any trial so he couldn't involve them.

"My father and mother, who was a Barbato, had to postpone their marriage for a couple of years until he could bring her to America after the Civil War My father was well-received here by the Patornos, who had been friends of our family in the old country. In fact, Sal Patorno is my attorney today." Bewf drank it all in, figuring he had hit the jackpot as far as this story went. Take it easy.

They sipped their brandy. Bewf looked around admiringly. "This building is magnificent," he said, marveling at the ornate detail and opulent detail. "Was it built for the Elks?" The doctor smiled broadly. "No. No. It wasn't built for the Elks. It was built for a friend of my father's, Kate Townsend, and was once the grandest house of ill repute in the United States." Bewf blinked, "I know of Kate Townsend; her name is legend in the South. This was her place?" The doctor nodded bemusedly. "This is it. Things are not always what they seem down here."

Bewf shook his head, then went on. "Doctor, among all those business types at the viewing, didn't I see Sylvestro Carolla, the head of the local…crime group?" "Sam was a supervisor at the French Market for my father after the First World War. When Prohibition came in, he wanted to get into it, as did many of the so-called gentry around here. He wanted to make my father a partner. My father was already in his '70's and considered it a young man's game, not that he had anything against it. So Sam went on his own and became a millionaire. Silver Dollar Sam, the newspaper calls him. But some people resent a Sicilian with too much money and Sam never lived down that "crime boss" tag and they're trying to deport him now. He has remained a close friend of our family and we will never disown that."

"Tell me more about Kate Townsend," Bewf said. "Well, my father set sail from Marseilles in the Spring of 1862. The previous year, Louisiana had seceded from the Union and Lincoln had blockaded the Southern ports and arranged for Admiral Farragut, assisted by the infamous General Benjamin Butler, we call him "Spoons" Butler down here because of all the silverware he looted, to invade New Orleans, coming up the Mississippi from the gulf.

"My family hadn't known how dicey things would be over here. My father got as far as Havana and got delayed. It was there that he met Kate, who was in the same situation coming from England by way of New York". They ordered another brandy. "Doctor, I've got a feeling that you've missed your calling. You're quite a raconteur," Bewf said. "Please continue."

The doctor sipped his brandy and replied. "All my life I've been very proud of my father. Many years ago, he was falsely accused, arrested, and nearly executed by a lynch mob even after the charges against him had been dismissed. I still have bitter memories of that episode even though I was only a young boy when it happened.

"My father was never compensated; never even apologized to. Yet he stayed on and made a huge success of his life. We had friends elsewhere. Our family was invited to relocate to Chicago. But my father felt a responsibility to the people who depended upon him and to the families of the eleven men who were murdered. That was the kind of man he was and now that he's gone, I would like to see his story told, if it's told fairly. Because it's a story of prejudice and hatred against the Italian people which still exists today, although to a much less degree.

"We deserve better. I've got a son in Italy right now with the Fifth Army marching on Rome and his blood would bleed as red as anyone else's." A vein stood out in the middle of the doctor's forehead; not ordinarily one to show emotion, he reined himself in. "Well, enough of that. Let me take you back to my father's voyage here."

SICILY, 1862

The Matranga family was one of the noble Albanian families, along with the Schirros, the Stasis, and the Barbatos, who had settled in Sicily in the area around Piana dei Greci over three centuries earlier: Dr. Carlo Matranga was sought out with great respect by the villagers, as had been his father before him, not only for his medical skills, but also for advice, and the wise mediation of disputes, of which there were many.

The doctor had married a Sicilian woman of Guiscardian descent, who had borne him three children: a girl, and two boys. The oldest, Carlo, Jr., was 14 when Salvatore Miceli, of neighboring Monreale, came through the village beating the drums of rebellion three months before Garibaldi's landing. Carlo, Jr., had followed Miceli and joined his squad on the 24th of May, 1860, when Miceli, Garibaldi, and his Red Shirts triumphantly arrived. Dr. Matranga had only objected because of the boy's age since he, himself, believed in the uprising.

The emotional Albanians had learned over the years to be suspicious of their absentee landlords and the land leases to the *latifundia* they inhabited. This had made them rebellion-prone and their proximity to Palermo had caused them to be in the vanguard of even larger rebellions at certain times--- May of 1860 had been one of those times. But two years had passed and it was time the boy resumed his education. After all, He should be in medical school soon, someday to assume the doctor's place of respect in the village. The doctor was becoming concerned and thought it was about time to have a chat with Miceli, or even Crespi, Mazzini's chief lieutenant.

PIAZZA VIGLIENA (QUATTRO CANTI)
MAGISTRALE DES CASSAEO & VIA MAQUEDA
PALERMO, SICILY
MARCH, 1862

Piazza Vigliena (Quattro Canti)

Carlo Matranga, Jr. stood with two other young men before squat, barrel-chested thirty-five year old Salvatore Miceli, and received his orders. Miceli's back was to one of the ornate fountains laid out on each of the four corners of the Piazza at the beginning of the seventeenth century The water of the fountain purposely muted his voice.

At the south end of the Piazza, near the Basilica San Giuseppe dei Teatini, stood Rosalino Pino, the young Sicilian nobleman who had served as Mazzini's advance agent prior to Garibaldi's invasion. He would later confirm to Francesco Crespi that Miceli's mission had been set in motion as Crespi had ordered.

Miceli motioned to the two other boys to move off to the side, then said intensely, "Carlo, these are orders from the top. We must defend our honor or perish. The Fratuzzi of Bagheria are cosci of ours, tied to the Stoppaglieri by blood oath. Yet one of their members sent here by a friend of ours for safety because he had killed two well-connected guardiani of an orchard over there, has betrayed his oath. His boss reached out to Crespi and Crespi sent him to me. His name is Giuseppe Provenzano.

"After his arrival, he seduced the wife of the farmer with whom I had arranged for him to stay. They both left the farm and haven't been seen since. Crespi and Pino have traced them right here to Palermo --- a flat off the Via Napoli, 14 Via Antonio, second floor. The three of you go there and kill them both. Make sure you aren't recognized. I have big plans for you. Provenzano is a small guy, receding hairline, hawk nose, early thirties". Carlo nodded, "I'll take care of it." Miceli looked at him warmly and put a firm hand on each shoulder, kissing him on one cheek, then the other. Satisfied, Pino left the Piazza for Crespi's office.

Miceli had picked a young man from Monreale, Frank Romero, to work with Carlo.. They had been together on a few other missions, but never any killings. Carlo liked and trusted Romero. The other youth, a boy of only twelve or thirteen with hazel eyes, was a Palermo street urchin and familiar with all the city's streets and alleys. His name was Giuseppe Esposito.

The boys spent the night at a friend of Miceli's located off the Corso Tukôry in the south end of the city. At seven o'clock the next morning, they were heading north into town. Romero carried a sack containing a shortened lupara. They cut north to the Via Alberghiera, then up the Via Ponticello to Piazza Bellini Santa Caterina, where the bright red dome of the Church of San Cataldo shone in the morning sun next to the Byzantine magnificence of La Martorana.

Carlo made the sign of the cross in front of La Martorana because it was Greek rite and a sister church of San Demetrio at home in Piana dei Greci. They continued into Piazza Pretoria. Carlo always marveled at the 40foot-high fontana with its beautiful statuary, steps, and railings. Surely, Palermo is the most beautiful city in the world, I will never leave it, he thought to himself. He had no idea how wrong he was.

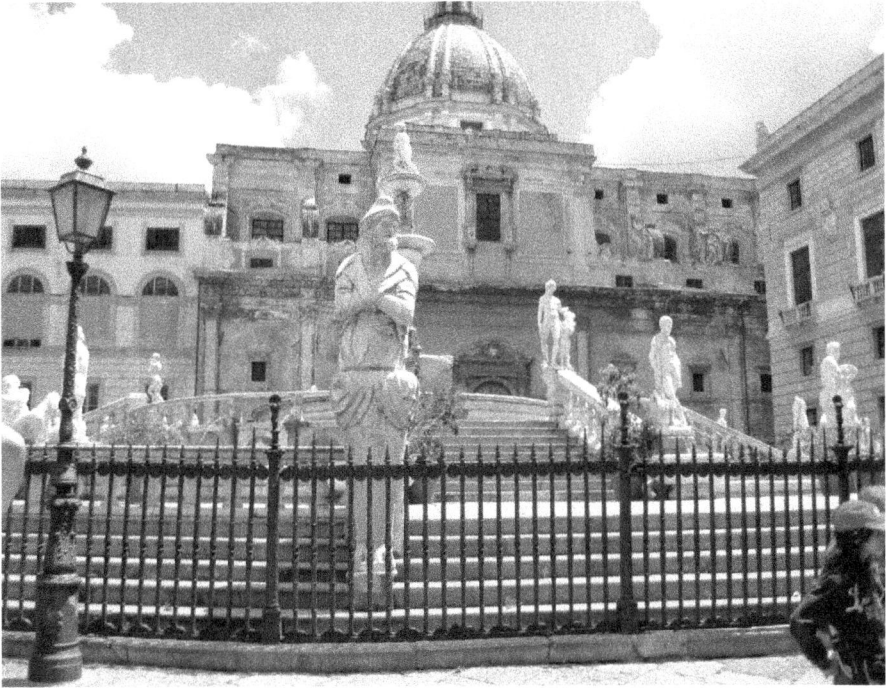

They descended the small set of steps into the Via Maqueda and continued north to the Via Napoli, then turning into the Via Antonio, a winding cobblestone alley about ten feet wide. Number 14 was a three-story apartment building facing identical houses. It had a small balcony on each floor in the front. Leaning out from one balcony to the one opposite, the tenants could have touched hands. Below the lower balcony, was an arched entry into a courtyard which contained an open stairway to the apartments above.

About an hour later, young Esposito knocked on the second floor apartment door of Number 14. When a full-bodied, flowsy woman in her late twenties answered, he held out his hand and begged for a few lire for his widowed mother and six sisters. The door was promptly slammed in his face. Now armed with the woman's description, Carlo, the boy, and Romero lounged at the corner of the street, caps pulled low on their faces.

About two o'clock in the afternoon, a woman answering the boy's description was seen leaving the building, a wicker shopping basket on her arm. "Ecco!', smiled young Esposito, and with that, Carlo thanked, paid, and dismissed the boy, although Esposito wanted to stay for the action. Frank

Romero followed the woman and Carlo stayed by the corner to make sure no one answering Provenzano's description emerged.

Romero soon returned and said, I followed her to La Vuccaria market. She'll be shopping for a while." "Good. Let's go," answered Carlo. "We'll take him. I don't want to disregard orders, but I'm not for killing a woman. Let her cuckold husband take care of her." Romero nodded. "I'm for that. We'll just say she wasn't home. It's true, no?"

They entered the courtyard and climbed the outside stairway. There was a landing, but on it were two doors, one for the front apartment and one for the rear. Carlo frowned. Salvatore didn't say which apartment, only second floor and we didn't ask Giuseppe; too bad I let him go so early. So now we don't know which." "Let's call it off," said Romero. "No!", said Carlo sternly. "Salvatore said this had to be done immediately. So we'll wait and take a chance that it's her. I've got a feeling that it is anyway."

They hid in a mop closet in the front of the hallway. With the door cracked, they could view both apartment doors. About twenty minutes later, an elderly man emerged from the rear apartment and started down the steps. "That's certainly not him," whispered Carlo, "so it must be the front one. Just as well, anyway. Provenzano probably wouldn't have answered the door if we had knocked."

After an interminable wait, there was the sound of footsteps ascending the stairs. "Get ready," whispered Carlo. "Might be the old guy." "I don't think so", Carlo said, pulling the bandana around his neck up over his nose. Romero did likewise. The woman had both arms around the wicker basket. A loaf of provolone and some produce was sticking out the top and she was trying to peek around the basket in order to see. She almost slipped on the steps and released one hand to grab the iron railing at the top of the stairs. She set the basket down on the top step, bending forward and revealing a deep cleavage. Carlo felt a surge of excitement.

Pulling herself up to the landing, she then fished her housekey from the tightly-fitting housedress she wore. Then she picked up the basket by the handle with the other hand. She shuffled up to the door and gave it a small kick at the bottom. "Giuseppe!", she called. No answer. Carlo nodded at

Frank Romero. She put the key in the lock and turned it. The bolt slid back and she grabbed the knob. At that moment, the two youths burst from the closet. She was only a few feet away, but managed to get off a small scream before they pushed her in the door.

It all happened in a flash. The man inside wore a sleeveless undershirt and trousers and had already jumped from the bed he was on and was making for the open balcony door at the front. Romero pulled the lupara from the bag and started to bring it up. The woman, who had been pushed in the same direction as the balcony, had stumbled but had regained her balance. Her eyes shown liquid brown fear. Provenzano had reached the two-foot-wide balcony as Romero raised the shotgun. "Nooooooooo!", shrieked the woman as she dove between the blast and her lover.

The blast was deafening; she was hit dead-on by both barrels at point blank range. Provenzano, without allowing himself the luxury of a backward look, agilely leaned over the balcony railing and swung himself over, gripping the balcony floor tightly for a moment to break his fall. Carlo had dove for him but tripped over the dead woman. Provenzano dropped to the street, rolling on impact, and came up running.

A few spectators stopped to watch as he raced to the back of the street and shimmied a low wall. The boys looked at each other in panic. "Leave the gun," Carlo said. They emerged back onto the landing and at the top of the stairs pulled down their bandanas. Carlo's cap had fallen off in the apartment when he dove for Provenzano. At that moment, an old woman emerged from the rear apartment door The three stared at one another for a moment. Then the old crone screamed, "Assassinos! Assassinos!"

Via Antonio today

The boys rushed down the steps and onto the street where people were emerging from doorways. The boys raced toward La Vuccaria. with a small band in pursuit at a respectful distance. The boys rushed down the steps and onto the street where it was late on a Saturday afternoon and the open-air market was jammed.

They were immediately lost in the crowd and made their way as quickly as possible through the maze of stands, exiting at the south and recrossing the Cassarô past the Oratorio San Lorenzo and the Gothic spires of the Church of Francisco d' Assisi, out the Paternostro and down the Via Roma, which was then under construction. It provided the best route south to Tukôry, the construction workers paying them no attention whatsoever.

At the house off Corso Tukôry where they had spent the night, a wagon was waiting to take them south. They laid in the back between bales of hay while the horse wended its way onto the Via Benedittini, then turned left onto the Via del Bastoni past the Capella Palatina at the rear end of the massive and ancient Norman Palace, past the Palazzo Aurnale, and onto the Corso Pisani toward Monreale. Three miles down this panoramic vista, Pisani intersected the Via Altofonte toward Piana dei Greci.

At the crossroads, Carlo told Romero, "Go to the Cathedral at Monreale. Salvatore will be there at five o'clock. He will wait until you get there. Tell him what happened. I have a place where we'll be safe. You'd better come there, too, until we see how things lie. A lot of people saw us. First, I must stop and see my father". Romero nodded and got up in the wagon with the driver. Carlo set out on foot toward his house, secure in his faith in Miceli.

Carlo entered his pleasant, yellow stucco house to find his father sitting at his desk, deep in thought. Carlo walked into the study and closed the door. At the sight of him, the doctor brightened. "Ah, Carlo," he said, smiling, "it's good you are home. I've just been thinking about you. We must have a long talk".

The doctor had made a lifelong study of people's faces, both patients and those who came to see him with personal problems. And he knew his son's face better than any of them. "Carlinu!", he cried. "What's wrong?!" "Nothing, Papa. Just that I had to do someone a service and there could be trouble. I am going to need to stay at the Abbey until I hear from Salvatore."

The doctor was already putting on his coat. "I will take you there myself. And on the way you will tell me the whole story." It took a while, but eventually the doctor got all the details from Carlo on the ride from Piana dei Greci. He wanted to cry out at the news of the woman's killing, but he stopped himself so as not to interrupt. He wanted to hear it all. He did not recriminate against his son. All he could do at the end of the tale was to stop the wagon and hug the boy tightly. "Carlinu. Carlinu, what kind of a stew have they put you in?", he said softly.

The doctor promised Carlo that he would get word to the boy's sweetheart, Rita Barbato, that Carlo was all right but would be away for a few days. Their wagon headed south to Corleone where the road forked. One fork went southeast past Lake Prizzi toward Cammarata and eventually Girgenti (Agrigento). They took the other fork, climbing up to Bisaquino, then heading west down into the quaint village of Contessa Entellina, another Albanian enclave like Piana dei Greci.

In the village, the doctor stopped at a friend's house, politely declined an invitation inside, held a hushed conversation in the doorway, then got back in the wagon and drove the short distance to the Abbey of Santa Maria del Bosco, settled by the Olivetan Order about the same time as the original Albanian settlement two-and-a-half centuries prior. He introduced Carlo to the Abbott and pressed some money into the holy man's hand. "You will be safe here, my son. My friend, the Mayor of Contessa Entellina will look in on you every day until I return. I must go now. I will be home very late and there is much to do tomorrow."

He hugged his son tightly and went back to the wagon. Tears streaked down the doctor's cheeks on the way home and a feeling of impending doom overwhelmed him. All the plans and dreams and hopes of his life were evaporating. He knew Carlo's situation could be and probably was much worse than the boy realized. He arrived home in the wee hours of the morning and spent a sleepless night. Early the next morning, he sent someone to Monreale to make an appointment.

At noon, Dr, Carlo Matranga made the short trip to Monreale.In the distance he could see the famous Cathedral of Monreale towering well over one hundred feet into the air on a promontary overlooking the Conca d'Oro and Palermo. This magnificent structure, one of the greatest in Europe, was the Norman King William II's supreme defiance of Papal claims of hegemony over his kingdom in twelfth-century Sicily. William installed his own Archbishop over the Papal-appointed English one in Palermo and named his site Regal Mountain: Monreale.

The doctor made his way to a small café on the Via Archimede where Miceli awaited him. He stoically endured Miceli's embrace and, at the doctor's suggestion, they strolled around the corner to the Piazza Castrense. Miceli was talking intensely; the doctor, tall and stooped, was listening and nodding his goateed head gravely.

Finally, on the Piazza, he faced Miceli. "Is this how men of honor operate, sending boys to kill women?" His eyes flashed at Miceli, who wasn't used to being talked to this way but let the doctor finish. "Dottore." Miceli said placatingly, "I don't make these decisions; I merely carry them out. Carlo does the same. I'm sure our friends in Palermo will straighten out this inconvenience. However, you should   be aware that there are witnesses and Carlo and the other boy could be identified and arrested. But rest assured they won't be convicted."

"No, because before trial, you'll get an order from Crespi to kill them before they become an embarrassment." Miceli started to protest but the doctor put up his hand. "Look, Salvatore, let's talk straight. You must tell Palermo that I'm sending my son out of the country. And the other boy, too, if he wants to go. I thought about it all night and although all my plans for the future of my family will be dashed, it's the only way I can see of saving my boy's life."

Miceli frowned, "I'll hate to lose him." The doctor ignored him. "Just tell Crespi to keep the dogs called off for two weeks. By then, Carlo will be gone." "Crespi? Why do you use Sr. Crespi/s name, Dottore?" Dr. Matranga gave him an icy look. "Ci vediamu, Sr. Miceli. Send the other boy to my home today. Alone." With that, he turned on his heel in the direction of his wagon.

Salvatore Miceli was a hot-headed gang leader and he had never really let anyone talk to him like that before. Oh, he took orders from the likes of Crespi, Mazzini, and Garibaldi, but only because it suited his purposes. This was different. He was truly awed by the quiet, patrician bearing of the tall, gaunt stooped figure with the slow, measured gait whose back he watched crossing the Piazza. He shook his head slowly. "There is a man", he thought. And he better understood what it was he had seen in young Carlo.

Dr. Matranga was a busy man in the next two weeks. He had Romero escorted to the Abbey by a couple of trusted villagers; he promised Rita Barbato that he would take her to see Carlo; he made a trip to Corsica from Palermo, not trusting anyone else with the mission; and he made another painful decision by having a long talk with his remaining son, Antonio, fifteen.

"Fighiu miu," he said. "I can finally answer your many questions about your brother. He must leave the country because of some unfortunate dealings he had with Signore Miceli. I am arranging his passage to New Orleans in America. Some of our people have gone there and report that it is a very agreeable place, with a climate much like our own. I know a friendly family over there, the Patornos, and Carlo is being accompanied by another young man, but as far as his own family, he will be alone, Antonio, I want you to go with him. Your mother and I will make the trip over within a year. I believe Carlo and Rita are engaged. If her family permits, we will bring her with us. Your sister, too, will visit."

Tony's face had a look of troubled apprehension at the thought of leaving his parents and sister. But along with it was the steadfast and faithful resolve to do anything necessary to help his brother. This blind loyalty between them, the doctor knew, would serve Carlo well against the pitfalls of this strange new land to which he would be going. "Whatever you say, father," answered Tony, "Carlo shouldn't go there alone." A large lump formed in the doctor's throat. He reached over with a bony hand and tousled his son's hair, then held him close. "You are a good boy, Antonio, and I am very proud of you."

Two weeks later, all was in readiness. The doctor had scheduled one last meeting with Miceli, hoping against hope that by some miracle, his sons wouldn't have to leave, although he kept all the details of their departure a closely held secret. They sat in a pew of one of the three aisles on the interior nave of the Monreale Cathedral. Next to them an exquisite Corinthian column supporting an ogival arch hid them from view of the one or two parishioners, who were deep in prayer in any event.

"And what news have you for me, Signore Miceli?," asked the doctor gravely. "Nothing has changed, Dottore," answered Miceli. "There are at least a dozen witnesses although there is a good chance that Carlo may never be brought in, and even if he is, he still may not be identified." "It's a chance I don't want to take." "I understand, Dottore, There is also an ironic twist to the story. Provenzano, the intended victim, has been identified as one of the killers and is being sought." "And what of this Provenzano? This man who was so important that my son had to give his life up for your revenge?"

Miceli lowered his eyes." A settlement has been reached on that, Dottore. Provenzano's boss from Bagheria came to Palermo and worked it out with Sr. Crespi. Provenzano's family has paid an indemnity to the farmer…" *And to Crespi*, thought the doctor. '…and since Joe Provenzano is now a fugitive anyway, it was worked out that the whole matter will be settled if all the Provenzanos leave the country and never return. Joe, Peter, and George have already left the country for New Orleans. If they ever come back, they are all dead men."

At the sound of New Orleans, the doctor's stomach tightened. "Do the Provenzanos know the identity of the attackers?", he asked. "No, Signore, assolutamente, no. No one knows."

"And this was the settlement of this debt of honor that had to be repaid in blood, was it? Worked out with the payment of money?" Miceli shrugged uncomfortably.

"Do you know what this has done to the lives of my whole family, man?" the doctor rasped lowly, the veins bulging in his neck. Miceli put his head down and said in a low voice, "I'm sorry, Dottore. When does Carlo leave?" "Two more weeks," the doctor lied. "I'll be going now. Make sure you convey my feelings about this matter to Sr. Crespi." Miceli heard the sound of the doctor's footsteps echoing on the marble floor of the Basilica.

At three o'clock the next morning, Doctor Matranga, his wife, son, and daughter, quietly departed their house by wagon, and, stopping by the Barbato house to pick up Rita Barbato, set out in the darkness for Contessa Entellina and the Olivetan Abbey. In the wagon were all the worldly possessions of Carlo and Tony Matranga, except for the few reminders their mother had kept.

It was approaching the noon hour at the Abbey when Carlo saw their wagon approaching. He and Romero were sitting on a small decrepit wall near the Abbey, in caps, vests, and suspenders. Romero had another lupara he had brought with him slung over his shoulder. Carlo threw his cap into the air with joy and ran to meet the wagon. Rita jumped into his arms and they embraced. It was a pleasant late-March day and the doctor had brought the makings of a family picnic. They spread out a large tablecloth on the hillside and to the casual observer were just a happy family having a Sabbath together.

The doctor and Carlo walked to the side and the doctor told Carlo of the events to date including the Provenzano settlement. "But Salvatore told me, 'we must defend our honor or we will perish,'" Carlo said. The doctor gave his son a wan smile of resignation. "You have learned an important lesson, my son. Words are only to hide true meaning. Fellows like Miceli are not icons to be blindly obeyed. Always make your own assessment of a situation and people's motives. The Micelis are only used by the Pezzo Novante; in turn, they use those under them. It was not Miceli's fault, it's just the way things are. It's too late for hindsight now.

"I have arranged for some Corsicans I know, who have no connection over here, to pick you, Frank, and Tony up the day after tomorrow at Marsala. They will take you to Marseilles. From there, a ship will take you to New Orleans. Once there, look up my friends, the Patornos. Next Spring, your mother, sister, and I will come over for a trip, and, if you both wish it, we will bring Rita and you can start a new life and family there. Her family thinks very highly of you and they have been close with our family since before anyone can remember, so they will certainly sanction it."

Carlo's head was down, and he was nodding assent to all this. Suddenly, a look of concern crossed his face. "Father, I know how you feel about all this, but don't openly defy Crespi or the Stoppaglieri. They are dangerous."

The tall, gaunt man shrugged his stooped his stooped shoulders. "Anything they could do to me, they have already done. No, they won't be a problem. They know they are wrong and I am worth no profit to them. Late tomorrow, a village boy whose family are friends of my friend the Mayor here, will come to take you to Marsala. His name is Vincenzo Traina, he's about ten.

"Meanwhile, after you make your goodbyes to your mother and sister, we will be leaving. I've arranged for the Mayor to escort Rita home tomorrow". Carlo reached out with both arms and pulled his father close.
"Go with God, fighiu miu, until we meet again," the doctor said hoarsely, "and remember the Provenzanos are somewhere in New Orleans. Beware." Carlo sobbed softly on his shoulder for a moment. Then they parted.

Santa Maria del Bosco

Santa Maria del Bosco

Contessa Entellina map

UNITED STATES OF AMERICA
APRIL, 1862

In the same two years since Garibaldi's landing, the United States of America was undergoing a major upheaval. Despite close ties to the Union, Louisiana came out in favor of the Secessionist's candidate for President against Lincoln in the 1860 Presidential election. That December, South Carolina seceded from the Union. Louisiana followed the next month, January, 1861, and Governor Moore seized Forts Jackson and St. Philip on the Mississippi at Plaquemines Bend, seventy-five miles south of New Orleans.

Also seized were the Mint, Arsenal, and Customhouse, along with Forts Pike, Macomb, and Livingston. Lousiana, on March 15, 1861, ratified the Confederate States of America Constitution, and ten days later joined the Confederacy and ceded to the Confederacy the seized property. On April 12,

1861, the Louisiana Creole Brigadier General P.G.T. Beauregard attacked Fort Sumter in Charleston Harbor. The fort surrendered. On April 15th, Lincoln declared a blockade of Southern ports.

In New Orleans, companies of volunteers were rapidly formed, among them, the Louisiana Tigers, later to be commanded by Major Roberdeau Wheat, who had served with Garibaldi in Italy.

In early May, Union troops invaded Virginia and on May 27th, the Union Man-of-War, "Brooklyn", blockaded Pass a l'Outre, one of the two navigable passes from the Gulf of Mexico to the Mississippi River below New Orleans. The "Brooklyn" then began seizing commercial vessels trying to get to New Orleans. On May 31st, seventy-one year old General David E. Twiggs was dispatched by the Confederacy to New Orleans to command Department Number 1. New Orleans, already defenseless against any major attack, was being stripped of its local troops who were dispatched to Pensacola and Virginia. Also, the blockade caused apprehension of a sea invasion from either down or up the Mississippi. Locally, the building of warships was hastily commissioned.

On July 1st, the daring sea raider, Captain Raphael Semmes, ran the Federal blockade into the Gulf aboard the "Sumter", thereafter to conduct a swashbuckling career that took him from the Caribbean to Gibraltar, to the China Sea, during which time he would capture 450 enemy craft and sink sixty-five.

Late in September, at the urging of the Mayor and the populace of New Orleans, President Jefferson Davis replaced the aged General Twiggs with a newly-appointed Major General, thirty-nine year old Mansfield Lovell, a former New Yorker and West Point graduate. New Orleans sea defenses continued under the command of the crusty and able old Commodore George N. Hollins.

Four days before Christmas, 1861, sixty year old Captain David Glasgow Farragut was enlisted by Union Secretary of the Navy, Gideon Welles and Under-Secretary Gustavus V. Fox to carry out a daring sea invasion of New Orleans from the Gulf, previously approved by President Lincoln and General McClellan. On January 8th, 1862, Farragut was officially appointed Commander of the Western Gulf Blockading Squadron, which reached from St. Andrew's Bay in Florida to the Rio Grande, and given the flagship, "Hartford". On February 20th, 1862, Farragut arrived at Ship Island, off Biloxi, and recently evacuated by the Confederates to the Union forces, there to begin his command.

Coinciding with Farragut's arrival was the arrival on Ship Island of Major General Benjamin Franklin Butler with a force which would soon number over 15,000 to handle the land part of Farragut's invasion. With Farragut's fleet assembling at the Head of Passes, martial law was declared in New Orleans on March 15th, 1862. Four Provost Marshals were appointed and an eight o'clock curfew was imposed on establishments dispensing liquor. Work was raised to a fever pitch to complete two ironclad warships, the "Louisiana" and the "Mississippi", to meet the challenge. Mardi Gras, that year, was unusually subdued.

HAVANA, CUBA
APRIL, 1862

Once on board the steamer from Marseilles, the Corsican captain informed Charlie Matranga that Havana, Cuba was as far as the ship could take them due to the Union blockade of the southern coast of the United States. Two weeks from the day they exited the Mediterranean through the Pillars of Hercules at Gibraltar, they sighted the tower of megalithic Morro Castle guarding the entrance to Havana harbor.

Havana was a hotbed of political intrigue. Warships bearing French and Spanish flag lay in Havana harbor, part of a fleet sent to forcibly collect the debts owed by Mexico, and on the French part, to promote the accession of Maximillian as Emporer; Confederate blockade-runners were docked alongside them, either planning to make a run through the Union blockade, or just having made one. Farragut had even stopped there on February 15th, on his way to the rendezvous at Ship Island.

Carlo, Tony Matranga, and Frank Romero, carrying their own baggage, followed some sailors down the gangplank of their ship to the waterfront cantina nearest the wharf, a beehive of strange-looking characters. Carlo was quick to notice that many of the men at the bar were clustered around the prettiest-looking girl he had ever seen.

She was wasp-waisted (with the aid of a tight corset), and her square, low-cut blouse revealed huge, voluptuous breasts. One of her tiny feet was up on the rail of the barstool next to her. White lace petticoats plainly showed above her high-buttoned shoes, as did a goodly bit of milky-white calf and thigh. Her face was oval with a delicately pointed chin, turned-up nose, high cheekbones, and large green eyes. Her complexion was fair with a trace of freckles across the bridge of her nose and above all that was extremely thick, curly, titian-colored hair. She had a drink in one hand and her other forearm was resting on her raised knee. She was laughing infectiously at something a swarthy Spanish sailor had whispered in her ear, revealing white, even teeth and dimples.

The three Sicilian boys were mesmerized by her looks for a few seconds, finally ordering tequilas from the barman and watching how the Cubans drank it, licking some salt from the back of their hand first and sucking a lemon after. The boys had enough sense to only have one and make it last.

It was early on a pleasant Spring evening and the trade winds were rustling the tall palms outside. Somewhere in the back of the cantina a guitar was playing La Cucaracha and people were singing, "*Pero no quiero, porque mi falta, marijuana que fumar*!" Through a window behind the bar with green shutters flung outward, wafted the pungent odor of marijuana coming from a Cuban couple sitting outside, backs to the wall, smoking it.

At that moment, a group of hardened, weathered, and heavily-armed American seamen strode through the open portal, led by a tall, rawboned man, with a long, heavily-waxed orange moustache. They commandeered some space up the bar from Carlo, away from the pretty girl. The bartender was very deferential. "Ah, Captain Semmes," he crowed, "another victory. How many prizes have you captured so far?" Semmes answered him in Spanish, "Diez y ocho.." The bartender grinned through a drooping moustache and a gold tooth. "Magnifico, Senor!"

Semmes was standing right next to Carlo. Drinks were bought all around and offered to the Sicilians, who declined politely. One of the sailors uttered a slur about Dagoes and Semmes reached across two other sailors to give him a hard, open-handed slap to the back of the head. "They're only boys," he said ominously.

Carlo could pick up most of the Spanish, which he had studied in Sicily, but he knew no English. He did know that the interplay concerned him and his friends, though. Raphael Semmes downed his drink and looked at Carlo with intense China-blue eyes. "Do you speak English?" he asked in Italian. "No. We are Sicilian," answered Carlo. Semmes smiled, causing the overhead light to flicker on a two-inch horizontal scar across his right cheek. "In that case, we've got a problem. I understood what you just said, but I'm not too familiar with the Sicilian dialect," he said in Italian. "I am fairly fluent in Spanish," smiled Carlo, "studied it in school." "That's what we'll settle on, then, young man," Semmes answered affably. "I know Spanish well. My brig was sunk off Vera Cruz in the Mexican War and later I was on the march to Mexico City. Did some interpreting for them, too."

Semmes went on to tell Carlo of his Maryland birth, entering the Old Navy at age seventeen in 1826, and making his permanent home in Mobile. He could tell this youth was educated and intelligent and it was a welcome relief from his rough-and-tumble crew. "I've also found the time to get a law degree," he laughed.: Something to fall back on if my sea legs ever give out. I'm fifty-three and getting a little creaky," he said with a laconic grin. He looked to Carlo to be the most rugged-looking man he had ever seen.

"How about you boys, are you coming, going, or staying?" We are trying to make it to New Orleans where my father has friends," said Carlo. Semmes replied, "That should be arranged easy enough…".

At that moment, the Spanish sailor who had been whispering in the pretty girl's ear, let out a yelp and jumped back, his hand holding his belly. In a lightening motion, the girl had pulled a six-inch straight razor from the top of that raised high-button shoe that her forearm had been resting on during the conversation, and sliced it across the sailor's stomach.

Lithely, she hopped to the floor, breaking her beer bottle in her left hand and clutching the neck of it. When Carlo looked at her, the pretty face was contorted in rage, the green eyes flashing, a snarl on the lovely mouth, as she faced four Spaniards, the razor in one hand, broken beer bottle in the other, waving them defensively. "Quien quire mas?!" she hissed, circling backward, like a cornered she-wolf.

Semmes immediately took command, motioning with his head to his men. "Throw the Spaniards out," he ordered. "Doc, see to the one that got cut." The ship's medic went into action pulling his supplies from a pouch slung over his shoulder, glad that for once it was other than his crew that was injured. Meanwhile, four of Semmes' largest seamen had fallen upon the Spaniards, guns drawn. "Alto!" hollered Semmes. "No mas! Vamos!"

Suddenly, the Spaniards moved toward the front entrance where Doc was doing what he could to stanch the blood flowing from the wounded man's belly. When he finished, the four of them left. The girl resumed her seat, eyes still flashing. Semmes called down to her, "Good thing we saved you, little lady, before you killed the lot of them." He and his men laughed heartily.

"I asked for none of your help," she said, with what Semmes recognized as a distinct Liverpool accent. "I can take care of myself."

"Oh, I can see that," Semmes drawled, :but you looked so chummy with that feller. What happened?" "He was a pig. That's what happened. And he made a filthy suggestion that I found insulting. So I opened him up," she said defiantly. "All I want to do is to get to New Orleans."

"Well," drawled Semmes, winking at his sailors, "you've got the same problem as these young fellers here. Whyn't you move on up here with us, if you promise to hold that Limey temper a' yores. Doc don't stitch too good after six drinks and he's had five already."

The girl hesitated. "C'mon," Semmes smiled. "the drinks are free and my men are harmless. I don't know about these hot-blooded young Sicilians, though," he winked. "And if you behave, I just might get you to New Orleans." Slowly, the sweet look reappeared on the girl's face, and she smiled, getting up and moving toward them.

She knew this man was somebody with authority; reading men was her avocation. Coming up to Semmes, she looked up at his handsome, weathered face, and said, "My name's Kate Townsend. What's yours?" "Captain Raphael Semmes, Ma'am, at your service," Semmes bowed exaggeratedly to guffaws from his crew. To Semmes' surprise, Kate was impressed. "The famous sea raider," she said, "I just came from New York and your exploits are all the talk up there."

Semmes shrugged. "Well, I'm flattered to hear that, Ma'am. Now let me introduce you to my young friends here. They don't speak English. Would you know any Spanish?" "Enough," Kate said, motioning to the Spaniard's blood on the floor. Semmes let out a loud laugh and stroked his wax moustache. "Yeah, I guess you do. Sure enough. More than that fella thought you did anyway, eh?

"*Miguelito! Bebidos por todos!*" Carlo didn't understand the words of their conversation, but got the general gist of it, catching a few words here and there. From then on, they spoke in Spanish. Semmes told them that he was sending one of his men back to New Orleans later that night on a small packet steamer with some dispatches, and that a Union invasion of New Orleans was imminent.

Captain Raphael Semmes

"You're welcome to make the run with him, if you like," he said. "If the blockaders don't blow you out of the water, the worst that's going to happen even if you get caught is the ship gets confiscated and you get taken prisoner. But being civilians and foreigners at that, they wouldn't hold you long. Your chances are good, though, my man has run that blockade a dozen times." It sounded adventuresome to all of them and all agreed to go, thanking Raphael Semmes. Kate went upstairs to a room over the cantina and returned with a carpetbag containing her clothes. "Good luck to you," said Raphael Semmes, "I'm off to the Mediterranean. There's some ripe Union pickings over there right now."

Kate whispered to him in English, smiling angelically, "Captain, if you'd care to follow me upstairs, I'll thank you properly." Semmes was taken aback. He clucked her chin with his thumb. "You're a reg'lar little vixen, aren't you? Well, Honey, I hate to miss out on a good thing, but at sea whatever I get, my men get." Kate turned up her nose. "That's what I figured," said Raphael Semmes, smiling sardonically.

"By the way, exactly where in New Orleans are you headed, if I might ask." "You might not ask," she replied petulantly. "After turning me down. But I'll tell you anyway. I have an invitation to Clara Ward's place on Phillippa Street. You know it?"

"Know it?" Semmes roared. "My crew practically spent the winter there." He looked at her again and shook his head admiringly. "You're some handful," he said. "Now, don't teach these young fellas anything they shouldn't know." Kate batted her dark eyelashes and smiled innocently. By that time the boys had joined in the revelry as much as the language barrier would permit.

About midnight, Semmes courier, the captain of the blockade-running packet, came in and at two o'clock in the morning the ship sailed, carrying Carlo, Tony, Frank, and Kate.

Before noon the next day, the small packet steamer was off Key West, which it gave a wide berth, Key West being a stopping-off place for the Western Gulf Blockading Squadron. Visibility was poor and it was raining, which was fine with everybody aboard the packet. The packet headed west, keeping well below 24° latitude. Eventually, it turned northwest.

Carlo learned more about Kate. Her real name was Katherine Cunningham, she was twenty-three, the daughter of a Liverpool stevedore. She had become a waterfront barmaid at fifteen. Eventually, she left Liverpool and came to New York. What Kate didn't tell Carlo was that she had left twin infant sons in Liverpool, something whose guilt haunted her every day; she also didn't tell Carlo that she was going to New Orleans as an inmate of one of its most notorious whorehouses.

GULF OF MEXICO
WEDNESDAY, APRIL 9, 1862

The little packet steamer plowed through a choppy Gulf, holding to her northwest course. Kate spent as much time as she could on the bridge with captain Gerard, a short, wiry man with a weather lined face. Kate questioned him incessantly, then relayed his answers to her three new-found Sicilian friends.

They had all known in advance about the southern blockade, but compared to what the captain told Kate, the blockade seemed a minor obstacle to overcome. Invasion of New Orleans by a Federal fleet, Captain Gerard said, was so imminent when he had left less than a week ago that it might have already happened.

"Well, thanks a lot to Captain Semmes for sending us into this!" Kate said sarcastically. The captain shrugged. "Look at it this way, the invasion will come through the southern passes and up the Mississippi. The Union ships have to go under our guns at Forts Jackson and St. Phillip, seventy-five miles below the city. At that point, we have a chained float barricading the river and we know they are coming and are ready for them.

"They believe with their steam power that they can outrun our guns; I doubt it. If they do reach the city, however, New Orleans probably will have to surrender. The Federals have three or four dozen gunboats already in the river and more available from the blockading squadron if they need them.

"They have captured our telegraph station at Pilot Town at the Head of Passes, twenty miles below the forts, and cut the wires, stopping direct wire service to New Orleans. They also have a land force on Ship Island, off Biloxi, which we estimate at between 10,000 and 20,000. The land invasion won't succeed without the sea invasion, but those fools in Richmond have picked our city clean of ships, shells, and troops to be pressed into service elsewhere. So if that fleet gets past the forts, it's probably all over for New Orleans.

"Either way it goes, I don't see the city itself getting shelled, it's too strategic for them, if they get it, to destroy it." Kate was amazed at the captain's fatalism, mistaking it for diffidence. She gave him a fiery look. "And we're going up that river past fifty warships?!" she asked.

The captain smiled, "Not hardly, honey. In fact, we're goin' in any way but that. We could go into Berwick Bay and into the city on the New Orleans, Opelousas, and Western. That's how most of the commerce has been conducted since the blockade, or, we could go into Barataria Bay, Jean Lafitte's old stampin 'grounds, and in through the bayous, or into Lake

Borgne, taking Chef Menteur Pass into Lake Ponchartrain. Lake Borgne was the way your British cousins tried fifty years ago in the War of 1812. They weren't too successful," he said with a lazy smile, "but we got friends waitin' for us, not Old Hickory."

Kate had no idea who or what Old Hickory was, but she tried to be optimistic. "You think that's the best route, then?" she asked doubtfully. The captain was enjoying the game. He gave a doubtful look. "Only thing is, Lake Borgne is just west of Ship Island, the Yankee headquarters," he deadpanned.

Kate was getting annoyed. She began to realize that he was playing with her. "So which way are we going to try?" she asked sharply. The captain gave a laconic grin. "Lake Borgne. But don't worry! When I say just west of Ship Island, I mean about thirty miles west. With this weather, and the Yankees busy at the Passes, we'll slide in with no trouble." Kate looked doubtful but the captain just smiled and chased her off the bridge.

When Kate went below and explained the situation to Carlo, he replied with black humor. "Maybe it's not a good thing you and I know the same language, I think I was better off ignorant of the facts." He then explained the situation to Tony and Frank.

Unbeknown as yet to the captain, Admiral Farragut, the chief of the Federal naval expedition, had tested the forts on April 5th with a five-boat convoy and was confident he could outrun their guns. David Glasgow Farragut was born July1, 1801, near Knoxville, Tennessee. His family moved to New Orleans while he was a child and there he was adopted by Commodore David Porter, and made a midshipman at the age of nine. Four years later, he was with the Commodore fighting the War of 1812.

The Commodore's son, Commander David Porter, Farragut's half-brother, had been on blockading duty at Southwest Pass and had been put in charge of the twenty-ship mortar squadron that was to assist Farragut in getting past the forts. Both Porter, Jr., and Farragut knew the waters surrounding New Orleans thoroughly.

On the afternoon of the tenth, the little packet, carefully skirting Ship Island in rough seas and fog, ran up between Errold Island and the

Chandeleurs and made the ten-mile dash from the tip of those islands safely entering Lake Borgne and docking at Proctorsville for fuel. Then they passed Fort Macomb into Chef Menteur Pass to Lake Ponchartrain. By that night they were in a New Orleans girdling for attack.

Along the Levee marched Soaves, Chesseurs, Rangers, Rifles and Guards, resplendent in their hastily-made uniforms with bright colors and brass buttons. The marchers deftly skirted bales of cotton vainly awaiting shipment to foreign ports, thwarted by the blockade.

To a much lesser degree than before the war were lined other crops, many of them perishable: hogsheads of sugar, kegs, boxes, and crates of apples, bacon, beans, beef, and butter; corn, cottonseed, cheese, flour, glassware, and hemp. There was also lead, leather, molasses, oats, onions, and oil; pickles, pig iron, potatoes, port; rice, rope, and rosin; soap and shingles; tobacco and twine; wool, wheat, and whiskey.

Much of the foodstuffs that couldn't run the blockade and was perishable was donated by the owner to the Free Market on Canal Street near the Levee which provided free food for the poor, the war widows, and their children. Atop City Hall on St. Charles Street across from Lafayette Square, the Louisiana state flag: thirteen red, white, and blue stripes with yellow star in a red field, snapped in the brisk spring breeze. Below it, wagons clattered hastily by, bearing donated bells from the estates and the churches to be forged into cannon.

Kate and the three boys had bid Captain Gerard a grateful farewell and were hurrying down a riverfront street in the "Irish Channel." Carlo was heading for the Patorno residence on St. Claud Street and Kate to Clara Fisher's house on Phillippa Street. They passed two burly-looking toughs holding an inebriated man with a bruised face by each arm. They were on their way to collect a two-dollar bonus for this new recruit to a rifle company.

Carlo had gotten to like the mercurial Kate but was leery of bringing her into the Patorno house or even letting her know exactly where it was., but he wanted to maintain contact with this strange girl, so they stopped at a coffee house near St. Claud Street and Kate agreed to wait while Carlo and

Tony went to meet the Patornos. Frank Romero volunteered to stay with her, figuring that three new arrivals with no advance notice might be a bit much, even for close paesanos.

The Matranga boys were greeted warmly at the substantial clapboard house that the Patornos had converted into a two-family dwelling. The elder Patorno, also a Charlie, was an abattoir at the French Market, whose business up until the blockade had been thriving, and since the blockade, had become even more so with the price of fresh meats skyrocketing.

Mrs. Patorno was a handsome, matronly woman who fussed over the new arrivals and insisted that they eat. She called her only son in from the dining room where he had been studying with a neighbor boy from down the street. Charlie Patorno, Jr. was a tall, well-built, athletic looking youth of eighteen. He had a handsome face with aquiline nose. The young man accompanying him was a year older, a bit portly, with a round and affable face on which there was a constant smile. He was dressed more expensively than anyone there.

"Charlie and Tony," young Patorno said after warm handshakes and embraces were exchanged, "meet my friend and our neighbor from down the street, Joe Macheca." And so Carlo was henceforth 'Charlie', too. Before long, the conversation got so intense that Charlie had to interject the fact that they had brought along another boy. The elder Patorno extended his hands, "For the dottore, a dozen would not be too many. I will have to find other quarters for him tomorrow, because we don't have room on a permanent basis. Tonight, of course, he can stay here. I will go and get him with you," Charlie gave an imperceptible frown to Charlie Patorno and Joe Macheca, and they immediately interjected, "No, Pa. You stay here. We'll go with Charlie and Tony and bring him back." "Bene", answered the elder Patorno, "but mind the curfew."

The five boys stayed in the coffee shop with Kate as long as they could prudently explain. Joe Macheca was dazzled by her looks. They arranged to meet in the same place in a few days and Charlie arranged for a cab for her before they left. "Since last May, all persons entering the city must get permits from the Provost Marshal," he explained.

"Habeas corpus has been suspended for New Orleans and the surrounding Parishes, so it's better to be off the streets at night until you've seen to that." Kate wasn't sure what habeas corpus meant but she thought twice about the reference to 'off the streets', before dismissing it as innocuous. "If you have any trouble, I'll fix it for you," Joe Macheca said as they parted.

The boys returned to the Patorno house for a huge welcoming dinner. When all the elder Patorno's questions about Piana dei Greci, the Matranga family, and other friends from home, had been answered and the family's curiosity quenched, they went to bed, leaving the boys to talk all night. Joe Macheca, they learned, had Sicilian parents who died years before of Bronze John, the yellow fever that made an annual decimation of the populace.

Joe had been adopted by a family friend, a Maltese man named Macheca, who was a pioneer at importing fruit from South America, a business that had made him very wealthy. Joe was being groomed to take over the business in a few years. Joe was an intensely curious young man and pressed Charlie Matranga for details about Garibaldi's invasion of Sicily. Charlie could sense that Joe was a fervid patriot looking for a cause to follow, and he immediately warmed to the beefy young Macheca.

BUFFALO BILL HOUSE
FRANKLIN & PHILLIPPA STREETS\
[AMERICAN SECTION]
NEW ORLEANS, LOUISIANA
WEDNESDAY, APRIL 23rd, 1862 7
P.M.

The previous Sunday had been Easter in an ever-more-jittery New Orleans. It had been two weeks since Kate had become an inmate at Clara Fisher's, but it was enough for her to determine that she wouldn't be staying long at Clara's. The girls were a rowdy bunch and she'd had to give one a bad beating.

Kate would have cut her except that she had come to Clara's on the recommendation of a mutual friend. Also, Kate hadn't made enough connections in New Orleans yet to go off on her own. Kate had met with the Sicilian boys the week before and was very fond of them. They had a date to meet again the next day.

This evening, Kate and two of the other girls, Jumpin' Jenny, and Lulu White, had taken a couple of hours off and had walked down Phillippa Street to Franklin Street, location of Bison Williams' Buffalo Bill House, one of the most notorious concert saloons in New Orleans. The girls were hoping to drum up some business.

The name concert hall should have been more aptly arena because the entertainment consisted of head-butting contests, boxing and wrestling matches, and rat-and-dog fights, with some pantiless can can dancers providing the entertainment between bouts. Bison Williams, a huge, bearded man with hair all over his body, bore more than a passing resemblance to his namesake, but he was nice to Clara's girls and Kate had begun coming in daily for a coffee around noon.

Bison had given her a guided tour of the "distillery" behind the saloon which interested her due to her days as a barmaid in Liverpool. "Irish Whiskey" was neutral spirits and creosote; "wine" was colored and flavored water with a little alcohol; "brandy" had a more intricate formula: neutral spirits, water, dried fruit, burnt sugar, sulfuric acid, and a plug of chewing tobacco. Kate opted for the 'wine" on her nighttime visits as the least toxic. "You know, Kate, you sure backed that fresh bitch Lily off last week," said Lulu. "She likes to test the new girls out and if they back down she steals any decent john they might get off them. With you, she might as well have fucked with Bricktop. You remind me of Bricktop anyway."

"Who's Bricktop?" Kate asked. The other two girls glanced at each other. "Who's Bricktop?!" repeated Lulu. "Bricktop Jackson's the toughest whore in this city, that's who. Bricktop was born here in New Orleans…worked in Archie Murphy's dance hall in Gallatin Street for a while. She killed two men while there. Stabbed one to death with her custom-made knife, double-ended with the grip in the middle."

"How'd she kill the second one?" Kate asked. "Beat him to death with her hands," answered Lulu. "Beautiful girl she was, too. But too hard to handle. She'd get into fights everywhere she went. Worked at Clara's for a couple of weeks, but all the girls were afraid of her.

"She hooked up with Button Lizzie's sister, Ellen Collins, Big America Williams, and Bridget Fury. Bridget got life for murder three years ago and the same year Bricktop, Ellen, and Big America were drinking at Joe Siedensahl's beer garden on Rampart Street, and the three of them stabbed a guy to death who had slapped Bricktop. She eventually got out of that one.

"Finally, she got tied up with a jailer who she had met while awaiting trial. A one-armed street fighter from Gretna. Last year he tried to cut Bricktop, but she took the knife off him and stabbed him to death with it. She's in Parish prison now, poor thing, with Bridget. Place is overrun with that 500 Yankee scum they brought down here from Manassas."

"And *I* remind you of her?" asked Kate "Oh, I didn't mean nothin' bad by that, Kate. It's just that you got the same sand as her, right, Jen?" Jen nodded appreciatively. "What was Bricktop's right name, Jen?" "Mary Jane….. It didn't seem to suit her."

At that moment, Bison sat down, turning a chair around and resting his huge forearms on its back.. "Wal, ladies, whaddayuh think of these invasion rumors?" Before they could answer, Bison continued, "Them Yankees gotta get by Fort Jackson, not to mention Fort St. Philip. 'Been shellin' Fort Jackson for the last five days.

"They'll never make it past, take my word for it. Ol' Johnny J.K. Duncan is commandin' Fort Jackson. Four years ago, I was on the Vigilance Committee after General Beauregard, he was the Mayor then, ran for election. J.K. was our leader. He was a captain then. J.K. seized the Arsenal, the Cabildo…jail, to you," he winked at Kate, "…and all of Jackson Square and held it with 1,000 of us for five days until an honest election was held."

Bison let out a whoop. "And the God-damned Know Nothing was elected anyway. Mayor Monroe, the Mayor now, is a Know Nothing, but a good ol' boy. But J.K. is a real soldier. West Pointer. Big, good-lookin' fella. He's only about thirty-six. He entered our army as a colonel.

"General Lovell knows how good J.K. is. Had Jeff Davis make J.K. a buck general last January. J.K.'ll hold 'em, ladies. There's a reporter from the Daily True Delta who drinks here. They're runnin' a telegram from J.K. tomorrow that he sent today. Says the Yankees'll wear themselves out sooner or later, and I quote, "We can stand it as long as they can." Don't worry about ol' J.K.," Bison said confidently

"Nice show," Kate said facetiously. Bison was unfazed. "Oh, yeah. We get some good people in here," he said, pointing. "There's Sam Gorman over there, the distinguished-lookin' old gent. Hails from New York City but spends his winters here. He's about sixty-five." "What line of work was he in before he retired?" asked Kate. "Retired?!" Bison let out a knee-slapping whoop. "Hell, he ain't retired. Best burglar in the country!

"Speakin' of burglars, there's our two best local talent just came in: Pierre Bertin and Jean Capdeville." "Who's that well-dressed couple sitting with Gorman, Bison?" "Oh, they're New Yorkers, too. Ned Lyons and his wife, Sophie Levy. Ned's the best safecracker around," Bison smiled.

"And we got Carl Hobgood and Gene Bunch, crackerjack train robbers, tonight, and Maggie Murphy," Bison pointed to a fiftyish woman with a sad face. "Helluva pickpocket. Works mostly funerals, that's why she's got that perpetual sad look on her face. Oh, we get the best, all right. And plenty of politicians, too. That's why I ain't gotta pay too much attention to the curfew."

"Get us a couple of live ones to take back to Clara's with us, will you, Bison?" Lulu said. She gave him a familiar dig in the huge stomach with a bony elbow. Bison smiled. "I think those Frenchmen are pretty flush. Get 'em to buy some champagne afore you leave, honey....Hey! Pierre!...Jean! C'mon over!"

When the evening had ended and Kate had finally gotten rid of the burglar, she went back to her favorite pasttime, planning for her financial future. Clara's was a straight five-dollar house and Clara got one-third of each of the twelve girl's earnings. Kate figured Clara was taking in about $1,000 for the house, less expenses.

But Kate had already learned that the real money was to be made in the ostentatious, upper-crust salons where ladies wore evening gowns and entertained by appointment only. Kate reckoned a smart madam with a couple of dozen girls could take in as much as $5,000 a week, "God, give me just four or five years," she whispered to herself, "and I'll have the finest house in New Orleans."

THURSDAY MORNING
APRIL 24, 1862

Kate turned down Franklin Street on her way to the coffee house on Esplanade by St. Claud to meet Charlie and the boys. She paid little attention to the grim and anxious faces of the passersby until she heard a distant thunder. She stopped and cocked up an ear.

Then she heard it again. Then it came in a faint staccato. Cannons, she thought. And she thought of Bison's confident words of the night before, "J.K.'ll hold 'em, ladies." Well, J.K. had jolly well tried. His double garrisons at Fort Jackson and St. Philip were held by 1,100 men and over 100 guns. But the month before, the heavy anchored and chained cypress barrier raft at the forts had given way before the current and debris of the Mighty Mississippi.

The barrier raft's replacement was weaker, a line of anchored schooners; it gave way as well and was hastily replaced. Porter's mortar squadron had begun peppering Fort Jackson on April 18th, and continued for five days.

The so-called "invincible" ironclad, "Lousiana", was sent to assist the beleaguered J.K. Duncan, but her captain refused to move her below Fort St. Philip, in range of Porter's mortars. At three-thirty o'clock that morning, Farragut's lethal procession had begun up river, penetrating the barrier and finally bypassing the forts.

They continued up to Quarantine Station after a night of fierce gunfights from the forts and the River Defense Squadron, including the ironclad Confederate ram, "Manassas" and numerous fire rafts. The final tally: Farragut had 37 dead and 137 wounded; the losses on the Confederate side were 73 dead and 73 wounded. At Fort Jackson there were 9 dead and 33 wounded; Fort St. Philip had 2 dead and 4 wounded.

New Orleans herself was to surrender before General Johnson K. Duncan finally gave in on midnight of April 26th, and only after a mass mutiny of his troops at the fort. Bison had not misjudged his man.

At St. Claud, Kate heard the fire alarm bells clanging twelve strokes four times repeated, signaling assembly of all military units at their armories. Kate finally reached the coffee house on Esplanade to meet Charlie and the boys.

Only Joe Macheca was there, explaining that with the invasion, Charlie, Tony, Frank, and the Patornos were busy at the French Market and would see her tomorrow. "I've got a buggy outside. Let's ride down to the docks and see what's going on." The Levee was a frenzy of activity. General Lovell had ordered the burning of all cotton, ships and shipyards, and the removal of all supplies that would give aid to the enemy.

Thirteen thousand bales of cotton were rushed to the docks, loaded onto barges, set on fire, and set afloat. Any boats capable of carrying passengers and freight were quickly boarded and took off upriver. It was open season on any commodities already at the docks and whatever could be carried away on wagons, or people's backs, was. Better them than the Yankees.

Men, women, and children sat on the wharves and cried, their faces contorted with rage and frustration. Joe offered Kate to spend the night at his house and she accepted. The elder Macheca was in Colombia on business. The portly youth and the voluptuous young prostitute clung to each other and made love while the sky outside was ablaze from burning rafts and barges, the conflagration creating a proud city's personal Hell.

The next morning, a heavy drizzle saturated New Orleans in a grey wreath. Farragut's squadron, having spent the night at Quarantine Station, reached English Turn at 10 o'clock. Token resistance was made by the Chalmette batteries, which had been so effectively used by Jackson against the English fifty years prior.

This time the batteries were leveled in twenty minutes, as was another fortification below Slaughterhouse Point. By one o'clock in the afternoon, the "Hartford", Farragut's flagship, and the rest of the squadron, anchored in the river at New Orleans, their broadsides facing the Levee on this black day of drizzling rain, flashing lightning, and clapping thunder. Thousands of grim faces watched in awe and disbelief, among them Kate Townsend, Charlie Matranga, and Joe Macheca.

Two hours later, two emissaries of Farragut --- a captain and a lieutenant --- were rowed to the wharf at the foot of Laurel Street in a small boat under a flag of truce. The crowd, upon seeing them disembark, was becoming an ugly mob. It was with some difficulty that the officers were taken to City Hall to meet Mayor Monroe and his delegation.

Eventually, General Lovell rode up ramrod straight on horseback. At the meeting, the Mayor said it was not in his power to accede to Farragut's demand that he surrender the city. The general said that he would not surrender, but would withdraw, thus leaving the city in the hands of the civil authorities.

Kate, Charlie, and Joe were pushed along by the angry mob, some of whom were kicking the locked doors of City Hall and vowing death to the Yankee officers. Finally, some of the town fathers and \ General Lovell went out and made speeches while the Union officers were hustled out a back door.

At ten o'clock the next morning, Saturday, City Council met to consider accession to Farragut's surrender demands. At the same time, Farragut seized the Mint and flew the U.S. flag over it. A crowd gathered outside and a local man named Mumford climbed up and took the flag down as the crowd cheered.

At noon, Mayor Monroe agreed to surrender the city to what he termed, "the power of brutal force". He refused to raise the American flag over city buildings, however. Charlie and Joe offered Kate a ride home. She accepted and on the way asked them to take her to the Buffalo Bill House.

The place was packed and the gossip was hot and heavy, but Bison got them a table in a far-off corner, as Kate had requested.

She looked squarely at Charlie as she said to Joe, "Joe, you'll have to interpret; I've got a few things I want you both to know, but I want to be sure that Charlie understands every word I say." Joe nodded. "Sure, Kate. I'll tell him just like you say it." Charlie's grey eyes were studying her and she felt uncomfortable. Kate proceeded.

"I came to this country for one reason, to make a lot of money any way I could. Before I came here I was a barmaid in Liverpool as you know. There is a very limited amount of money to be made at that trade. I met you fellows and I took a liking to you. I like to be around you because there are no strings attached. We can be ourselves and have a laugh. that's a welcome relief for me.

"You see, I went to work in Clara Fisher's and Clara Fisher's is a whorehouse. I say that not in boast and not in apology, it's just the way things are. I would like to keep your friendship, if possible, and I understand now that you know, you won't invite me to meet Charlie Patorno's family or you, Joe, your stepfather."

Joe's jaw had dropped but Charlie was still studying her. I'll leave you to think it over," Kate concluded. "If you still want to keep in touch, you know where to find me. I figured this is not the time for us to have secrets from each other." Kate got up to leave.

Joe looked undecided and looked to young Charlie, but Kate wasn't out of the chair before Charlie extended his hand and put it over her wrist. "Sit down, Kate," he said in Spanish. "You are our friend and what you do for a living does not concern us. Tony, Frank, and I consider you the first friend we met here and you will not lose us so easily," Charlie smiled.

Joe, taking the cue, nodded. Kate was a shrewd judge of character and she could tell that this boy was wise beyond his years and would be a good person to have as a friend in the years to come. She retook her seat; the subject was changed and not ever brought up again.

On the way home in Joe's buggy, Joe said, "Can you believe that? I never figured Kate to be a…" Charlie's look stopped him from continuing. "Joe," he said, "I was taught not to make friends lightly and I don't. Kate is the real stuff. She's our friend and how she makes a living is her own business. Do you agree with that?" Joe, remembering his night of passion, said, "Sure, Charlie, …sure." Joe was surprised at the deference he was showing this youth, three years his junior.

The buggy clattered south on Franklin in the damp and desperate night of the Crescent City's surrender.

SUNDAY, APRIL 27th, 1862
FRENCH MARKET
NEW ORLEANS, LOUISIANA

Charlie, his brother Tony, Frank, and young Charlie Patorno were just finishing helping the senior Patorno to load his supply of meats on a wagon. Charlie Patorno, Sr., intended to store them in a secret location for a day or two while he disposed of them and awaited the outcome of the Yankee occupation.

The market had been built a half-century before and was simply a long, pitched slate roof supported by stout columns in the Doric style. It contained three sections: for meat; dry goods; and the third for fish, game, flowers, fruit, and vegetables. It was an important part of the city's commerce, a bustling place that reminded Charlie of La Vuccaria when he first saw it, before the invasion. Now the merchants were all in the process of clearing out until it became known what was going to happen next. After the meats were hidden away, Charlie, Tony, and Frank returned to St. Claud Street; the two Patornos stayed behind to sell as much of the meat as possible that day.

Charlie went by Joe's house and Joe invited him to go down and see the offices of Joe's father's Louisiana Steamship Lines. Macheca's offices were on the second floor, overlooking the docks from large windows. "Charlie," this fruit-importing business of my father's is really starting to grow." Joe said. "When I finish school next June, I'll be here every day. I love it. Maybe you come in with me. We'd make a good team." "We'll see, Giuseppe. We'll see," said Charlie. "Call me Pepe, like my father does," smiled Joe. "Yeah, Charlie, there's real possibilities here."

On Monday morning, April 28th, 1862, Farragut again ordered Mayor Monroe to lower the Louisiana flag or he would fire upon the city. He ordered the removal of the city's women and children within forty-eight hours. Monroe replied with another refusal, saying, "There is no possible exit from this city for a population which still exceeds 140,000, and you must, therefore, be aware of the utter inanity of such a notification. Our women and children cannot escape from your shells if it be your pleasure to murder them on a question of etiquette."

Farragut, finally, had his own officers haul down the flag while a force of Marines with bayonets at the ready and two howitzers kept the angry mob at bay.

THURSDAY, MAY 1, 1862
HEADQUARTERS OF THE UNION
MILITARY COMMANDER OF NEW ORLEANS
MAJOR GENERAL BENJAMIN FRANKLIN BUTLER

Flag Officer David Glasgow Farragut had just completed the official ceremony, turning the city over to the military command of General Butler. Butler, a squat, hawk-nosed man, cross-eyed and bald headed, had been a criminal lawyer in Lowell, Massachusetts. Before turning to politics in 1853.

He owed his present assignment to his old friend and classmate, Gustavus V. Fox, Assistant Secretary of the Navy and also a native of Lowell. Farragut, about to depart for Vicksburg, had just finished apprising Butler of his adventures of the past week, finishing with the tale of Mumford hauling down the Union flag from the Mint. Butler's eyes narrowed. "I'll promise you this, David. I'll find him and I'll hang him. It was a promise he would keep.

Butler walked Farragut to the door. "Again, Admiral, allow me to congratulate you on your gallant conquest. I'm sure further glories await you in the north." As soon as Farragut was gone, Butler summoned in his brother,

A.J.. His brother wore an officer's uniform with no insignia, but was referred to by Butler as "the Colonel" and carried on the payroll as an "aide" to the general.

Butler breathed a sigh of relief. "Now, we can get down to business and put these rebels in their place. Maybe get rich doing it, too, eh, brother?" The colonel smiled. "Brigadier General Algernon Badger and Lt. General Godfrey Weitzel of the First Louisiana Cavalry, that's a Union outfit, brother," he smiled, seeing Butler's concern, "are waiting to congratulate you." Butler smiled expansively, "Send them in."

Butler invited Badger and Weitzel to accompany him on a tour of the Vieux Carré. They were escorted by Weitzel's aide, Corporal David Hennessy, and a squad of Butler's men.

While walking through Lafayette Square, outside City Hall, they passed three or four well-dressed New Orleans housewives, each of whom carried a small Confederate flag and gave the soldiers hateful looks as they passed by. "Nervy Rebel tramps," hissed Butler, "I'll get around to them before long." "This is going on all over town," said Badger, "I've gotten many reports from my men. The women are bolder than the men."

TWO WEEKS LATER
THURSDAY, MAY 15th,1862
BUTLER'SHEADQUARTERS

Ben Butler sat at his desk, livid with rage. There had been numerous instances of confrontations between his troops and the women of New Orleans over the last two weeks and just this morning, General Weitzel's aide, Corporal Hennessy, had been spat upon.

Next to Butler was his Chief-of-Staff, Assistant Adjutant General George C. Strong. Butler waved a piece of paper in the air "George, have these put all over town. And have these posters with my picture on them put right underneath so they'll know who I am." The two officers reread General Order 28:

"AS THE OFFICERS AND SOLDIERS HAVE BEEN SUBJECTED TO REPEATED INSULTS FROM THE WOMEN CALLING THEMSELVES LADIES OF NEW ORLEANS, IN RETURN FOR THE MOST SCRUPULOUS NON-INTERFERENCE ON OUR PART, IT IS ORDERED THAT WHEN ANY FEMALE SHALL, BY WORD, GESTURE, OR MOVEMENT INSULT OR SHOW CONTEMPT FOR ANY OFFICER OR SOLDIER OF THE UNITED STATES, SHE SHALL BE REGARDED AND HELD LIABLE TO BE TREATED AS A WOMAN OF THE TOWN, PLYING HER AVOCATION".
By Command of Major General Butler, George C. Strong, A.A.G., Chief of Staff

"Let's see how those bitches like that, George. And the procedure will be that upon the complaint of any soldier, without more, they shall be arrested, held overnight, and taken in front of a magistrate in the morning and fined $5.00."

Strong saluted and had an aide take the bale of circulars and posters. "We'll have them all over town by tonight, sir." With that, he left. Butler summoned his brother, "Colonel, bring in that gambler, Devol." George Devol was a colorful character who operated Oakland Race Track just outside town. In the grandstand, he ran games of chance. He was also famous for his prowess as a head butter and street fighter and was a town wit as well, known for his dry sense of humor.

Devol entered the room behind the Colonel, accompanied by two armed guards. Butler bid them wait outside. Glaring at Devol, Butler said, "Devol, you have been found to have been illegally operating games of chance at your track. Now this could have been handled by the Provost Marshal, but since you are a well-known citizen in this town, I've afforded you the courtesy of seeing you personally. What have you got to say about it? I, ah, believe the Colonel has spoken to you as well." A..J. nodded.

Devol wiped a meaty hand over his huge bald head and smiled. "Look, General, all the big gambling houses in town have been closed for a year. Jim Sherwood, Henry Perritt, Price McGrath, Gus Lauraine, and

Charlie Cassidy --- all closed by General Lovell. Price went home to Kentucky to work his horse farm…"

"And his partners, Perritt and Sherwood equipped companies of men that are fighting against us in Virginia right now," yelled Butler.
"I know all about them! It's you I'm talking about, Devol. Now, what do you want to do?" Devol looked him straight in the eye. "General, I don't mind paying a fee to your Yankee Provost Marshal, and I am from Ohio but I consider New Orleans my home.

"I've lived here for twenty-five years and I've worked the riverboats, and I'm not forty yet. No , I don't mind that. But as far as taking in the Colonel in as a full partner --- and he's as much of a colonel las I am, he's your brother, is what he is --- I'll close up first!"

Butler jumped to his feet, his face purple with rage. "You are closed!! As of right now not only are you closed, but all your gambling equipment is confiscated as are all the horses at your track. Additionally, as the Military Commander of New Orleans, I hereby sentence you to one year in Parish prison. How does that suit you, Devol?"

George Devol shrugged. "Win some…lose some. I'll be here long after you're gone, General." "We'll add $1,000.00 fine to that sentence for that last remark. Get him out of here!!" yelled Butler to the waiting guards.

After Devol had gone, Butler sat down with his brother. "It was better to make an example of him. You can sell his equipment to some of the other gamblers and after seeing what happened to Devol, I don't think you'll get many arguments in the future. Either you're their partner or they don't operate." A,J, nodded appreciatively. "Also," Butler continued, "I've telegraphed Washington that I'm confiscating any excess wealth that some of these monied families possess. The silverware, for instance, can be melted down and made into Federal coin at the Mint to help meet the payroll…. After we've taken our 'finder's fee" of 50%. But you've got to coordinate one major strike at their houses Once they get wind of it, everything will be hidden." "I'll have it done within two weeks, Ben, because I'll be busy disposing of Devol's stuff first." Butler smiled.

"Yes, you're going to be a busy fellow. By the way, what are you going to do with his racehorses now that I've confiscated them as you requested?" "There's a Confederate camp on the other side of Ponchartrain and they're desperate for horses to head north with. I've got them sold for $50,000." Butler let out a raucous laugh. "Oh, you're bad, Colonel. Only you would have the audacity for a deal like that…..Or maybe me."

They laughingly slapped each other on the back. Two weeks later, Mayor John T. Monroe held a demonstration outside Butler's headquarters. Leading the delegation were some of the most notorious madames and prostitutes.in the city, who, curiously enough, were more outraged than anyone at the General's Order 28.

Among them was 35-year-old Fanny Sweet, the colorful and infamous courtesan and practitioner of voodoo, who stood six feet tall without shoes. Fanny had a voodoo amulet in one hand and a shrunken image of Butler's bald head in the other.

Butler went outside and faced them. By his side, were the Colonel, General Badger, Adjutant General Strong, and a squad of armed guards.
Mayor Monroe raised his voice above the crowd. "General Butler, we're here to protest your infamous order of the 15th. President Davis has labeled you an outlaw because of it and put a price on your head and the people of this city won't stand for it."

Butler pushed his chin forward and looked at the hapless mayor. "Let me tell you something, Monroe. First of all, a renegade is in no position to label anyone a 'outlaw'. You are hereby relieved of your duties as Mayor in favor of the military government that is now in possession of this city

"And I recognize that tall strumpet over there as the notorious murderess and poisoner, Fanny Sweet. Strong, have four of this squad escort her to the city limits. And don't return, whore, or I'll have you hung. The rest of you disperse while you can or face the same. This is nothing short of an insurrection! Now get out!!"

Slowly, and amid much mumbling, the crowd dispersed. Back in his office, Butler savored the moment. "I've been meaning to get rid of that

Monroe since I got here. He's been a thorn in my side. Well, he gave me a good chance to do it. Strong, you look as if you have something to say. What is it?" A.A.G. Strong faced his commander uncomfortably.

"Well, sir, there is something that has been brought to my attention that I think you ought to know about, although it is so vile that I hesitate to even mention it." Butler was getting impatient. "Out with it, man! We're all friends here." "Well, sir, you remember the posters with your picture that you had me place under Order 28?" Butler nodded. "Yes, yes. I remember. Have they been ripping my picture down, is that it?" "Worse than that, sir. The whores have all come into possession of the posters and have glued your picture to the inside of their chamber pot bowls and are urinating on it."

"WHAT?!?!?!?!" Butler was on his feet. A vein down the center of his forehead looked about to burst. In one motion he leaned forward and pounded on the desk. "GET THAT SQUAD READY!!!" "We're going to hit every whorehouse in this city and take every chamber pot and smash it and I'm going with you to do it in person. Let's go! On the double!!"

By the time the potty brigade finally got to Clara Fisher's on Phillippa Street, the girls had gotten wind of the expedition and it was the joke of the town. Still, no girl had removed the poster and some drank as much beer as they could so that they would have at least one last shot at Butler before he arrived.

There was no poster in Kate's chamber pot. She considered it bad for business in case any Federal troops or officers came in, as they sometimes did. Besides, she was English and felt she couldn't afford the luxury of a once-removed patriotism in a city in which she had lived for such a short period. Sure enough, Clara sent most of the Union officers to her. The enlisted men mostly approved of the chamber pot idea since they had no love for Butler either. Late in the afternoon, Clara's door was stove in and a search of the rooms was effected amid much giggling, Butler right with them.

When Butler finally got to Kate's room, he marched straight to the pot and looked in without having given her a look. When he did, he encountered

Kate's large green eyes innocently blinking at him in feigned confusion, the picture of innocence. "Hello, General, I've heard a lot about you. It's a pleasure to meet you." Butler was taken aback by this beautiful girl.

"Corporal Hennessy," he said to Weitzel's aide, who had been loaned to him for the day "proceed to the next room with your men." Hennessy suppressed a smirk and did as he was told. Butler kicked the door shut for privacy. "Do you know why we're here?" he asked. Kate shook her head up and down. "Well, in any event, it doesn't seem to apply to you. You certainly are a lovely girl. English, aren't you?"

Kate nodded. "I'm English descent myself. How long have you been here?" "Only a short while. In fact, I'd like to leave." "That's a good idea," Butler said appraisingly. He looked Kate up and down.

"How'd you like to go into business for yourself?" "That's my intention," Kate said. "Splendid," replied Butler. "I just padlocked a place at Villere and Customhouse today. Some of the girls might resent you reopening it, but if you can handle it, it's yours....of course, there will have to be financial arrangements to be made. You can see my brother, the Colonel, on that."

"Nothing's free," replied Kate fatalistically. "Exactly!" Butler exclaimed. "I'm a good judge of horseflesh," he said, smiling at his own joke and thinking of Devol, "but aside from everything else, I'd like to have a place where my officers and I can go to relax without fear of violence or tales being carried. Do you understand? I've been so mesmerized by those eyes that I didn't get your name."

"Kate Townsend, General, and I understand perfectly. You'll find that I'm the soul of discretion." Butler stroked her thick, titian hair a moment and looked into her eyes. "We are going to get along famously, Kate. Come to my headquarters in the morning.?" Kate smiled innocently. "I'll be there, General."

Kate took the General in as a partner in the house on Villere but she shrewdly got more from him for renovations than she ever paid him for his weekly take. It was a large frame house and Kate, with Butler's approval, made an inordinately large part of the ground floor into a sumptuous lounge, with leather chairs, plush carpet, and an oak bar. There was always a buffet of delicious fresh food and the Federal troops who could afford it --- the officers and a few more successful of the profiteers among the enlisted black marketers, found a congenial home-away-from-home at Kate Townsend's house.

This was to be Kate's theme in all her future endeavors: luxury, discretion, and satisfaction. Those three words, she often thought, could be her coat of arms. Butler brought to Kate's all the visiting politicians and military brass he was trying to impress, and they, in turn, eventually brought in all the high-level carpetbag politicians who came in to run the city after the war was over. The ever-thrifty Kate salted away $5,000 a week for the five years she ran the house.

Butler and the "Colonel" were finally run out of town due to the furor over Order 28 and rampant reports of their two-fisted graft, and the two of them were transferred back to Washington a week before Christmas, 1862.

A jeering mob saw them off at the dock and their rowboat was pelleted with rotten fruit as they were rowed out to the waiting steamer. If not for their heavy guard, their fate would have been much worse. As they passed, newly-released George Devol smiled and repeated his earlier promise, "I'll be here long after you're gone, 'Spoons'".

After their departure, General Nathaniel P. Banks, Butler's successor as commander of the Department of the Gulf, allowed everything to remain on status quo, including Kate and all the 'licensed' gamblers and they all prospered mightily minus their involuntary 'partner', the 'Colonel', who was said to have taken in two million for himself and his brother during their six and a half month sojourn in New Orleans. Only after the Southern gamblers had gleefully fleeced so many of the Union army in New Orleans that it verged on bankruptcy, were the gambling houses shut down for good in 1864.

During this period, Kate always maintained her friendship with Charlie and the Sicilians. In fact, they came to her aid when the former proprietor of her house tried to put a claim against it upon Butler's departure.

When the war ended, Kate put the money up, very quietly, of course, for Charlie and Tony Matranga to buy a saloon near Canal Street called Pizzini's. Charlie renamed it the "Stopp Inn", a sly reference to his Stoppaglieri sect in Sicily.

FIVE YEARS LATER
NEW ORLEANS
APRIL, 1867

Charlie Matranga was an up-and-coming young businessman in postwar New Orleans. He was involved in many things in the French Market, from supplying fruit to loaning money and, though only 21, Charlie was known as the man to see if there was a problem, a favor needed, or a dispute to be mediated.

Charlie was on the payroll at the Macheca family's steamship company, where Joe was now general manager. Apart from the original nucleus of Frank, Tony, and Charlie Patorno, Charlie's leadership qualities had been quickly recognized by newly-arrived Sicilians, especially the young ones, who wanted something more daring than lugging meat or working the fields.

To supply jobs for some of these followers, Charlie had branched out into running church-sponsored lotto games, rondo games, and faro banks, along with the traditional Italian card and dice games.

It had been decided that Charlie's family would wait until after the war to come over and bring Charlie's fiancé, Rita Barbato, who had waited faithfully for him. The trip was made in 1865 and Charlie and Rita were married in New Orleans. The Provenzanos had finally surfaced and had been found to be living on the other side of the river, in Barataria. Additionally, although it was more of a meeting-place than a major money-maker, Charlie and Tony operated the Stopp Inn. Thanks in large part to Kate, it had become a popular pub-crawling spot for swells out on the town.

On this particular evening, Kate had brought in two spenders and they were guzzling champagne with Kate and one of her girls at a frenetic rate. Kate had put on a few pounds from many nights spent in a similar fashion but she was still lovely as ever, Charlie thought, as he watched her from the bar, her white, even teeth bared in a captivating smile.

"That Kate's something.", Tony said. "What a guy she would have made," Charlie marveled, "coglioni like cannonballs." Kate winked up at them from behind her escort's back, and motioned with her head for Charlie to join them at the table. When he did, Kate introduced her companions.

"Charlie, this is one of my new 'associates', Abbie Reed. The tall good-lookin' fella with her is Joe Shakspeare. Joe's got a big iron foundry here in town. And this is Charles Howard, the founder here last year of the Louisiana Lottery, biggest money-makin' scheme I ever heard of. Even bigger than mine." They all laughed. As the night wore on, Charlie could see that Shakspeare was very taken with Abbie, a beautiful strawberry blonde. Shakspeare himself looked the part of a stage actor, tall and slender with black, wavy hair.

Charlie was careful to keep his distance and not spoil Kate's game with Howard, whom Charlie was well aware of. The Louisiana Lottery, which Howard founded with the backing of a Westchester County, New York, financier and the blessing of the local carpetbag administration, was off to a promising start. After its charter by the legislature in 1866, a 25-year monopoly was granted for a $40,000 annual contribution to Charity Hospital and untold bribes.

Howard had the acumen to appoint Generals Pierre Gustave Toutant de Beauregard and Jubal A. Early, Civil War heroes, as directors at $30,000 apiece per year, for two days work per month, a public relations coup.

The Lottery, which then opened a headquarters at St. Charles and Union Streets, opened 108 offices in New Orleans, some in cigar stores, but many leased to state legislators. It took in two million dollars a month and paid out $1,054,600 in 3,134 prizes of from $100 to $300,000.

Winning numbers were picked from a six-foot-long mahogany drum with a hand crank on each side. Orphans picked the winning numbers from small cylinders inside the drum. $.25 tickets could win $3,750 doubling up in equal increments until at its height, a $20 ticket could win $300,000.

Before it would finally be closed in 1907 through the passage of federal laws prohibiting interstate transportation of lottery tickets, the Louisiana Lottery would be sold nationwide and reach an annual volume of $20,000,000, by far the largest in the country.

It was late in the evening when Kate gave Howard a big kiss, and said, "Let's go back to my place. You, too, Charlie. Bring Tony. It's time to close anyway. You've never seen my new house. You can all fit in my carriage and I'll have my driver bring you home whenever you say."

"No, Kate," Charlie replied, "I'd like to, but I have things to do early in the morning." "Don't give me that", Kate said, green eyes flashing. "I never asked you before but now that I did, you aren't going to embarrass me, are you?"

Charlie saw the two men smirking; he hadn't liked either one of them on sight. He had heard much about Kate's new Basin Street mansion; it was the talk of New Orleans. "Okay, Kate, we'll come over for a little while."

The Stopp Inn was nearly empty anyway. "Close up, Tony. We're going to Kate's." Tony smiled. As the carriage pulled up at 40 Basin, Tony nudged Charlie in the ribs. "Some swell place," he whispered of the threestory marble and brownstone palace.

After they had entered, Kate had a liveried butler serve them drinks in her first-floor apartment which was entered off Common Street. Then she took Charlie and Tony by the arm and said to Abbie, Shakspeare, and Howard, "Make yourselves comfortable. I want to show my friends around."

Kate's Place: 40 Basin Street (later redesignated 121 S. Basin Street), redone in 1917. Now Tulane U. School of Social Work.

Basement Pool

Front entrance

Smoking & reading parlor

Kate in her prime

Kate after gaining some weight

The Girls

When they had left, Shakspeare said to Abbie, "She really likes those Dagoes, doesn't she?" "Well, they were smuggled into New Orleans together on the eve of Farragut's invasion," Abbie said, "so they're old friends."

Kate led the brothers into the main part of the house. Pretty girls in prim Victorian dress sat demurely in one of the parlors on damask-clad French sofas. Heavy aubusson carpet covered the floors and around it the solid black walnut floors were highly polished. The fireplaces were fronted with ornately carved white marble mantels. The walls were adorned with huge gilt-frame paintings and mirrors.

Kate ushered them into a lounge with small oak bar tended by a liveried black man. One couple sat at the bar and another was at a corner table listening to a harpist. The men had on evening wear. "That's the only way I let them in," Kate said. "Keeps the riffraff out." They sat at a table. Charlie said, "You're amazing, Kate. This is magnificent."

"I do okay," she replied, "I've got twenty girls here. My maids greet the johns at the door and they have to wait in the drawing room you saw as we passed. While there, they are expected to buy anyone in the room good wine at $15a bottle. That's if I know them. Otherwise, I interview them myself to make sure they're good enough to get in. If not, I throw them out bodily." Charlie remembered Cuba again and nodded with a smile on his face.

"Then," continued Kate, "they get the girl for $20 an hour. The girls turn five to ten tricks a day. The girls get to keep 50%, the house 50%, plus they pay me $50 a week room and board. The bribes account for about half my take but I still make $10,000 on a good week.

"You're the only two people in the world I'd admit that to, mind you." The Matrangas were impressed. "If you don't mind my asking, Kate, what did this place set you back?" Kate smiled. "One hundred thousand," Kate replied. "Not counting my own apartment, which was another forty. And that's not peanuts when carpenters only get two dollars a day."

Her pretty face was flushed from the drink and Charlie realized why it was so important that he and Tony come there. She was really proud of the elaborate whorehouse and Charlie felt good for her. "Anytime you've got something you can't handle, Kate. Remember, we're always on call," said Charlie.

Kate gave him a big hug. "I know, boys. But I can handle anything. I appreciate it, though. C'mon, I'll show you out the front door. You don't want to go back to those boring guys I'm stuck with. But business is business. I'll see you soon.."

Charles T. Howard spent the night in Kate's apartment. The huge bed was surrounded by lace mosquito netting and baskets of fresh flowers hung from the bedposts. Mammoth armoires in the room held bedclothes of the finest quality.

Silverware shone from a large oak sideboard beside a white marble fireplace. The glow of the fireplace reflected off the big, French gilt-framed mirror above it. Fine paintings lined the walls. It cost Howard three hundred bucks at $50 per hour, and at nine A.M., he was ushered politely by a liveried maid to a hearty breakfast and shown the door as Kate slept peacefully, the money stashed under the gold chamber pot beside her bed. The next morning, Charlie read in the newspapers about the shooting death of a member of the hated Reconstructionist Metropolitan Police Force. His name was Hennessy, a former wartime scout and aide to Union General Godfrey Weitzel during the war.

After "Spoons" Butler's ouster of Mayor Monroe in 1862. Weitzel had been named occupation mayor and General Algernon S. Badger had been appointed head of the newly-formed and mostly black Metropolitan Police Force. When the war ended, the three men, all northerners, decided to stay on in New Orleans, and at Weitzel's intercession, Badger named Hennessy an officer in the Metropolitans.

The previous evening, Hennessy had been drinking in a St. Ann Street bar and had gotten into an argument with Arthur Guerin, an ex-cop , and a member of the white supremacist White Magnolias. Guerin called Hennessy a nigger-lovin' son of a bitch and Hennessy drew his revolver.

Patrons ducked for cover as Guerin also drew a gun and shot Hennessy dead. Hennessy's ten-year-old son, David, who had been waiting on the outside porch of the bar, watched in horror from beneath the bar's swinging doors. The case was later declared to have been self-defense, but Guerin's face was indelibly etched into young David's mind.

General Badger, at the widow Hennessy's intercession, gave the boy a job on the Metropolitans as a messenger, and made his older cousin, Mike Hennessy, a patrolman.

****

Of the five military districts provided for in the Reconstruction Act of March 2, 1867, the fifth, covering Texas and Louisiana, came under the command of Gen. Phil Sheridan. Those who had been guilty of insurrection in the eyes of the Federal government were disenfranchised as voters while all Negroes over 21 were newly registered to vote.

The resulting electorate was two/thirds black. Upon the adoption of a new Constitution, Louisiana was re-admitted into Union on June 25, 1868. Control of the Metropolitan Police Force was switched by the legislature from General Badger to the new governor.

In 1874, the White League was organized in New Orleans. White secret societies like the Knights of the White Camelia and the White Magnolias had been around since New Orleans' occupation. The aim of the White League was the overthrow of the despised Reconstructionist government.

The White League had the support of the 1st Louisiana Infantry Regiment, State Militia. Heading Company B of the 1st was Captain Joseph P. Macheca. The Italian "Innocents", including Charlie Matranga, also supported the White League. On Sunday, September 13, a notice appeared in the newspapers, signed by 50 leading citizens, decrying the government's "trampling" on the Constitutional rights of the citizenry and calling for a mass meeting the following day at the Clay statue, on Canal Street.

A crowd of 5,000, mostly armed, and with military support from the state militia, assembled at the Henry Clay Statue at the intersection of St. Charles, Royal, and Canal Streets.

Charlie Matranga watched the scene from the window of Moody the Shirt Man, across the street at Canal and Royal. It had been arranged by wealthy members of the White League who were also members of the Boston and Pickwick clubs, New Orleans' most exclusive, that a shipment of arms would be picked up in New York City and placed aboard one of Joe Macheca's steamers, the *Mississippi,* late Saturday. Charlie's *Innocents* had been unloading them all weekend.

Reconstructionist Governor Frank Kellogg got wind of the shipment and ordered it confiscated, which triggered the impromptu call for the mass meeting; the Clay Statue had been traditionally used for such gatherings ever since the mass meeting recruiting Confederate enlistments to a chorus of the Marseillais in 1862.

Charlie watched as the citizen's Committee of Seventy appeared across the street on the porch of the Crescent Billiard Saloon at Canal and St. Charles. They introduced resolutions affirming the citizen's right to keep and bear arms, and condemning Kellogg as a usurper.

The citizens were then told to go home and arm themselves and return at 2:30 that afternoon. Meanwhile, White Leaguers were barricading the surrounding streets. White Leaguers seized City Hall and the telegraph office, stopping all outside communications. So began what came to be called the Battle of Liberty Place.

The Battle of Liberty Place

General Algernon S. Badger, a native Bostonian who had relocated after the Civil War, was now in charge of the city's mostlyblack Metropolitan Police Force. He set out from the Cabildo with a force of 500 Metropolitans. They marched down Canal Street toward the Customhouse.

Someone fired a shot and the Metropolitans opened up with artillery and a Gatling gun. White Leaguers fired from behind barricaded cotton bales. General Badger was hit four times; his horse was also hit and fell on him, causing the eventual amputation of his leg. As he lay on the ground, the leaderless Metropolitans began to flee. He drew his revolver and shot one of them.

A gutless member of a surrounding mob approached Badger with a bayoneted rifle pointed at Badger's chest. Suddenly, a stout militia officer rode up and whacked the man with the flat of his saber, quickly dismounting and standing between Badger and the mob until the Leaguers reached him. It was Captain Joe Macheca.

Joe and the others tried to carry Badger on a mattress but it wouldn't hold. Joe then ran across the street to the Chattanooga Railroad Depot and ripped a door off its hinges. Then Joe and seven others carried Badger to Charity Hospital. The irony of this rescue wouldn't become apparent to Joe Macheca for eighteen years.

The fighting had lasted less than half an hour and resulted in a total rout of the Metropolitans, most of whom threw down their arms, ripped off their uniforms, and fled. Seventeen-year-old Dave Hennessy had been left at the Customhouse and never got a chance to fire a shot. There were a dozen or more killed and four or five times that many wounded on each side. Those Metropolitans who didn't get in the Customhouse or desert, retreated to Jackson Square, hiding in the Third Precinct Station. They now numbered about two hundred.

Remarkably, no black Metropolitan was killed. At ten P.M., Joe and his B Company of Italians were granted a leave of absence for the night, to report the next morning. Joe headed for the Stopp Inn to release some of the tension. When he got there, a large party was going on, even Kate was there. She had ballooned to 300 pounds and her enormous boobs were now legendary. She let out a whoop when she saw Joe come in the door. "Captain Joe of the Horse Marines!" she cried, giving Joe a bear hug and dragging him back to her table. Then she ribaldly sang,

"I'm Captain Jinks of the Horse Marines,
I often live beyond my means, I
sport young ladies in their teens,
To cut a swell in the army.
I'm Captain Jinks of the Horse Marines,
I give my horse good corn and beans; Of
course its quite beyond my means, Tho a
Captain in the army.

My Tailor's bills came in so fast
Forc'd me one day to leave at last,
And ladies too no more did cast
Sheep's eyes at me in the army.
My Creditors at me did shout, at

me did shout, at me did shout, My
Creditors at me did shout,
"Why kick him out of the army!"'

Charlie and Charlie Patorno were at the table along with a strangelooking little man named Treville Egbert Sykes. Kate picked up Sykes and sat him on her huge knee."This is my fancy man, Joe." Sykes, a little drunk, smiled uncomfortably. Kate squeezed the breath out of him, saying, "Go on home, Syksie. I want to finish getting drunk with my old friends here. Take the carriage. I'll get a ride, okay?" It was an order.

Sykes shrugged, got up, bowed, and left. "Little twerp's from an aristocratic family here. I don't know how I got tied up with him. He couldn't protect a flea. 'Must be something I like about him, though. He's been hangin' around me since we got here. Wants to move in but I won't let him. He annoys me so much I'd probably kill him if he lived with me. No backbone. Won't stand up for himself. Ah, fuck him. How was the battle, Joey?"
.

Joe shrugged. "Short is the best way to describe it. By the way, I saved old Badger's life. Some trash wanted to kill him." "Ah, he's not the worst guy there is. Funny thing is that the worst ones are my best customers." Kate laughed, "There's always room for you, though, Joey dear. Remember our night of passion?" Joe's face was reddening. "I haven't seen much of you since you got married, Joey dear," she continued. Joe remembered the beautiful girl he had made love to and spent the night of the invasion with and looked at the grotesque bloated painted face before him. *Mother of God!,* he thought, and depression fell over him.

Kate read it right away. Ignoring it, she turned to the two Charlies. "Well, what do you think? Are we going to be better off or worse off?"

Charlie Matranga shrugged. "Kate, one's the same as the other to me. We organized the *Innocents* because we've got to live with these people. But remember nobody confiscated any off our property because we weren't Confederates. Nobody killed or maimed our sons. We don't have the same motives as these Orleanians, but I understand that and sympathize with them. If it had been my land and my family,

"I would feel the same way. As it is, the carpetbag government and the Negro legislators can be dealt with as easy as the others, so businesswise it doesn't matter who rules. Let's face it, to Northerners or Southerners, we're just 'Dagoes'. I know that and I treat them accordingly; as long as nobody bothers our family or friends." Charlie Patorno nodded in agreement.

Charlie continued, "It's been a big day, Kate, and Charlie and I still have some unfinished business to attend to, so we're gonna have to leave you. Have fun. And when Joe leaves, I'm gonna have Tony take you home, okay?" Kate blinked her bleary eyes innocently.

"Whatever you say, boss. You're the only four chaps in this town that I respect." When she had blinked her eyes, a vision of the night in Cuba with Captain Semmes flashed through Charlie's brain. And he was sad for her.

He and Charlie Patorno kissed Joe on both cheeks and he said softly, "I know how much you love America, Peppino, and I admire you for it. You did a great thing today and you can be proud." With that, the two Charlies left. Kate put a beefy arm around Joe's neck. At her insistence, they had three or four more drinks.

"Kate. I got to get out of here soon. I have to report early in the morning." Tears formed in Kate's heavily-mascaraed green eyes. "Don't want to stay with a fat old whore, is that it, Macheca? Well, don't feel bad. I'm getting what I deserve. Do you know that I left twin infant sons in Liverpool to come here?"

The sad face was distorted with grief and rage. "That's right. They're eighteen years old now. I have never seen them since they were a couple of months old and never will. I can't bring them to this kip, can I now? And I'm too grotesque-looking to go to England. They have a picture of me when I was young and beautiful and that's all they're ever going to have. But I've set up trusts for their education. They're in Oxford right now."

Joe stroked her hand and said softly, "I never knew, Kate. But you should see them anyway. They'd still love you. You're their mother."

Kate took a belt of her drink and tears came to her eyes again. "No. It would never work. I'd have to leave them and come back here and they'd never understand. And leaving them after I saw them would kill me…Oh, what am I telling you all this for? I'd rather go to Sykes' house and beat him half to death." She got up and called for Tony to take her home.

The following day, President Grant gave the citizens involved in the rising five days to disarm, return government property, and give up political office. Actually, it didn't take that long. Federal troops arrived on Saturday and reinstalled Kellogg as governor. However, Thomas Boylan had been installed by the insurrectionists as chief of police.

Since General Badger was hospitalized and would eventually lose his leg as a result of the horse falling on him, and since the Metropolitans were completely discredited, Boylan was permitted to retain his post.

On Monday morning, the 21st, Officer David Hennessy reported to Boylan's office to file a complaint that he had seen one of the Leaguers who had shot General Badger and could identify him. The name he gave was Arthur Guerin, the man who had shot his father to death seven years prior. Guerin was arrested and appeared in the Civil Court building to answer the charges. David Hennessy didn't appear and Guerin was released.

As Guerin descended the courthouse stairway, Hennessy was passing in the other direction. Hennessy looked up at him and said, "This is from Dave Hennessy, father and son," and put a bullet in Guerin's heart. Hennessey kept walking as Guerin tumbled down the stairs. Hennessy was never arrested but the seventeen-year-old's reputation was established.

He was immediately appointed special officer with the pay of patrolman on the demoralized Metropolitans. The following year, Badger disbanded the Metropolitans except for two men: Boylan and Hennessy, with Boylan as Badger's successor, and Hennessy as an eighteen-year-old detective on the new Nicholls Police Force.

In November, 1876, after some back-room maneuvering, presidential candidate Rutherford B. Hayes, secured the electoral votes of three southern states, including Louisiana, handing him the election over Samuel T. Tilden, who had had a 300,000 lead in the popular vote. In repayment of the gift, Old Rutherfraud, on April 21st, recognized the government of White League candidate and Confederate hero Frank T. Nicholls over Republican Yankee Marshall Packard. On the 24th, Hayes withdrew federal troops. Reconstruction was over.

****

TUESDAY, NOVEMBER 2, 1943
NEW ORLEANS ELKS CLUB
121 S. BASIN STREET (ELKS PLACE)

Bewf and Dr. Matranga had met for the last five days straight, including the weekend, except for the morning of the 29th, the day of Charlie Matranga's funeral. Bewf was amazed at the amount of information the doctor had provided, both from a diary he kept since a boy, documents, news reports, and his own personal knowledge.

Today the doctor faced him amiably. "I hope I haven't been exhaustingly detailed in what I've provided you, Mr. Alley, but I think it's important that you are fully briefed on the background in order that you understand what ultimately led to the later outrage." "No, doctor, I'm a detail man myself. Good to know the facts even if you don't use them all. Keeps you on the right track." The doctor smiled graciously.

"Thank you, sir. I'm glad we see things alike. Well, as you might recall, when my father went after Provenzano in Sicily, a young boy was sent with him, Giuseppe Esposito. This boy didn't have to leave the country but instead joined up with a ferocious hill bandit named Antonino Leone, Il Leone, as he was known.

"Giuseppe first ran errands but over the next 15 years, he became Leone's right hand. One of their specialties was kidnapping and they kidnapped a young Englishman named John Forester Rose, a clergyman whose family owned sulfur mines in Sicily. Supposedly it was triggered by

Rose deflowering a young girl, the mine manager's daughter. He in turn asked Leone's help.

"Whether this is true or not I do not know. But Leone and Esposito definitely kidnapped Rose. When the family balked at paying ransom, Leone and Esposito sent more ransom notes accompanied by body parts: the ears, one at a time, and then the tip of his nose. This barbarity set off an international incident.

"The British Prime Minister Benjamin Disraeli threatened to send troops to invade Sicily if the carabinieri didn't act decisively. Both men were caught but Esposito escaped and was able, with help, to ship out of Marseilles, France for New York. He ultimately came here and out of loyalty, my father helped him get settled. Here is his story in this country as I know it…"

CHAPTER TWO
ESPOSITO'S END

NEW ORLEANS RAILROAD STATION
APRIL, 1879

Vincenzo Randazzo, formerly Giuseppe Esposito, disembarked the monstrous black and red steam engined train from Memphis, hazel eyes scanning the platform. With him were two other Sicilian fugitives who had accompanied him from Sicily, Pietro Natale and Charles Poitza. Charlie Matranga, resplendent in white suit, high collar shirt and tie, and spats, approached. With him was three-year-old Carlo, Jr.. As Esposito neared, Matranga opened both arms; they kissed on both cheeks. "Greetings, ah, Vincenzo. Come to my house. There are friends of ours waiting to meet you." Esposito introduced Natale and Poitza.

Once settled on the porch of the comfortable Matrnaga house on the shore of Lake Ponchartrain, Esposito gave Charlie a rundown of the Rose affair and his journey over. "Even the newspapers here made it a big thing, this Rose kidnapping.

"Over here, it hardens the prejudice against us. But the best thing we've got going is that the plantations and docks need labor. And they love the Italian labor because they know Italians are good, reliable workers. And the workers listen to men of their own breed, not some Anglo *chadrool....Ah, ecco l'amico nostri, Signore Macheca/!"*

A carriage pulled up to the porte cochére drawn by a fine black horse. A heavy-set man in his forties alighted. He had a straw skimmer, bow tie, and a heavy gold watch fob across his vest. As he approached their chairs, he stopped to remove his hat and wipe the perspiration from his brow with an immaculate white linen handkerchief. He then shook Esposito's hand warmly.

"Signore Randazzo," he said knowingly, *"mi piace conoscerlo."* Turning to Charlie, he said, *"Don Carlo, bon jornu."* "Bon jornu, Mr. Joe.. Sit down, my friend." Macheca flopped into a big wicker porch chair. Soon they all walked down to a garden picnic table. Charlie's brother Tony arrived and joined them along with five more trusted Sicilians, John and James Caruso, Salvatore Sinceri, Charlie Patorno, and Rocco Geraci.

Rita Matranga supervised the service of a sumptuous dinner of antipasto, fresh fruit, lobster Savannah, and fettucine was served along with a few bottles of white Sicilian wine. Introductions were made all around and eventually Esposito/Randazzo's companions were given transportation to a hotel in town by some of the other guests.

The five men remaining, Charlie, Tony, Joe, Charlic Patorno, and Randazzo, sat on the porch until well after midnight in friendly conversation reminiscing on the ways of the old world and the complexities of the new.

Poydras (French) Market c. 1890

In the months to follow, Vincenzo Randazzo's fortunes improved considerably. He was a frequent visitor to Joe Macheca's Louisiana Steamship Lines and, along with Charlie Matranga, who wisely preferred to remain in the shadows, was proceeding to tie up all the business connected with the Italian immigrants who now composed ten percent of New Orleans' population.

They had a good piece of the Poydras "French" Market with its fruit, produce, meat, fish, and flowers. They branched out into "sweat shops" producing cheap clothing. Randazzo bought a lugger, a small boat used in the transportation of produce and oysters. He named it "Il Leone" for his old boss. He set up business on Customhouse, between Burgundy and Rampart Streets on the Lower Coast.

The three friends were seated in the office of Joe's steamship line one day discussing prospects for the future. Joe Macheca leaned back expansively in his red leather desk chair, his vest buttons straining against his girth. He clipped the end off a Havana cigar and flicked it into a gleaming brass cuspidor.

"You know, Charlie, the legitimate profit alone here is phenomenal, New Orleans brings more cargo down the Mississippi bound for the international market than any port in the country. We're second in volume only to New York City."

Charlie looked back at him, "What are you trying to say, Joe? That we should go legit," he asked, with a crooked smile. "What do you say, Vincenzo?" Randazzo smiled. "Just give me all the swag that we pilfer and all that we smuggle, and the shylocking."

"You're both right," said Charlie, "but the real strength, mark my words, is going to be in controlling the labor force. We'll set up unions whose power will be unbreakable. Then nothing will move in or out of here that we don't want. We'll have a monopoly, my friends, a monopoly."

****

Joe Macheca was named 1879's Man of the Year at New Orleans' leading *sujita* or *fratellanza.* That was the evening Randazzo met Felicia Datillo, a 22-year-old Sicilian widow with two young children. Her father had started out as a farm laborer, went on to buy his own farm, and had become a well-to-do member of the Sicilian community. Her father was also a friend of Joe Macheca, who happily played Cupid for Randazzo and Felicia.

By the end of the year, Randazzo was keeping steady company with Felicia.In January, 1880, Randazzo sat in Charlie Matranga's house before a blazing hearth.

"Carlo, I have some serious business to discuss," said Randazzo. "Nothing can be so urgent that we can't make some small talk first, my friend. How's Felicia?" "That's what this is about, Carlo. And I want to resolve it before Joe gets here", Vincenzo said animatedly. Charlie looked back quizzically. "Go on then, Vincenzo, if it's that important."

"It's Felicia. She's pregnant." Charlie smiled knowingly. "Her old man's gonna shoota you' balls off if you don't do the right thing," "That's no problem, Don Carlo. I'm nuts about her. But in Sicily, I've got a wife and two kids." Charlie thought for a few seconds. "You think you'll ever go back, Vincenzo?"

"Not in a thousand years, Carlo. The only thing there is my kids. I kidnapped my wife when I was seventeen and made her pregnant to get back at her family for doing the same thing to my first cousin. There was never any real feeling between us. And there is no way I'd ever be able to go back anyway."

"And have you ever thought about bringing your wife and kids over here?" "My wife would never leave Sicily, Carlo. She's from a big family and she loves it there. It's all she knows. Her family hates me anyway; they wouldn't let her leave even if she wanted to. And the kids: they're all girls. What could I do with them? They'd be lost without their mother."

"You have put it exactly as it is, Vincenzo. Sicily for you was another life. It's over. You have a new name and you must start a new life here just as if nothing existed before New Orleans. So if you are asking my advice, Vincenzo, I would tell you that there is no reason why Vincenzo Randazzo should not marry Felicia Datillo." *"Grazie, Don Carlo.* That's the way I see it, too.

"When Joe gets here I am going to ask him to stand for us at our wedding. Felicia's father would expect that. Your connection with me is more private and more close. So I ask you to be my *compare,* godfather to our child." "I would be honored, Vincenzo."

Joe Macheca was entering the driveway. When he came in they omitted all of the conversation except that Vincenzo and Felicia were to marry and would he honor them by standing up for them? Joe was gratified by the invitation. "It will be my extreme pleasure, Vincenzo. We'll show these greaseballs the best damned wedding they'll ever go to!"

MACHECA FARM
METAIRIE, LOUISIANA
FEBRUARY, 1880

Carriages lined the white post-and-railed driveway of Joe Macheca's comfortable antebellum estate. Inside, members of the Louisiana political structure rubbed elbows at the huge Italian crystal punchbowl with prominent members of the Sicilian community.

Friend and foe alike had received invitations to the wedding of the man who was said to be Joe Macheca's protegé , Vincenzo Randazzo, and his pretty bride, Felicia Datillo. Charlie sat at Randazzo's right at the long table at the head of the ballroom with Joe Macheca at his left, each fittingly bedecked in evening dress with a bottle of vintage port between them.

Joe looked approvingly at Vincenzo's uncomfortable countenance as his dickey threatened to burst from the muscular, knotted neck it contained, causing the hazel eyes to appear pained. "Don't let the monkey suit get to you, cumpari," said Joe. "You're an established member of the community now and everyone will recognize you as such."

A quizzical look was back on Charlie's face as he surveyed the crowd and settled on two faces at the punchbowl. He softly elbowed Joe. "There are some strange birds mating tonight," he said, "look at that little sewer rat Provenzano palling up to the smart-ass detective Hennessy." Joe smiled and shrugged, "You said to invite him so we could see what he was up to and not let him know our true feelings."

"I know, I know," Charlie answered. Provenzano, Miceli's old nemesis from Sicily, was now an aging streetwise Mafioso who led a group in competition with Charlie and Joe.

Up until that day, Provenzano had only had a nodding acquaintance with Hennessy. Signora Felicia Datillo stopped at the head table and bent down and kissed her new husband. Joe Macheca beamed. At the punchbowl, Provenzano assessed Hennessy as the band played a lively tarantella. The wily old Sicilian was careful to appear humbly deferential to the egotistical Hennessy. He decided to break the ice. He had felt for a while now that this Hennessy could be manipulated to his advantage. He had kept up on any news from Sicily and he had a strong suspicion about the newcomer, Randazzo.

"Ah, Signore Hennessy. How are you? Lovely wedding. Mr. Joe seems to think the world of this, what's his name, Randazzo." "Come on, Provenzano. I've seen you at a couple of meetings with Matranga and Randazzo. And now you don't remember his name?"

Provenzano flashed him an oily smile. "Not that name I don't." "What are you trying to tell me, Joe?" "It is not my place to tell you anything, Signore Hennessy. You're a good detective." "So I should start checking on your competition, is that it?"

Provenzano shrugged exaggeratedly. "That's a lot of work, Joe," Hennessy smiled, "It would mean a lot of overtime without pay. We police don't have a union. And don't tell me you'll be happy to organize one for us. I've seen some of your labor consulting work." Hennessy gave a lop-sided smile, blue eyes twinkling beneath his brilliantined curly black hair.

"I'm sure we could reach an accomodation regarding your compensation, signore," Provenzano said, sure now that he had been right about this pompous young upstart. "You don't like competition, do you, Joe?" "In Sicily we have a saying, 'He who plays alone can't lose'," Provenzano replied, holding up his punch glass. "Salute, signore," the two men grinned at each other and clinked their glasses together.

OFFICE OF CHIEF OF POLICE TOM BOYLAN
NEXT MORNING

Dave Hennessy and his cousin, Mike, arrived at the Chief's office bright and early. Dave faced his boss, "Chief, I think I'm on to something big. One of my informants gave me information that a Matranga man is very likely a wanted fugitive from Sicily." "What's his name?" Boylan inquired.

"The name he uses here is Vincenzo Randazzo, but we have good reason to believe that's not his right name." "You got a file on him?"

"Yeah, Chief. He's got a produce store near Burgundy and Customhouse. Lives over top. He hangs around Raphael's saloon up the corner from his store, often in the company of two unidentified Sicilians.

"Mike and I would like to watch him and hopefully have a sketch drawn of him to send back to the Italian authorities." Boylan pondered a moment and said, "Not now. It's too cold and you've got other work to do. Within the next couple of months, try to rent a room across from the produce store. Then when the weather warms up, if you're not busy on some real work, we'll give it a go."

By April, the room was secured and the following month a fulltime watch was set up on the produce store with Dave, Mike, and two relief men. As the summer passed, it became apparent that Randazzo was in the daily habit of going up to Raphael's saloon and later, of sitting outside his store at a table.

On the way down Customhouse towards Randazzo's store, they saw an artist displaying his wares on the sidewalk. Dave stopped him and asked, "Hey, you, how would you like a job sketching somebody for us?' The artist eyed them warily. "My specialty is landscapes. For portraits you want Carl Hoeppner, he's the best around."

"All right. Give him this address and ask him to stop up and see me. Tell him to make it on a nice day in the early afternoon."

Two days later, Dave Hennessy was spelling Mike at the window of a front room on the second floor of a building across the street from Randazzo's store, when there was a knock on the door. Hennessy answered. A thin, intense German looked back at him. "I'm Carl Hoeppner. You had some work for me?"

Hoeppner wore spectacles and had a wisp of blonde hair in the center of his otherwise bald head. In his delicate hands, he carried a folded easel and the other tools of his art. Dave Hennessy appraised him and, satisfied, replied, "Indeed I do, Carl, if you're as good as they say you are. Come over to the window. You see that short, stocky fellow sitting outside the produce store? I need a good sketch of him. Do you think you can handle that?"

Hoeppner looked puzzled. "From here?" Hennessy nodded. "Police business, Carl. Not to worry. You'll be well paid." "I suppose so. When do you need it?" Hennessy smiled at him. "How about right now, Carl, if you have the equipment to do it? "

Hoeppner moved to the window and sat at his easel. Randazzo was telling Poitza and Natale a Sicilian parable that he had learned from Il Leone. "There are many fishermen at sea and there is only one way a fish can swim through all those fish hooks without getting snared. What is it?" He looked at Poitza who smiled and shrugged, then at Natali who shook his head. "Keep his mouth shut!" Randazzo replied. All three enjoyed a raucous laugh.

Hoeppner studied him a few minutes, then sat down at his easel. In an hour, he handed Hennessy a finished sketch. Hennessy studied it. "Great, Carl. You meet me at police headquarters and you'll be well-rewarded. Come tomorrow morning at nine o'clock. One more thing, Carl. This is strictly secret. What you did here today is not to be repeated to anyone. Understand?"

He looked at the trembling Hoeppner and knew he didn't have to worry. Across the street, Randazzo's wife was playfully cuffing him on the ears to come in and work on the produce as he put his hands over his head in mock terror and his two friends roared in laughter.

ROME, ITALY
POLICE HEADQUARTERS
AUGUST, 1880

The sketch that arrived had a written description of Randazzo, along with a written inquiry as to whether he was a fugitive from Sicily. It had been delivered by Chief Boylan personally to the Italian Consulate in New

Orleans marked confidential. Then it was forwarded to the Italian Embassy in New York from where it traveled in a diplomatic pouch.

The two detectives to whom it was assigned, looked at each other and then back to the sketch. Then both raced for the file on Giuseppe Esposito, which contained a four-year-old sketch by one of Il Leone's kidnapping victims. The two sketches were identical. The older detective said to the younger one, "Get Marshal Candelorio in here immediately."

That week, a reply was sent through diplomatic channels and marked "Confidential" to Chief Boylan of the New Orleans police. *"Thank you for your recent comminiqué. The man, Vincenzo Randazzo, is indeed Giuseppe Esposito, the most wanted man in Sicily. There is a reward for his capture. We would ask that you have him watched closely until his extradition can be officially arranged. I shall personally bring the warrant to your country. Michele Candelorio, Marshal, Polizia Italiano."*

Prior to his marriage, Vincenzo Randazzo had taken a small flat on Chartres Street, between St. Philip and Dumaine, adjacent to Decatur Street's "Vendetta Alley." Later, he moved above the produce store just off the corner of Burgundy and Customhouse Streets.

It was there, in September, 1880, that Felicia gave birth to their son, christened Giuseppe after Joe Macheca, but also after his own father. At his baptism, Charlie Matranga stood as godfather. A small gathering was held afterwards, at the Randazzo flat and Joe Macheca proudly made an announcement.

"This is no place for such a wonderful boy to grow up. I've cut off two acres at the top of my driveway in Metairie. Here is the deed. Build yourselves a fine house there." Felicia kissed the stout man on his moustache and Vincenzo hugged him. "It was a lucky wind that blew me to this place and to friends like you and Charlie. Felicia, baby Giuseppe, and I are all forever in your debt, Mr. Joe. We will live out the rest of our lives there."

Christmas Eve found Dave and Mike Hennessy in their surveillance room across from the produce store, watching through the window as

Randazzo smilingly helped his customers select some fine produce for the holiday meal. "Look at the murderin' little Dago, thinks he's the Italian ambassador. Yesterday, he half-killed one of Provenzano's men for trying to work one of Matranga's jobs. Today, he's Santa Claus," Dave said drily.

"And now he's got a bunch of his goombahs working building him a big house out in Metairie next to Macheca, while we sit up here freezin' our arses off." "When is that extradition going to come through?" asked Mike. "It will come, Michael. Rest assured of that."

Dave reached inside his oevercoat pocket and found a flask next to the envelope he had received from Provenzano that morning. It contained $500. He withdrew the flask. "Merry Christmas, Michael," intoned Dave Hennessy and they passed the flask back and forth as they continued to watch the produce store.

INDEPENDENCE DAY PARADE
BOURBON STREET
JULY 4, 1881

Dave and Mike Hennessy stood among the crowd in shirtsleeves watching the festive parade celebrating the 105th anniversary of the nation's independence. Directly across the street, equally intent on the festivities, were the Matranga, Macheca, and Randazzo families: young Carlo and Dolores, Marco and Dominic, and little Giuseppe watched in rapt attention as the Marine band marched by in step to a stirring march, their horns gleaming in the midday sun.

Three days earlier, three men had presented themselves to the Italian Consulate in New Orleans, flashing credentials. The latin-looking one of the three, a handsome, athletic man of thirty-five with a strong, determined chin, announced, "Signore Consul, I am Marshal Michele Candelorio of the Polizia Italiano.

"These are detectives James Mooney and Donald Boland of the New York City Police Department, specially deputized by our Ambassador with the concurrence of the Department of State, to assist me in the extradition back to Italy of Giuseppe Esposito, a resident of this city." The consul responded, "May I see your warrants, Signore Marshal?" "Of course," replied Candelorio.

Within an hour, they were at the office of Chief Boylan. "Yes, Marshal. I'm the fellow who sent you the original communiqué on Esposito, but the original tip and all the surveillance afterward was done by two of my men, Mike and Dave Hennessy. I'll bring them in here." Seeing the 23-year-old Dave and 25-year-old Mike, Mooney and Boland, two hardened New York cops in their early forties, exchanged a pained wince. "Watch these two nickel rockets blow it," whispered Mooney. The Hennessys, for their part, remembering the promised reward, wanted to make sure that it remained *their* case, and convinced Candelorio to leave the New Yorkers at their hotel during the Independence Day Parade, assuring him that the appearance of two strangers, who had "cop" written all over their weather-beaten faces, might spook the Sicilians, whereas the appearance of one more Italian, Candelorio, in this neighborhood, would go unnoticed.

Candelorio stood slightly behind and to the side of Dave Hennessy at the parade. He took a step forward and whispered in Hennessy's ear, "There is no doubt about it, Signore Hennessy. That man is Giuseppe Esposito, wanted in Italy for eighteen murders, one hundred extortions, and the kidnap/mutilation of John Forester Rose."

"Well, Signore Marshal, if you say so, I'll arrest him, but I hope you're sure because his goombahs are going to raise bloody Hell if you're wrong." "I am here unofficially, Signore, until he is turned over to me by your courts. But there is no mistake. I interviewed him as a prisoner personally."

The morning following the parade, July 5th, 1881, dawned on what appeared to be a glorious day. Vincenzo Randazzo made love to Felicia, after which she happily cooked him a big breakfast. It would be his last ever as a free man.

He picked up ten-month-old Giuseppe, and raised him high in the air, kissing him as he lowered him and handed him to Felicia, whom he kissed in turn. In shirtsleeves on the warm Summer morning, Randazzo started out the door. "I'm going to take a walk along the river, Cara. I'll be back by lunchtime."

Randazzo walked down St. Philip Street to the riverfront, then strolled the bank of the "Mighty Mississippi" to the foot of Canal Street, where he ran into an acquaintance from the Poydras Market nearby. As they chatted, the four men fifty yards behind slowed their stroll.

Eventually, Randazzo turned back in the direction from which he had come and started to head for home. The four men stopped and the New Yorkers shielded the Hennessys with their backs to avoid recognition as Randazzo passed. Randazzo decided to take a short cut through Jackson Square and get back to Felicia as quickly as possible. He wanted to bed her one more time before the day got too hot. He could see the Gothic lines of St. Louis Cathedral looming up across from the Riverside Gate of Jackson Square. He turned in toward the gate just as the four men closed in on him with weapons drawn.

"I'm James Mooney and this is Don Boland, New York City detectives deputized by the Italian government to arrest you on charges of murder, Esposito. These are detectives Mike and Dave Hennessy, New Orleans Police Department. Don't try anything or you're dead."

Randazzo's eyes warily sized up the seriousness of the threat presented. In animated broken-English, he answered, "Try anything? My name is Vincenzo Randazzo and all you're going to get out of persecuting Italian-Americans is a lawsuit. How much is Provenzano paying you?"

Dave Hennessy lunged forward and brought down the barrel of his revolver across Randazzo's temple, opening a nasty gash. "We don't need to be offered any money to eliminate scum like you, Esposito." Randazzo crumpled to the ground and Hennessy prepared to strike him again. Mooney grabbed him.

"Hey, kid. This guy's our prisoner. You remember that. If we're going to get blamed for his condition when we deliver him to New York, then we'll have the fun of working him over. Not you!" They cuffed Randazzo's hands behind his back and dragged him across the Square to the police station.

On the way over, Mooney said, "He struck a nerve there, huh? Who is this guy Provenzano and how much *is* he paying you?" Boland snickered. Hennessy made a move toward Moody but Mike Hennessy grabbed him. Mooney just laughed. Inside the station, the sergeant began to book Randazzo.

"That won't be necessary, sergeant, we're holding this guy incommunicado for a while until his transportation can be arranged, so his friends don't try to break him out. Put him in a single cell. I don't want him talking to anybody". "I've got just the spot for him," said the sergeant.

The following morning, July 6th, Felicia Randazzo was at Louisiana Steamship Lines, with Joe Macheca and Charlie Matranga, who had been hurriedly summoned. "My Vincenzo has done nothing wrong to anyone. Why was he not come home last night? He don't fool with no other women. What has happened to him? Please, Mr. Joe and Mr. Charlie, you've got to tell me."

They stared at each other blankly, which caused Felicia to wail. Her baby and two young children became frightened; they began to cry as well.

Joe Macheca came around from behind his desk and stroked her hair. "Felicia, I'm sure it's nothing. Let me and Charlie talk for a minute. It'll be all right." Her children following, she was led out the door. As Joe closed the door behind her, he smiled and winked at Charlie. "That old dog! He must be shacked up somewhere down on Bourbon Street. Didn't he used to see a girl down there?"

Charlie looked back seriously. "That was before he met Felicia. I don't think so, Peppino. Something stinks here and it smells like Provenzano." "If he's hurt Vincenzo, he will roast like the pig he is." "Let me look into it. Get ahold of Charlie Patorno and have him set up a meeting between me and Joe Provenzano for tomorrow. Meanwhile, you try to pacify Felicia. I'm going out the other way."

BAGHERIA COFFEE HOUSE
JULY 7, 1881

Charlie entered the small dark room and approached one of the little round tables near the window. "Don Giuseppe," he said,taking a seat. "Always a pleasure, Charlie," Provenzano replied carnivorously. Matranga was serious. "Look, Joe. We have our differences, but we don't let these 'Mericani run all over us."

Provenzano stared back in seeming non-comprehension. Charlie continued, "In case you haven't heard already, Joe. Vincenzo Randazzo hasn't been home in two days. I did some checking yesterday and my people tell me he's being held at the Jackson Square police station incommunicado by your new pal, Hennessy, and some cops from New York. If they get away with Randazzo, it'll be open season on all of us."

"You think so?" asked Provenzano, fingering his spoon. "Personally, I'm not worried about it. I made it my business to become a citizen and so are most of my men.I wasn't going to get involved in this, but seeing as how you asked. Yes, I did hear about it, and I also heard that Randazzo accused Hennessy of working for me. That's only one step from saying that I informed on him. And then I'm supposed to help him?"

"Joe. Of course no one thinks that you had anything to do with Vincenzo's arrest. It's just that the people who told me know that Hennessy's on your pad and they thought it was a shakedown." "Of who? You, Charlie? I don't need to shake anybody down, my old friend. I've probably got more money than you have. This is something Hennessy got into entirely on his own. I knew nothing about it until after it happened and then it was too late."

He looked at Charlie with a hint of mockery and said, "I would, of course, like to help my *paesano* , Charlie. After all, Piana dei Greci and Bagheria are so close to each other. We are probably cousins, no?" Charlie clenched his jaw as hard as he could before replying, "What do you suggest, Joe?" personally satisfied now that it was, indeed, Provenzano who orchestrated the whole thing.

Provenzano looked wounded. "Suggest? Who am I to suggest when a man's freedom is concerned? However, Hennessy obviously has a hard on for the guy."

"What can be done about him?" "All I could tell you is that I get along with the guy because I pay him. Not directly…but he knows it comes from me. I have never personally handed him any money and I still won't even on something as important as this. That is one condition that must be known. But with him, it's more than just money. He gets his rocks off by thinking he's important enough to deserve tribute from what he considers lowlife Dagoes like us."

Charlie spit on the floor. "That don't solve the problem, Charlie. He's a cop. He can cause trouble. So we gotta try to live with him." "Tell him Joe Macheca will give him $50,000 if he proves that Randazzo isn't Esposito at the hearing. Tell him we will also help him get appointed Chief of Police. "Chief Boylan is retiring real soon." "Me tell him? Why don't you tell him?" "I thought you were his friend." "Yeah, Charlie. But like I told you, we don't talk no business directly. You'll have to go through his bag man, Attilio Abruzzi. And that's going to coast you ten percent whether Hennessy accepts or not. Another 5 G's."

"Is there any chance he'd try to set me up for bribery?" "Not if he knows it's through me. He's already on my pad, ain't he?" "Ok. Where do you want the money?" "I'll be here tomorrow. Same time."

ABBIE REED'S RED LIGHT CLUB
257 DELORD STREET, NEW ORLEANS
JULY 9, 1881

Joe Provenzano entered the gilt façade of the famous bawdy house and saloon, the brownstone mansion containing it had been a gift from the politician/racketeer Joseph Shakspeare to his main squeeze, strawberry blonde Abbie Reed, former inmate of Kate's house and currently the town's most celebrated madame.

Abbie greeted Provenzano at the door in a low-cut red velvet gown, luxurious hair piled atop her head. "Mr. Provemzano, nice to see you so early in the day. Dave is waiting in a private booth. I thought you'd like it better that way." Provenzano was led to a semicircular chesterfield booth also done in red velvet. Abbie pulled back the beaded curtain and a pretty whore slid out from next to Hennessy on Abbie's signal.

"Well, Mr. Joe. What's interesting today? Have a drink and we'll order some lunch." Provenzano slid into the booth facing Hennessy and ordered a glass of chianti. He looked at Hennessy impishly." Our dear friends, Joe and Charlie, want to offer you a bribe."

Hennessy hooked his thumbs in his vest, revealing his shoulder holster, and asked expansively, "How much?" "Five thousand." "Five times five thousand, maybe." "Dave, you couldn't take it if it was $50,000. They'd own you. And everyone in New Orleans would know it. I told 'em you weren't interested." "You did?" Hennessy said dejectedly. "Don't worry, my friend. We got a taste. I told 'em you had to be approached by a bag man who had to get two grand, win or lose. So we'll cut up a thousand apiece," Provenzano purred, "and you can buy lunch."

Hennessy laughed as Provenzano passed him the thousand under the table. "With pleasure, you old fox." Provenzano acquiesced to the praise, then got serious. "Now, Dave, remember to have those reporters at the pier tomorrow when Esposito's ship leaves for New York. This should make you a national hero."

"It's all taken care of, Mr. Joe, all taken care of," said Dave Hennessy. "and Tom Boylan has arranged for me and Mike to accompany him to New York, too."

MISSISSIPPI RIVERFRONT
FOOT OF CANAL STREET
JULY 10, 1881, 6:00 A.M.

Giuseppe Esposito stood, shackled hand and foot, between Dave and Mike Hennessy, in the early dawn. A reporter asked Dave, "What led you to identify this man as the famous Sicilian bandit, Detective?" Hennessy yanked Esposito around to face a photographer, "Hard-nosed police work," he said. Mooney looked at Boland and rolled his eyes.

Two reporters from the New Orleans Picayune and the Republican turned and ran toward some approaching figures, "Here she comes!" one of them called back.

Joe Macheca was hustling Felicia Randazzo through the clutter of journalists, police, and dock workers agape at the proceedings. With little Giuseppe in her arms, one daughter by the hand, and the other tugging along at her skirt, she spotted Esposito and let out a soul-piercing wail,

"Vincenzo!! Vincenzo!! Cara mia, merciful Mother of God, what are they doing to you?!!! Oh, someone help us. Someone please help my poor Vincenzo!" Esposito bit his lip at the sight of her, and the hazel eyes filled with tears. As Felicia approached, he made a move toward her, but was restrained by the manacles. He lowered his head. Joe Macheca walked up to the detectives. "Have you no compassion? Can't you see what this poor woman's going through? Let them have their farewell, for God's sake." Hennessy tightened his grip on Esposito's arm. "Fuck you, Macheca,"he started to say. Mooney sidled up beside him.

"Listen, kid, and remember this. This guy's *our* prisoner. You wanna get us writ up in the press as heartless flatfoots? Now take the irons off him for a minute or two and let him hug his wife, and don't embarrass yourself by giving me any lip or I'll do it myself. If he makes a move for the water, I'll plug him and save everybody a lot of time and trouble."

Hennessy began unlocking the shackles. Felicia jumped into Esposito's embrace and they clung to each other desperately. "This terrible mistake will be corrected once I get to New York, mi vita, Mr. Paul will help us. Joe and Charlie will contact him for me," ("Paul Kelly" was the pseudonym of Paolo Vacarelli, a Sicilian New York mobster connected with the Whyos, a New York Irish gang). "I shall see you and the children soon, my love. I must go now." He thrust her back to the waiting arms of Joe Macheca, who tried to speak.

"Nothing from you, Dago," said Mike Hennessy, "you won't be giving this guy any signals; his goose is cooked." Dave began to relock the shackles. "No!!" cried Felicia in English, "no take-a my husband!! No!!" The sound of her wailing accompanied the skiff into the fog as it pulled out into the harbor toward the New York bound steamer which awaited them.

The America of 1881 was becoming an increasingly violent place to live. In the South, there were a hundred lynchings in a steadily increasing spiral. President Garfield is shot while boarding a train in D.C. and would only survive ten weeks. During Esposito's voyage to New York, Pat Garrett would shoot down Billy the Kid. In three months, Wyatt, Virgil, and Morgan Earp, and John "Doc" Holliday would meet the Clanton brothers at the O.K. Corral in Tombstone, Arizona, leaving three of them dead.

Giuseppe Esposito was shackled to the floor, manacled hand and foot between two double-decker bunks, which held the detectives. Mooney and Boland sat one one of the bunks, cups of rum in their hands. "Hey, Esposito, that's a pretty nice wife you got there," taunted Mooney, "think she'll wait?" Esposito's eyes flashed green-and brown hate. *"No spika de English, Signore. Mi chiamo e Vincenzo Randazzo."* "You could speak well enough the other day, wop, Now don't aggravate me." Esposito stared back defiantly.

Across the stateroom, Dave and Mike Hennessy snickered at Mooney.Dave said, "You don't have the touch, Mooney. He'll only talk to me. Right, Joe?" Esposito eyed him sullenly. A young Italian under-steward entered with more drinks. Mooney said, "Hey, wait a minute. I want you to translate something." He walked over to Esposito and, with Boland's help, dragged Esposito to his feet. "C'mon, Joe. You're embarrassin' me in front of my partner and he don't like fresh Wops anyway. Now tell us your name."

Esposito looked at the young under-steward who looked back sympathetically. Mooney's knee came up into Esposito's groin followed by a right to the jaw from Mike Hennessy. Boland pulled Esposito's head up by the hair "What's your name, Dago?" "Mi chiamo e Vincenzo Randazzo." Mooney looked back at the under-steward and smiled maliciously.

"He don't feel like talkin' right now. I want you to come back every day at this time. Cabeesh?!" The under-steward looked back at him distastefully and nodded. He then went to hand Esposito a cold towel. Dave Hennessy grabbed it. "Thanks," he said, putting it over his head, "hot, ain't it?"

Back in New Orleans, Charlie Matranga and Joe Macheca were putting Felicia Randazzo and her baby on the train for New York City along with a trusted gofer, Antonio "Tony Bags" Bagnetto. Macheca's wife had volunteered to watch the two older daughters until she got back.

"Now, Tony," said Charlie Matranga, "when you see Paul Kelly, tell him it's very important to us down here, that Giuseppe's been like a brother to me and Joe Macheca, and that we will put up $50,000 to spring him, if it can be done, *Capito*.?" Tony Bagnetto's massive head nodded obediently as his thick brow furrowed.

"Sure, Charlie. But what happened to the connection Provenzano had with Hennessy through Attilio Abruzzi?" Charlie's face darkened, the grey eyes becoming the color of tarnished pewter. *"La Santa Mamma* will take care of it, Tony." Bags' face brightened perceptibly and he hugged Charlie like a huge bear. They then boarded the train.

SCREWMAN'S HALL
CORNER OF EXCHANGE PLACE & BIENVILLE STREET
SHORTLY BEFORE MIDNIGHT
JULY 20, 1881

Joe Provenzano pushed his chair back from the green felt card table and looked at Attilio Abruzzi. He smiled, "You little greaseball, you beat me pretty good tonight." Abruzzi winked, his bald head shining mahogany in the heat of the summer night. His eyes crinkled over his hawk nose.

"What the Hell, Joe? We're still spending Macheca's money, right? I'm going to head for home." Abruzzi opened the beaten, paneled door of the Hall and stood for a second on the second-floor landing. Then he descended the rickety stairway that led to the street.

As his first step hit the pavement a shotgun blast killed him instantly. Joe Provenzano opened the second-floor door and smashed the bulb in the swinging green fixture that illuminated the landing. He was just in time to see Salvatore Arditti, a friend of Charlie and Joe Macheca, running down the street.

NEW YORK CITY HARBOR
JULY 27, 1881

The steamer docked at the foot of Fulton Street, just below the half-finished Brooklyn Bridge. It was met by a Black Maria and a squad of heavily-armed, mounted policemen. As Esposito hobbled down the gangplank in shackles, Mooney gave him a vicious dig in the ribs. "Smile for the people, Joe," he said malevolently.

The young Italian under-steward was already on the quay giving an interview to the throng of reporters outlining the mistreatment of Esposito by the detectives. Dave Hennessy said to cousin Mike, "Look at that crowd; every paper in the country will carry this." He was right. As Mooney and Boland brushed past the reporters, one asked, "Was it a tough catch, fellas?" "All in a day's work," crowed Mooney. The understeward glared at him. "And don't believe anything this little Wop tells ya, either. For all we know, he might be in cahoots with Esposito; we're checkin' on that right now."

He gave the steward a shove and hustled Esposito into the back of the Black Maria; it then took off at a lively trot for the Tombs.

At the same time, having ensconced Felicia and little Giuseppe in a hotel off Washington Square the previous day, Tony Bagnetto was meeting with Paul Kelly in a little *fratellanza* on Mulberry Street.

Paul viewed the big man's hulking consternation across the small table, and said, "The papers have already picked up on this, Tony, but it's being worked on right now. Red Rock Farrell is supposed to send an alderman to see Senator Platt today and we'll see if anything can be done. Between us, though, it don't look good".

A hearing was scheduled for July 30th, before the Honorable Leonard Parker to determine if grounds existed to warrant the prisoner's extradition back to Italy. Scheduled for the same day in the Mayor's office, was a ceremony to commend Esposito's valiant captors, from both the New York City and New

Orleans Police Departments, at which time Dave Hennessy would receive a $5,000 (25,000 lire) reward from the Italian government.

FIVE POINTS, NEW YORK CITY
WHYOS CLUBHOUSE
JULY 28, 1881

The soles of Red Rock Farrell's size 12's faced Paul Kelly from atop the old walnut desk. Red Rock's thumbs were hooked into his plaid vest and a huge cigar framed the cocked derby hat he wore in a halo of smoke. A meaty hand, the back of which was covered with thick, orange-colored fuzz, held a gold pocket watch.

"Paul," he said, chewing on the cigar, "if it wasn't for you, I'd take this greaseball's money and keep it. This Esposito is the same wise little prick who thought New York wasn't good enough for him, right? If he woulda stayed here in New York like we told him to, he'd never be in this mess.

"And he would've made plenty of money over the last few years, just like you did, right?" Paul nodded glumly. Red Rock was just warming up. "But where was he when we were fighting the Plug Uglies, the Bowery Boys, and all the other gangs who were trying to muscle in on our rackets? Down in New Orleans sunning himself, is where.

"Well, I'll tell ya right now, Paul, I doubt if Platt'll touch it. He's a hot potato right now over getting caught with that hooker in Albany and he don't need any more bad publicity. And, frankly, I don't give a shit."

Both men looked around at the arrival of small, morose, blacksuited Alderman Cornelius McGillicuddy. Red Rock stuck the watch back into his vest pocket. "You're late, Gilly. What happened?" The alderman's face collapsed into a look of intense and anguished sorrow. It was the same look that had consoled hundreds of people at the McGillicuddy Funeral Home, the family business. He paused.

"Cut that undertaker crap, Gilly. Will he or won't he?" "In a word, Red. No. Not that he doesn't want to help. He appreciates all the help the

Whyos have given him at the polls over the years and he's not averse to making a dollar, as you know. But in his situation right now after those old bitches in Albany having the audacity to peek through the transom of his hotel room and …catching him with his pants down, so to speak, he said to tell you he can't afford anything which might bring adverse publicity right at this time.

"Not only that, but in the end it must get Blaine's approval at the State Department. Blaine not only hates Tom Platt with a passion but there's some English guy over here who's really pushing this. Seems Esposito once kidnapped a friend of Prime Minister Disraeli's. Tom says to try Matt Quay. He also sends you his best and says the Ellis Island project has been very satisfactory. That you'll know what he meant."

"Yeah, I know what he meant, all right. That he received his whack this month out of the laborer's money that I sent him."

Gilly waxed beatific. "Oh, he's a shrewd man, the Senator. He's got a deal now with the Senator from Tennessee where a company they formed is going to lease out all the convict labor in the state to private parties. At a nice profit, needless to say. A shrewd man, the Senator." Red Rock looked back at Kelly. "Well, Paul, there's your answer. Of course, there's no time to send anybody to Pennsylvania to see Matt Quay and I doubt if he could do anything anyway. Esposito is going on a voyage."

Red Rock stood up to his six-foot-two height, spread his arms and shrugged, "I did what I could for you, Paul." Kelly expressed his thanks and started for the door. "Get the fifty grand anyway, Paul", Red Rock called after him, not altogether jokingly. Paul took the steam-driven, woodencarred elevated train into Washington Square.

As Felicia Randazzo and her baby were escorted out of the visiting room, Giuseppe Esposito, shackled hand and foot, was told to remain. The visiting room door opened and a tall, aquiline-nosed man with wavy, dark hair combed straight back, entered. The cut of his Savile Row clothes identified him as a gentleman.

It made no difference to Esposito; he just gave the man a hooded stare. Clive Clifford dusted the stool that Felicia had occupied with a white linen handkerchief, and sat down. "Hello, Mr. Esposito, my name is Clifford. You don't know me, but I bring you a message from a very important person, the Prime Minister of England. I promised Prime Minister Disraeli on his deathbed three months ago, that if you were caught, I'd see to it that you never got out of prison…alive, that is.

"The Rose family? You remember Mr. Rose?" Esposito gave no sign of recognition. "Well," Clifford continued, "they are Scottish Jews, even though they became Anglican converts for political reasons, you know. And our Jewish Prime Minister took it as a personal affront, your attack on Mr. Rose. Very personal, indeed. He was aware when he died that they had located you over here and he cleared it with the current government that they would push to the fullest that you get your come-uppance.

"We located Il Leone, you know." Esposito's eyes gave a flicker of recognition. "In Algiers. Bloody Arabs didn't want to give him up. A couple of chaps set upon him on the street and slit his throat. Cut his ears and nose off, from what I understand. Bloody barbarians, those Arabs, wot?" Clifford smiled at Esposito's discomfort and arose. "Have a nice voyage, Giuseppe. I'll be waiting for you on the other side. *Ta."* Clifford rose, turned on his heel, and exited.

COURTROOM OFJUDGE LEONARD PARKER
CITY HALL, NEW YORK CITY
JULY 30, 1881

Giuseppe Esposito stood before Judge Parker, hands shackled in front of him, leg irons on his ankles, head bowed. He had just heard Marshal Candelorio identify him and summarize the charges on which he was a fugitive. Mooney and Boland had also testified, along with the cousins Hennessy.

Felicia sat in the front row, her young face haggard from lack of sleep and the strain of the proceeding which was being translated in part for her by Tony Bagnetto. Paul Kelly sat at his side. Felicia's haunted eyes looked down at the infant Giuseppe, cradled in her bosom. Large tears streamed over her high cheekbones and a sob escaped her throat which caused Esposito to turn and eye her painfully. He noticed Kelly and nodded to him grimly.

The judge began. From a seat in the rear, Clive Clifford leaned forward attentively. "Giuseppe Esposito, alias Vincenzo Randazzo, I find the testimony of the witnesses against you to have been credible. Under the law, extradition is warranted if we find a crime has been committed and that you were in that jurisdiction when the crime occurred. We have been furnished with full documentation of the crime committed against the Reverend John Forester Rose, and Marshal Candelorio has identified you as a suspect in the crime, that he personally questioned you in Sicily after the Italian police tracked you down and captured you. At some loss of life, I might add.

"I, therefore, find probable cause to believe that Vincenzo Randazzo and Giuseppe Esposito are one and the same person, and order you to be placed in the Tombs, from there to be deported to Italy on the earliest ship. And I understand that an Italian warship has been specially sent over for that specific purpose and waits in the harbor. Is that correct, Marshal?" Candelorio answered affirmatively.

The Judge added, "And let me take this time to commend the concerted efforts of our combined police work in both this city and New Orleans with that of the Italian authorities in bringing this brigand to bar. A fine piece of work, gentlemen."

Judge Parker glanced to the press bench where the reporters were scribbling furiously. He allowed himself a small smile of self-satisfaction. "I'll see you gentlemen in the Mayor's office shortly for the commendations." Remembering Esposito, he added to the Sheriff's officers, "Take him away!"

MACHECA ESTATE
METAIRIE, LOUISIANA
AUGUST 25, 1881

Charlie Matranga sat on Joe Matranga's front porch and listened to the angry Macheca. "Vincenzo's wife came to see me two days ago. She just got back from seeing Vincenzo being put onto that boat. A warship they sent over special for him. Can you believe it!? And poor little Giuseppe being carried around the country like an orphan. Which he would be except for Felicia's old man, and me and you, Vincenzo's *cumpari.*

"All because of that publicity-hungry rat, Hennessy. Wants to be police chief. I promised Felicia that Vincenzo would be avenged. Poor kid still believes it's all a mistake and that Vincenzo's coming back to her. Well, I put the first nail in Hennessy's cross this afternoon. He turned up his nose at our $50,000? Well, the Mayor didn't turn his nose up. Today, I made a 'campaign contribution' of $25,000 and he's going to appoint Bill Devereaux chief this month, not Hennessy".

"That's good, Joe," Charlie said, "very good."

OCTOBER 13, 1881 11:00 P.M.

Patrolmen Dave and Mike Hennessy had spent the evening pub crawling since going off duty at five o'clock as beat cops patrolling the waterfront. The new chief, Bill Devereaux, had come down heavily on the Hennessys since his appointment and he had forthwith demoted both of them from plainclothes to patrolman. Dave's beat took him past Louisiana Steamship Lines, Joe Macheca's company, and every time he passed under their second-floor office the portly Sicilian seemed to be at the window, looking down at him with a satisfied smile.

As they left the last pub, Dave said to Mike, "I can't take no more of it. Macheca was there again today. I'd rather break that stooge Devereaux's head than stay on that beat another day." Mike was feeling no pain, and smiled back at his cousin. "Well, let's do it, then. He's in Matranga's restaurant every night, slopping up spaghetti. Let's sit at the bar over there and if he says the first wrong word, let's stretch him and quit." Dave smiled back, "Right you are, cousin."

They entered the Stopp Inn, took seats at the bar and ordered Irish whiskies with beer chasers. Devereaux was seated in the rear with some political cronies. "There his Majesty sits in the back with his friends from City Hall," Mike said loudly. Dave laughed.

Upon hearing them, Chief Devereaux walked to the bar, facing the Hennessys at the other end. "I'm going to pretend I didn't hear that. But you two are breaking departmental rules against drinking in uniform. And you're drunk. You're both suspended until further notice. Now get out and go home. You're a disgrace to the force."

Mike's gun was out of its holster. "You're the disgrace, you Dago-lovin' traitor. And the penalty for treason is death!" He fired a shot at Devereaux, who narrowly missed being hit as he ducked under the bar. Devereaux drew his own gun, as did Dave Hennessy. Devereaux returned the fire and hit Mike Hennessy in the arm. Mike's gun dropped to the ground and he lowered his weapon, not seeing Dave Hennessy's.

Dave raised his pistol and shot Devereaux in the head. As the patrons of the Stopp Inn dive for cover, the Hennessys made a hurried exit.

"My God, Dave. You killed him," said Mike, as the realization of what had occurred began to sink in. Dave gave him a sideways glance as they jogged down the street. "Who pulled the gun, cowboy? You did. Dad always taught me that if you pull a gun on somebody, you better damn well shoot him. C'mon, I've got to see Provenzano."

****

"I'll see what I can do, Dave. You didn't get caught drunk and I don't think Charlie's bartender will testify against you; not if I know Charlie. It'd look bad. Then, if we can get Devereaux's dinner companions not to testify, it'd be your word against a dead man's that it was self-defense.

"Or maybe if it goes good, they won't even be able to prove you were there at all. First thing tomorrow morning, you got to turn yourself in with Arthur Dunn as your attorney. As soon as bail is set, we'll get working on this thing.," Provenzano advised.

"Thanks, Joe. I feel much better after talking to you. I knew you wouldn't let me down." "That's what friends are for," Provenzano replied, licking his lips. The following day, the cousins Hennessy were released on recognizance bonds on charges of second-degree murder.at their preliminary hearing; they were also suspended from the police force.

****

SAN STEFANO PRISON
LATIUM, ITALY CHRISTMAS
EVE, 1881
7:00 P.M.

San Stefano Prison

Giuseppe Esposito's squat, muscular five feet four inches stretched out on the straw bunk and he lay with his head resting on the palms of his hands, staring at the ceiling. Twelve days earlier he had been convicted of six of the thirteen murders he was charged with, after a six-day trial. He was sentenced to death.

Somewhere in the vast, murky distance outside the prison he heard the perpetual sound of the Tyrrhenian Sea lapping up on the shores of the prison island since all cells faced inward to the circled compound. His reverie was interrupted by the sound of footsteps approaching down the open concrete hallway.

It was more than one man, he thought and he steeled himself in case of the appearance of a "death squad", small groups of guards who, he had heard, either out of hatred or for payment, were said to bundle a prisoner in a blanket and beat him to death, leaving him to be found that way, having died of "natural causes." Esposito swung his short, stocky legs off the bunk and sat up.

When the door was unlocked, he saw a familiar face, an old jailer who had let him know he was willing to bring in food and wine from the mainland. For a price. Esposito relaxed a little. Then he saw the man *behind* the jailer. Clive Clifford. "Hello, Joe. Or I believe the proper salutation for today is *Buon' Natale:* isn't that the way you chaps over here say 'Happy Christmas'? I'm sure you noticed me at the trial, and I'll be staying in Italy over the holidays. Countess Della Torre invited me to be a guest at her villa in Rome while she's abroad. Still, I'm alone so I thought I'd pop down here and see how you were coming along."

Esposito glared at him, but managed a smile, "Fuck you, Clifford." Clifford crossed his leg and straightened the crease on his expensive trousers. "Indeed. Well, Joe, in Italy, a life sentence is about twelve years. You're what? Twenty-seven now? You'd be out before you're forty, wouldn't you?"

Esposito's lip curled. "What are you talking about, *cavone*? You know I've been sentenced to death." "No. You're not up to date, Joe. Over strenuous objection of our government, King Humbert I has granted you Christmas clemency and commuted your death sentence to life imprisonment. You are now an *ergostolani,* a lifer." "Are you joking? Why would you come all the way down here to tell me that?" Esposito asked, rising as the hope sprung up in his chest.

"No, Joe, I'm not joking. And that's not what I came here to tell you," Clifford answered calmly. Esposito let out a whoop. "I didn't believe it would happen although I was told there was a good possibility." His grinning face was set in animated satisfaction. "So what *did* you come here for, Englishman?"

"To tell you that our government…and I personally, for that matter… don't think that twelve years evens the score for Mr. Rose, let alone the other dozen or more men you've murdered, and the hundred you've kidnapped and extorted."

Esposito expanded his chest and sneered, "So what are you going to do about it, Clifford? Order the King to change his ruling?"

"No, Joe", Clifford said, rising, "but mark you well this: you will never leave this prison alive." Clifford's eyes were like burning coals. "Believe that, Joe. But first I'm going to let you serve most of your sentence." "You can do nothing in this country, pig," Esposito said, but doubt was already creeping into his newfound elation. "Get out!!"

"We won't be seeing each other again, Joe. Goodbye, and may God have mercy on your soul," Clifford said.

He rattled the tin cup that had been left for him on the bars to signal the jailer; he then walked toward the gate. Clifford made a long stop in the Commandanté's office, during which 2,500 lire changed hands. An hour later, the Commandanté finished by saying, "I will see that he gets the treatment he deserves, this dog, Signore Clifford.

"I have been Commandanté here for twelve years and am not in fear of these Mafiosi…as to the, um, final part, since you are in no hurry, I suggest that we wait until shortly before my retirement in '88." "That would be fine, Signore Commandanté," answered Clifford as the older man escorted him to the office door. The Commandanté shook his hand warmly. "Here in Italy, we have a saying, 'Revenge is a dish better served cold'..Buon' Natale, Signore".

"E Lui, Signore," Clifford answered. "The tokens of our appreciation will be sent to you each year at Christmas until we…consummate our arrangement." The Commandanté bowed graciously and a guard appeared and escorted Clifford to the small launch waiting to ferry him to the mainland.

NEW ORLEANS, LOUISIANA FOOT OF
CANAL STREET
FEBRUARY 5, 1882, 10:00 A.M.

As the passengers boarded the side-wheeler steamboat, *Robert E. Lee*, a festive air pervaded. The flat-bottomed shallow-hulled craft was the size of a football field, but had beaten the *Natchez* in the famous river race of 1870 and had made it from New Orleans to St. Louis in less than four days.

Her current owners, Joe Macheca and Charlie Matranga, had converted her to her present luxurious state: two upper decks of opulent salons, restaurants, bars, cabarets, and a gambling hall; and a top deck which sported sumptuous staterooms for the wealthiest passengers. There were sweeping gingerbread-railed observation decks fore and aft on all three levels.

As the *Lee* set off from the dock with an ebullient toot-toot of her whistle, a large, orange-and-green sign on the dock, proclaimed in bold, black letters:

SPORTSMEN'S SPECIAL
RIVER CRUISE ABOARD THE FAMOUS & RENOWN RACING
STEAMBOAT, *ROBERT E. LEE* TO MISSISSIPPI CITY,
MISSISSIPPI, FOR THE GREATEST FIGHT FOF THE CENTURY:
THE "TERROR FROM TIPPERARY", PADDY RYAN,
HEAVYWEIGHT CHAMPION OF THE WORLD VS. "THE BOSTON
STRONG BOY", JOHN L. SULLIVAN, FOR THE
HEAVYWEIGHT CHAMPIONSHIP OF THE WORLD, LONDON
PRIZE RING RULES. BOAT LEAVES CANAL STREET DOCK
FEBRUARY 5, 1882, FIGHT FEBRUARY 7, ARRIVING BACK AT
CANAL STREET FEBRUARY 9 - $20 US ALL-INCLUSIVE –

SPECIAL ACCOMODATIONS FOR SPORTING GENTLEMEN OF MEANS!

The Captain gave a wave from the small, cupolaed pilot house as the two wood-powered steam engines, sated by the frenzied feeding of the stokers, caused the huge, lateral flywheels to kick up a beautiful spray of green wake. The brisk, sunny February day was topped off with a cloudless sky of china blue and the invigorating sea air moistened the faces of the warmly-dressed passengers on the deck, with a fine mist.

In the private salon reserved for those with upstairs staterooms, Charlie, Joe, and Tony Bagnetto, shared a table with Antonio Scafidi, Bastiano Incardona, Charlie's brother, Tony, Charlie Patorno, and Salvatore Sinceri. Across the room sat Joe Provenzano, along with Vittorio Soli and Dave and Mike Hennessy. Joe Macheca was livid.

"Charlie, I can't believe you're letting that scum on this boat. And those two pig cops. If I hadn't moved fast we'd have been out one good police chief. Devereaux was a good man for us. It was lucky that I got Dominick O'Malley appointed in his place before the Mayor had a chance to back out."

Charlie gave Joe a perturbed look that he would speak so boldly in front of others, but understanding his friend's emotions, which he always considered a weakness, he was patient. "Excuse us," he said to the group, and he and Joe moved to another table out of earshot.

"Peppino", said Charlie, "you must understand. We can't do things whenever the mood strikes us. They must be timed. And now is not the time for us to attract attention upon ourselves. Until we consolidate the power of our union, for one thing, we are going to be at the mercy of the hordes of cheap Chinese labor that's going to be brought in here this year with the opening of the California rail line by the Southern Pacific from San Francisco.

"We are going to need the help of every politician in the state from the governor on down and the railroad's already throwing big money their way. The Federal government has already sold out. They granted the state two million acres of swampland between here and Texas for next to nothing on the condition that the Limey outfit, North American Land and Timber, would get first shot at it for twelve-and-a half cents an acre.

"Now, Watkins of North American is promoting the ground as good for farming – rice farming. And who farms rice? Chinese, that's who. If you need any further proof, Watkins is cozying up to Harriman of Southern Pacific, who, in turn, is backed by Jacob Schiff of Kuhn. Once these Chinese get here, our people are going to be in jeopardy, Joe."

"It's all got to be thought out ahead of time. We can't afford any splits right now, especially with Provenzano. Remember, there are things cooking that he doesn't know anything about. A young fellow named Eugene Debs is coming down next month to talk to me about giving us a charter for an American Railway Union lodge.

"If that materializes, we'll have plenty of say on the Southern Pacific, on their laborers, and on who the Hell they think they're going to transport in here. So cool off, Peppino. I'm going to talk to Provenzano and straighten out these pigs for the time being. To be really straight about it, it was the cousin, Mike, who drew his gun. He should carry the full blame. Dave only shot in self-defense."

"Like Hell he did!" blurted Joe Macheca. "The bartender said that Chief Devereaux had lowered his weapon after shooting Mike Hennessy."

"Maybe. But maybe Dave Hennessy didn't see him lower it. Anyway, the ruling I'm making is this with Provenzano: Mike has to leave town and we'll help Dave. In return for that, I'm going to demand a lot of concessions from Provenzano." Charlie called his brother to the table. "Tony, tell Provenzano to meet me in my stateroom before dinner."

MISSISSIPPI CITY, MISSISSIPPI FEBRUARY 7, 1882, 11:00 A.M.

A field outside the small river town near Biloxi had been made into a makeshift fairground for the big event. In the center of the field stood a roped-off twenty-four foot square. Around it, at a distance far enough back to give the spectators ample room were various and sundry tents and wagons festooned with gaily striped red-white-and blue and green-and-white buntings.

The largest of the tents had been turned into an enormous barroom, its ground covered with sawdust. A piano played loudly and at the bar near it stood Provenzano and his companions. Provenzano's silver hair showed thick under his derby, although thin on top, and his arm was around one of the "sporting ladies" who had come downriver from Chicago and St. Louis for the event.

"You know, Dave, besides what I told you about the case, Charlie tells me that this kid, Sullivan, will beat Ryan. They sent him word from New York. They said he fought Johnny Flood on a barge on the Hudson River by New York City last year and knocked him stiff with one punch; it took two hours to revive him."

"Joe, you listen to this Irishman. Nobody will beat Paddy Ryan. Christ, didn't Ryan just two years ago knock out Joe Goss, the champion of the world? Who'd Sullivan ever beat? A bunch of bums, right, Mike?" Mike nodded his assent.

Provenzano stroked the nape of the girl's neck, "Belle, you're a beauty. I'm gonna take you home to New Orleans with me." Belle fluttered her heavily-mascaraed eyelashes and reached over to give Joe a kiss on the cheek. Her curly blonde hair was cut short and the black woolen shawl was left open to show off her ample décolletage. Her deeply rouged cheeks hid perfect milky-white skin. She lit a Sweet Caporal and blew the smoke into the air adventurously, looking at the Hennessys.

She put a knee up as Provenzano sat on the empty stool beside her, causing her petticoats to open to reveal a well-formed dancer's calf. "Joe, you're so sweet. I just might go. If you're good to me, that is," Belle cooed. Vittorio Soli guffawed as Provenzano winked at him with an exaggerated lewdness.

Provenzano continued, "But wait a minute, fellas. That is just the point. It's true that Ryan did beat Goss. But Joe Goss was an old man. They were both in their forties, for Chrissakes. Goss was Ryan's first

professional fight and he has never fought since. And that's two years ago."
"Well, my money's going on Ryan," said Dave Hennessy.

A stout, muscular man next to him at the bar turned around, "You'd be throwing your money away, lad." Hennessy wasn't used to back-talk and stepped back in amazement. Belle, in the middle of a puff of her Sweet Caporal, let out a laugh that blew a cloud of smoke past Hennessy and into the stranger's face. The stranger looked angry. "Lady, put that blasted thing out. Only a cigar's fit for a man to smoke. Cigarettes are for Italians, Greeks, Spaniards, and Turks and they ain't no good nohow. And no ladies should indulge in such a filthy habit."

Hennessy's hand went to the grip of the nickel-plated Derringer in his vest pocket. The stranger's hand closed over his in a grip like a vice.

"Who the Hell do you think you are?" asked Provenzano. "I'm John L. Sullivan and I can lick any man in the world," Sullivan bellowed confidently, "Why, wasn't you just tellin' this thick Mick here the same thing?" he said, nodding at Dave Hennessy. The whole group, including Sullivan, broke up in laughter, except for a sheepish-looking Dave Hennessy.

"Well," said Joe, "the Boston Strong Boy, himself. How about a drink?" "Don't mind if I do," answered Sullivan. "Some way to train," Hennessy groused. Sullivan smiled. "I'm twenty-three years old. Trainin's for old guys like Ryan. He's thirty, you know."

John L. swigged down a large schooner of beer. Belle was purposely rubbing up against John L. now and marveling at the biceps that bulged through his coat as he lifted his glass. Provenzano kicked her in the shins and she hopped back over to him. Sullivan winked, first at her, then at Provenzano; he was used to it.

He stuck a finger in Hennessy's chest. "Remember what I told you, Mick; bet your money on me." He banged his schooner on the bar and stuck out his chest, "I can lick any man in the world!" he bellowed. Then, with another wink at Provenzano, he said, "It never hurts to blow your own horn.

Publicity, you know. Time for my warmup now. I'll be back in the bar here after I demolish old Paddy."

Belle looked adoringly as he strode out of the tent. Provenzano gave her another kick in the shins . *"Putana!* Get the fuck away from us." The others barely suppressed their laughter.

Soli said, "But, Joe, you were gonna take her back to New Orleans an hour ago." Provenzano gave a dour look. "That would be like taking a catfish to a lobster dinner." Belle drew herself up to her full five-feet-one height and said, "Well! I like that. I'm going." "Don't let the door hit you in the ass," Provenzano replied, turning his back on her.

Two hours later, the New Orleans contingent was gathered at ringside. Along with Charlie's entourage was Paul Kelly, Red Rock Farrell and two of Red's Whyo stalwarts, the brothers Connolly, "Slops", and "Baboon", all of whom had come down from New York by train. "What a friggin' trip, Charlie", said Paul. "The connection in Memphis was late and then we had a hell of a time getting a carriage over to here. You'd think these hicks down here would show some enterprise.

"Red Rock promoted that last fight of John L.'s on the Hudson. What's the purse here?" "Five thousand dollars a side," Charlie answered. "Well, Red and I want to lay whatever we can get on Sullivan." Paddy Ryan's handlers escorted him to the ring. He climbed through the ropes and did a few stretching exercises. Provenzano and Hennessy ambled over to Charlie's group and Provenzano said, "That Ryan's a bull, Charlie. Look at him! Two hundred pounds of fightin' fury. And you told me to bet the other guy? You wouldn't kid me, would you, Charlie?"

Joe Macheca looked at Hennessy. "You wanna bet a thousand of that reward money you got for Randazzo on Ryan, cop? You ain't spent any of it yet." Before Dave Hennessy could reply, a bunch of hard-looking Boston Irishmen flanked John L. as he approached the ring. Clinging to his arm was Belle.

Hennessy said, "Yeah, Macheca, matter of fact I do. Make it five hundred." "You're faded," said Joe Macheca. Provenzano looked at Belle looking at Sullivan.

"Charlie, I'm gonna have to ignore your advice. I'll put a grand on Ryan. Who'll take it?" Paul Kelly looked at Charlie. "Not me," Charlie said, smiling. "He'd tell everyone in New Orleans that I swindled him." Red Rock stepped over to Provenzano. "We'll take it. In fact, make it two thousand if you can handle it."

Provenzano looked up, annoyed, and hissed, "I can handle anything you wanna bet, redhead." "Charlie, hold the money." He reached into his pocket. "Đone," said Red Rock, handing Charlie a thick roll of bills.

The fighters stepped up to scratch. Prior to the fight, both had their hands soaked in brine to harden them. The referee gave the signal and Ryan took a swing that would have knocked the head off a horse. John L. deflected it with his shoulder.

Both bobbed and weaved, circling each other warily. The first time they got in close, John L. missed with a left hook and Ryan came over it with a right hand to the temple. Sullivan found himself on the ground and the first round was over. Thirty seconds later, both men were standing at scratch listening to the referee.

"All right, boys, you had eight seconds to get to scratch which is up right…now! Go to it!" John L. hit Ryan with a tremendous left hand to the solar plexus followed by a right to the jaw and the second round was over.

Seven rounds later, Ryan's handlers were carrying him, unconscious, out of the tent. John L. Sullivan was the new Heavyweight Champion of the World. John L. held clasped hands above his head as the diamond belt was placed around his waist. He shouted, "I can lick any man in the world!" to the cheers of his supporters, mixed with catcalls and boos.

At ringside, the Hennessys arose with disgusted looks on their faces. Sullivan spied Dave out of the corner of his eye, and winked him an "I told you so". He expanded his bull chest proudly and looked down at the glittering belt. Charlie handed Joe Macheca $1,000 and Red Rock $4,000.

The Hennessys headed into the departing crowd after arranging to meet Provenzano back at the boat, Provenzano was more philosophical, "C'mon, Charlie, we're supposed to meet John L. for a drink in the tent. Anyway, I want to repossess my girl," he said sarcastically, elbowing Soli, "right, Vic?"

Soli laughed, "I think she's a lost cause, Joe". Red Rock looked disparagingly at the tent. "I wouldn't be caught dead wit' dat bunch of yokels."

"We'll get Paul to tell John L. to meet us at your steamboat. How's that, Charlie?" "Fine," Charlie Matranga answered. The Mississippi sunset cheered the bleak winter landscape and the group headed back to the *Robert E. Lee.* Back on the boat, John L. was the center of attention with all the ladies He regaled the gentlemen at the ornate, gilt-encrusted bar with stories, in all their gory detail, of the street fights he had won in Boston before turning to the ring. John L. and the New Yorkers spent the night, left the next morning and, the *Lee* set out for New Orleans.

Upstairs, in Charlie's suite, Joe Macheca, Joe Provenzano, Salvatore Soli, and Charlie were having lunch served by a Filipino cabin steward. Provenzano and Matranga repaired to a small, corner table and talked in hushed tones. "Dave would like to hear for himself, Charlie, how about I bring him up here?" Charlie looked back at him and raised an eyebrow. "Don't push it, Joe. These two mugs come into my joint, kill the police chief, and then want me to fix the case so they don't have to take the consequences. Now he wants to hear it for himself? Any more and he's on his own, Joe."

"Okay, Charlie. You're right. So the trial will be held in the Spring. You're sending the bartender back to Sicily for a holiday shortly before that. And Devereaux's companions will testify that they were in the back and could see nothing. Good enough."

Charlie faced him somberly. "There's one condition, Joe." Provenzano faced Charlie across the table. Slowly, a smile flickered at the corner of his thin lips. "I knew it. What is it, Charlie?"

Charlie eyed Soli. Provenzano said, "Go downstairs, Sal. Please. I'll be down shortly." A flicker of resentment passed across Soli's eyes but he said nothing. Charlie motioned to Joe Macheca to accompany him. When they were alone, Provenzano said, "So what's the big condition, Charlie? What could two men's freedom depend on?"

Charlie raised one finger. Provenzano looked back questioningly. "One, Joe." "What do you mean, one, Charlie?" "Dave Hennessy is the one you're interested in, right?" "Well, yes…but…"

Charlie cut him off by raising his hand, palm forward. "No buts, Joe. I should have had both of them killed and not even let them go to trial. They show me no respect and then have the effrontery to ask --- no, *demand* --- my help. Well, as a favor to you I'm doing what we discussed, for your *friend* Dave Hennessy. But the cousin I'm holding fully responsible. He's going to receive a letter from Houston, offering him a job he can't refuse, Joe. When he goes there, Joe, he doesn't come back.

"You take care of it." Provenzano looked back, amazed. "Me? But these two kids are with me, Charlie. You can't ask that!"

"But I am, Mr. Joe. In fact, I demand it or you can forget the whole deal. Mike Hennessy is to leave for Houston immediately after the trial. And on your oath to La Santa Mamma, you will swear right here that he will be dead within a week after his arrival."

Provenzano looked back uncomfortably. Charlie's grey eyes were unflinching. A vision that he couldn't quite decipher subconsciously flashed through the back of his brain – two grey eyes above a bandana – a long time ago.

Provenzano shifted in his seat, then looked back to Charlie's gaze. Charlie held out his hands, Provenzano took them with his and looked Charlie straight in the eye. "I swear it. On La Santa Mamma, I swear it." They looked in each other's eyes for a long time, each knowing he would one day have to kill the other.

NEW ORLEANS, LOUISIANA
APRIL 3, 1882

On the day that Bob Ford shot Thomas Howard, alias Jesse James, in the back, at St. Joseph, Missouri, Dave and Mike Hennessy were acquitted in their murder trial in the Crescent City. Neither cousin testified. No one could identify them as having fired the fatal shot or, for that matter, even having been in the Stopp Inn on the evening in question, the bartender being unavailable in Sicily, and Devereaux's companions having testified that they were not in a position to have actually seen anything.

After the trial, both cousins went to reclaim their jobs with the New Orleans police. But the new Chief, Dominick O'Malley, refused to let them back on the force.

"You're nothing but a fucking puppet," Dave Hennessy snarled at him as they walked out of the office. As they headed down Rampart Street, Mike said to Dave, "Look, Cous, I didn't want to say with the trial coming up and all – and if we got re-hired here, I wouldn't have bothered – but I got a good job offer with a detective agency in Houston. I'm going to give it a try."

****

Three days after his arrival in Houston, Mike Hennessy was shot to death as he left his hotel. The crime was never solved.

Two months later, Joe Provenzano faced a distraught Dave Hennessy across two steaming cups of espresso. "Look, Dave, take my advice. Stop mooning about Mike. What's done is done. If anyone from here had it done we'll never prove it and who knows that he just didn't get into an argument with some Mexican or cowboy down there? Mike was a real hothead, you know that yourself."

"I know it came from here, Joe, and when I prove who did it, I'll kill them, just like I killed the guy who murdered my old man."

"Sure, Dave. Meanwhile, let's talk business. When I put you with the Farrell Police after the trial, I did it for a reason. I knew Farrell was in very poor health. You been bellyachin' ever since that he made you a bank dick. Well, he did that at my suggestion.

"The bank you've been workin' at, we're going to need help in. And just like I knew would happen, the Irishman that runs the bank took a liking to you. Now, Farrell's on his deathbed and won't live the week out. Who's handling the estate? Why, your friend, the banker, he's the executor. You've still got that reward money stashed away, I hope?" "Most of it. Why?"

"Because the new owner of the Farrell Police Force is going to be David C. Hennessy, that's why. As you know, Farrell specializes in keeping labor peace, that's how I got friendly with Farrell. I've purposely kept you away from that end of it these past few months with that in mind. Well, now, kid, we're gonna move in a big way."

Hennessy's face brightened, *"The Hennessy Police Force"* I like it!" "Not so fast, kid. I said you're the new owner and so you are. With the money you have, I'll put up the rest, and if we need any more the banker will advance it. But you've got to move easy.

"Your rep is that of a hothead and you're known to have a connection to me. What you'll do is to make your old Chief, Tom Boylan, a partner and we'll out his name on it, the Boylan Detective Agency, that's what we'll call it. Then we just lay low until the time comes. And when the time comes, we even the score with Macheca and Matranga once and for all, right?"

Hennessy's brow furrowed, and he gazed at Provenzano for a long minute. Slowly, his features softened into a broad grin. "Right!" he exclaimed. And he extended an outstretched hand across the table towards the devious little Sicilian.

STOPP INN
NEW ORLEANS, LOUISIANA
THURSDAY, NOVEMBER 1, 1883

Kate Townsend was roaring drunk. Rolls of fat poured off her now-300-pound body and onto the chair of Billy McLern, a young hustler and dandy to whom Kate had taken a fancy. Accompanying them was one of Kate's girls, Mary Buckley, known as Molly Johnson, and another man.

Kate had McLern in a stranglehold and was kissing him for the 1,000[th] time. McLern had had enough. "Leggo of me, Kate, or I'll break this champagne bottle over your thick skull!" McLern shouted. From out of nowhere, Tony Matranga and two other men had the champagne bottle and McLern's shoulders. His feet didn't even touch the floor for the trip out the door.

"What the Hell'd you do to my boyfriend?" Kate screamed, too drunk to get up. Tony came back and said to Molly,

"Take her home. She's had enough". Then, turning to Kate, "C'mon, Kate. You don't want Charlie to see you like this." Kate squinted her eyes. "Yeah, Tony. I don't. I'll go now. Don't tell him, all right?" "Sure, Kate," replied Tony. Kate turned to Molly and her friend. The once beautiful face had that old vicious look that they knew so well. Kate had always been her own bouncer at the whorehouse. "I've got to cut somebody," she said,

"I think I'll go home and open up Sykes's belly!" Treville (Bill) Sykes had been living with Kate for five years now. "Sure, Kate," placated Molly, "let's go."

When they got back to 40 Basin, Molly rushed to Sykes's room and told him, "Watch yourself, Bill, Kate's crazy drunk and out for your blood." "I'll lock myself in", replied Sykes, whereupon he locked and bolted his door. Kate slept for 30 hours, waking periodically to hold her head and groan.

At 9:30 A.M., Saturday, November 3rd, Sykes awoke and went to Kate's quarters. Mary Philomene, the negro housekeeper, heard a terrible commotion shortly thereafter and went in to find Kate and Sykes rolling on the floor. Sykes ejected her and locked the door. The terrified housekeeper remained outside her mistress's door and for a few minutes thereafter heard the sound of screams, curses, and a terrible struggle. Sykes then appeared in the doorway and said, "Well, Mary, she's gone." There were cuts all over Sykes's body and he held a bloody knife.

The Sunday Picayune carried a banner headline:

"CARVED TO DEATH!
TERRIBLE FATE OF KATE TOWNSEND AT THE HANDS OF
TREVILLE SYKES WITH THE INSTRUMENTALITY OF A
BOWIE KNIFE! HER BREASTS AND SHOULDERS
LITERALLY COVERED WITH STABS!"

The Daily Picayune, in its account of her demise (November 4, 1883), described her room: 'In the left-hand corner was a magnificent etagere, upon which were statuettes, the work of renowned artists, and small articles of verdu, betraying great taste both in selection and arrangement. A finely carved though small table stood next, while adjoining this was a splendid glass door armoire, on the shelves of which were stored a plethora of the finest linen wear and bed clothing. Next to the armoire was a rep and damask sofa and over the mantel was a French mirror with a gilt frame. A large sideboard stood in the corner next to a window on the other side of the chimney, and in this was stored a large quantity of silverware. Another armoire similar to the one described, a table and the bed completed the furnishings in the room. Saving the armchairs, of which there were a number, covered with the finest rep and damask, with tete-a-tetes to match. The hangings of the bed, even the mosquito bar, were of lace, and an exquisite basket of flowers hung suspended from the tester of the bed. Around the walls were suspended chaste and costly oil paintings. The bloodstained carpet was of the finest velvet'.

KATE MEETS HER HUSBAND IN LIVERPOOL. — MISS MOLLY JOHNSON THE PRINCIPAL WITNESS — THE VICTIM — KATE TOWNSEND — KATE BIDDING ADIEU TO HER CHILDREN

KATE'S FIRST APPEARANCE IN A PUBLIC HAREM IN NEW ORLEANS. — RETRIBUTION-MC LERN AS WAITER IN TEXAS

→ The TOWNSEND TRAGEDY. ←

Kate's funeral was Monday, November 5th, 1883. It was an elaborate affair with champagne served at the viewing in Kate's drawing room, as had been her wish. Twenty carriages accompanied the casket to Metairie cemetery. Among the most sincere mourners were six Sicilians.

At the cemetery, the vendors that had catered the promenade on Metairie Ridge for All Saint's Day, the previous Thursday, returned for Kate's burial and had a field day peddling the estomac mulatte (flat iced ginger cake), coconut and pecan pralines, candy tire (pulled candy), calas (rice cakes), La Biere Creole (beer from the juice and pulp of the pineapple). For them, Kate's funeral was two holidays in one. The Sicilians stopped at the cemetery gates for refreshments.

"Some end, eh?" said Frank Romero. Joe Macheca shook his large head and said sadly, "She was our friend." Tony nodded in agreement. They all had been looking at Charlie. Finally, Charlie Patorno asked the question that had been in all their minds. "What about Sykes? If he wins the case, are we going to let him get away with it?"

There was a pause before Charlie answered. "The thing is this," he had a habit of saying, "Sykes only did what Kate wanted him to do. I've noticed for a long time. Kate was more and more unhappy. And the worse whatever was deviling her inside got, the more weight she put on, and the more weight she put on the more miserable she got. No, Kate wasn't mentally, as she used to say, 'the full shilling'. She's wanted to die for a long time now. She just goaded that little miserable mutt into doing it for her.

"It's a terrible shame. Underneath it all, Kate was the finest, most generous person you'd ever want to know. But whatever was causing her pain started a long time ago, when she was a kid, probably. Who knows? But as far as Sykes is concerned, forget him. He did her a favor."

Joe scowled and thought it over. "You know, Charlie, you're right. I told her about her telling me about the twin baby sons she left in Liverpool. She was real upset about it. She told me that on the night of the battle. Remember, you and Charlie Patorno were there but you had left."

Charlie nodded grimly. "With a few of the right breaks, she could have been anything. Even so, she showed the people in this town a thing or two. They'll write books about Kate Townsend. And I think that would make her happy Yeah, she knew she was going. She just recently made a will providing for full funeral arrangements down to the last detail. And I'll tell you another strange thing. She made Sykes her executor." Treville Sykes was later acquitted of Kate Townsend's murder on the grounds of selfdefense.

ABBIE REED'S RED LIGHT CLUB 257
DELORD STREET
NEW ORLEANS, LOUISIANA
FALL, 1885

The soft pink lights of the bagnio basked the lounge in a soft glow. Scantily-clad waitresses padded softly on the thick red carpet. In a red velvet booth, Joe Provenzano counseled Dave Hennessy, partner in the Boylan Detective Force. "Dave, I think our time has come. This guy Shakspeare's got a real shot with his "reform" movement. Shakspeare's a bigger crook than you or I will ever be. This joint of Abbie's was formerly his mansion.

"He sold it to her to make this whorehouse and he's got a piece of it. He's also got a piece of the Louisiana Lottery. Believe me, this current Mayor is due for a fall. And he's much closer to Matranga and Macheca than he is to me. He never got you reinstated like he promised. And the voters are starting to get wise to him. Over the years that he's been in, I've been making a note of every slip he's made I'm gonna give you all of it. It's enough to have him tarred and feathered.

"Meanwhile, you go to Shakspeare and volunteer your services to 'investigate this corrupt administration' for him. Free of charge. Then, when you produce all the stuff I'm gonna give you, right before the election, he'll think you dug it all up yourself. Hell, Dave, you'll look like Allan Pinkerton. You'll be a shoo-in for the next Chief of Police. And that's where I want you." "You always come to my rescue, Joe. I won't forget you." "I won't let you forget me, Dave." The young detective and the old Sicilian laughed and slapped each other on the back.

After a well-planned smear campaign against Ring Mayor John Fitzpatrick, by the reform movement under Joseph Shakspeare, the new administration was elected by a landslide in November, 1888. At his inauguration, the tall, patrician-looking Shakspeare announced his new appointments, not the least of which was David C. Hennessy as Chief of Police.

That afternoon, the "States" newspaper quoted Chief Hennessy as declaring war on the city's Mafia. In the first six months of 1889, three Provenzano poll workers were murdered. Vincenzo Ottumno was found floating in the 16th Street canal; Giuseppe Mataino had his throat cut in his own house at Franklin and Bienville; and Camillo Victoria was shot in the head through a window while playing cards at 15 Philip Street.

SAN STEFANO PRISON
LATIUM, ITALY
SEPTEMBER, 1889

Clive Clifford sat with one long leg crossed over the other in the office of the prison Commandanté. The hair he wore in modishly fashion low over his ears, was mostly silver now.

The Commandanté said effusively, "Ah, Signore Clifford. You are a man of your word. My…stipends---arrived right on time every Christmas since we started our---arrangement." Clifford looked back at him bemusedly. "And your retirement is at hand, is it not, Commandanté?" "Si, Signore. I shall be a *free* man at Christmas, as they say," the Commandanté said with a smile of relief.

"And how is our friend doing?" "I have made it as tough on him as I could but he is a tough one, Signore. I am glad the game is over. I have received death threats over the years from his friends, you know."

He hungrily eyed the bulge in Clifford's jacket pocket. Comprehending, Clifford removed the thick envelope. "Of course, Signore. Perhaps this small token of my government's appreciation will help in ameliorating all the distress this has caused you." Clifford handed the Commandanté the envelope. Then, reaching into his left-hand pocket, he withdrew a small vial of prussic acid.

"Here. An aperitif for Signore Esposito's evening repast."

The Commandanté took it and put it into his desk. "Perhaps you would like to watch this, his last, meal, Signore Clifford." "Not necessary, old man. It would only alert him. I'll be off. I know you will not disappoint us." The following morning, 37-year-old Giuseppe Esposito was found dead in his cell at San Stefano. It was ruled a heart attack. A week later, the newly-retired Commandanté was found dead in his apartment. It was ruled a suicide.

CHAPTER THREE
WHO KILLA DA CHIEF?

In September, 1889, Charlie Matranga's Dock Workers Union No, 22 had its first confrontation with Joe Provenzano's Longshoremen's Local No. 7. The docks were bathed in sunshine on the clear September day and Provenzano had an audience of animated, rough faces gazing up at him as he stood on a packing crate and delivered a fiery address.

His shirt was open at the neck with sleeves rolled up to the elbows in contrast to his usual dapper appearance. A purple vein bulged down the center of his forehead and his arms waved. He exuded sincerity. "Men, I call for a general strike of these docks to be honored by all dockworkers until working conditions along this waterfront are upgraded and our personal demands are met. They include equal rights with the Longshoremen's Local on the morning shapeup lines. We're sick of getting the leavings, right, men?"

There was some hand-clapping and yells of assent. What Provenzano neglected to mention was that he had made another 'personal demand': a $20,000 under-the-table payment to him. Charlie had personally avoided the speech. Instead, he looked down on it from the offices of Louisiana Steamship Lines, hearing Provenzano's voice through the open window.

Joe Macheca looked concerned. "What do you think of it, Charlie?" "Think? Ignore him, of course. What do you reckon I should do? Let him hold us up?" Turning to his brother, Tony, Charlie said, "Tell all our men in Twenty-Two to show up for work tomorrow, just like always."

Turn-of-the-century New Orleans dockworkers

The next morning, bright and early, both Matranga brothers sat in the office of Local No. 22, next to Louisiana Steamship Lines, drinking coffee. There was a knock at the door of Charlie's office Vittorio Soli entered. At his entrance, Pietro Natale and Charles Poitza, Giuseppe Esposito's two companions on the tripfrom Sicily ten years previous sauntered into the room with Charlie's lieutenant, Giovanni Scarps. Soli looked around nervously and took a seat before thc Matranga brothers. "All Joe wants is an equal share of the hiring on the docks, Don Carlo."

"And a payoff of twenty thousand, is that it?" "Joe is willing to forego that," Soli said uncomfortably. Charlie's jaw tightened, grey eys like srorm clouds. "Oh, he'll *forego* it, will he? Well, let me tell you something, Soli.

For most of the 19th century, the banana trade, led by Chiquita (formerly United Fruit and United Brands), was eminent along the riverfront and in the economy of New Orleans. This scene at Erato Street Wharf offers a glimpse of United Fruit's operations at the Port of New Orleans in the early 1900s.

These docks belong to us. We got all those guys their jobs, staked them for a place to live until they got paid, and we're not stepping aside for Mr. Joe. Why didn't he come over in person? He too important now?" Soli shifted in his chair. "No, Don Carlo, it wasn't that. He said he wants to meet with you, if you want to talk turkey"'

"Not necessary. I can give you the same answer that I would have given Mr. Joe. How's that?" "Good enough, Don Carlo." Charlie looked at Scarpa. Scarpa nodded to Natale and Poitza. Poitza produced an axe handle, and, holding it with both hands, brought it down with full force, splitting Soli's head open. Soli crumpled to the floor. Charlie shrugged to his brother, Tony, "This had to come." Looking back at Scarpa, Charlie said, "Take him and dump him in front of Provenzano's office."

Later that week, an unknown assailant assassinated Giovanni Scarpa in front of his home. Matranga and Provenzano girded for an all-out war. Provenzano didn't relish it. He preferred skirmishes and negotiations; open warfare would disrupt his entire operation, not to mention that, at 62, he didn't relish the possibility of being a casualty.

One morning, a day or so after the Scarpa killing, Provenzano entered the offices of the New Orleans Police Department to see Dave Hennessy. Hennessy spied him from behind the half-glass partition of his office and waved him in. "I was expecting you, Joe."

Provenzano sat down. "Dave, you gotta arrange a sitdown between me and Charlie. We can't stand a war right now. Not if it can be helped." Hennessy considered the situation for a moment. "I am not the most popular guy in the world with Charlie, you know. But, okay, I don't want him coming in here. We'll invite him up to the Red Light Club on Friday. He can't hardly refuse an official request from the Chief of Police."

Joe Macheca, Charles Matranga, Charlie Patorno, and Rocco Geracci discussed the invitation over espresso on Macheca's porch. "This is a pressure play, Joe. I have to go to the meeting but we're not giving up anything."

The soft light from inside the house animated Macheca's features. "Charlie, this Hennessy is the devil incarnate. He's been behind all our trouble beginning with Vincenzo right up to today. Now, to top it off, there's this news from Sicily about Vincenzo," said Joe. Charlie scowled. "Yeah, eight years in that dungeon only to die there. And of a heart attack. Christ on the cross! He was only in his mid-thirties."

"Exactly! It was murder, for sure. Felicia doesn't know yet. And poor little Giuseppe. We gotta do something about that Irish son-of-a-bitch once and for all." "The Holy Mother lets no wrong go unavenged, Peppino. Bide your time. It will happen."

ABBIE REED'S RED LIGHT CLUB 257
DELORD STREET
NEW ORLEANS, LOUISIANA
OCTOBER 2, 1889
8:00 P.M.

Charles Matranga entered the Red Light Club, admiring its velvet and gilt, mirrored Victorian elegance. One of the girls, dressed in a gown, led him to a table where David Hennessy and Joe Provenzano were enjoying an aperitif. Joe Provenzano rose and extended his hand like a snake flickering its tongue. "Don Carlo! Buona sera. Comé va?"

Matranga gave the extended hand a loose shake and looked over at Hennessy who proffered a slight wave in his direction. "'Lo, Charlie." "Good evening, Chief…Mr. Joe." He sat down and ordered a glass of red wine. Provenzano broke the ice. "First of all, Charlie, I want you to know that I didn't have anything to do with what happened to Scarpa." Charlie eyed him coolly. "And I didn't have anything to do with what happened to Soli." "Good enough, Charlie. That's history. We both make mistakes. The thing is to join together now, Unite."

Hennessy got up from the table. "While you guys are uniting, I'm going to the bar. But I'm going to say this just once. You better straighten this out tonight. I've never had anything against you, personally, Charlie, but you got a bad choice of friends…that fat ass Macheca's got a smart mouth. So you could say I called this meeting for your benefit. But I warn you, if you two have any more trouble after tonight, I'm gonna land on you like a ton of bricks." Charlie smiled with his mouth and nodded. Hennessy turned for the bar.

Matranga and Provenzano talked for close to an hour, Provenzano doing most of the talking. At Provenzano's signal, Hennessy returned from the bar. "You fellows friends now?" "Of course we are friends, Chief," said Charlie Matranga. "Forever," added Provenzano. Charlie eyed him and said silently, "Cascittuni." *Informer.* Charlie bid them goodnight shortly thereafter.

As he exited quietly across the thick carpet, Provenzano whispered, "He won't budge, Dave, he's gotta be moved. And it's gotta be soon." "Do what you have to do, Joe. You know whose side I'm on." There were some small skirmishes and agitation on the docks over the next six months, with the Provenzanos coming out a little the worse for it.

THE STEAMSHIP "FOXHALL" NEW
ORLEANS DOCKS
MAY 6,1890, 4:30 A.M.

Tony Matranga and his crew of Local No. 22 dockworkers had finished unloading the final crates of Colombian bananas, and climbed aboard a horse-drawn wagon to take them home. The wagon rumbled slowly along and finally reached the intersection of Esplanade Avenue and Claiborne. Shots rang out from the weeds on a corner lot and one of the gunmen shouted, "Scabs! This dock is on strike!"

A bullet hit Tony Matranga in the leg. "Go to Hell!" one of Tony's men yelled. The driver whipped the horses and more shots were fired at the rear of the departing wagon; another Matranga man was wounded.

ABBIE REED'SRED LIGHT CLUB 257
DELORD STREET
NEW ORLEANS, LOUISIANA

Abbie solicitously escorted Dave Hennessy over to Joe Provenzano's table, her voluptuous hips swaying side to side in the process. As she approached, she gave Provenzano an acknowledging smile for the way he admired her half-exposed breasts. She collared a young, sexy-looking waitress and, smiling at Hennessy, said suggestively, "Take care of the Chief and Mr. Pro, Honey. First of all, give them a drink. On Abbie."

Hennessy patted her on the ass and slid into the booth. "I'll let y'all talk business, Chief honey. If there's anything Ah can do, you just call, y'heah?" When Abbie returned to the door, Provenzano laughed and said to Hennessy, "Where did she get that magnolia accent? She's from Frisco and before that Kansas City, I hear."

Actually, Abbie, formerly Mary Hines, had grown up in a dirt poor section of Brownsville, Texas and, at 15, had run away with a carpetbagger. He took her to the fanciest hotel in San Antonio for Christtmas of '69 and from there she never looked back (although she used to joke that she spent a lot of time looking up in those days).

She went to work in a bawdy house when the carpetbagger deserted her, but it wasn't long before her agile young brain showed her where the lion's share of the money went. And that was to the grotesquely painted old bag who ran the place. Abbie saved for two years and made her plans. She would open a place with class and with the best of political connections. And it wouldn't be in San Antonio, either. She considered San Francisco and New Orleans. She opted for San Francisco and decided to fatten her stake in New Orleans first.

However, there was one thing Abbie hadn't figured on: love. And she had fallen hard for the Crescent City. New Orleans was the only thing that Abbie ever truly loved although she could put on a convincing imitation otherwise when it served her purpose.

So she met Kate Townsend and stayed on. In a half-dozen years, she had formed friendships with many of the most influential men in the state When Joe Shakspeare moved from his big brownstone in town to a mansion on Carondelet Street, he made Abbie a gift of the house in reurn for a cut of the profits.

Abbie became known for her girls, her food, the elegance ofher house, and above all, her discretion. In another half-dozen years, Shakspeare was Mayor of New Orleans for the second time and Abbie, as his mistress, could do no wrong. She became a very wealthy lady with another house at 15 Burgundy Street.

Hennessy smiled and shrugged, then turned serious. "That wasn't smart, Joe." "What wasn't? This morning, you mean? Why, what'd you hear?" "I'll tell you what I heard, Joe. That was Tony Matranga that you hit in the leg this morning and could just as easily have killed. Charlie's coming for your head. Listen, Joe. This affects me, too, personally.

"I've got to take you and your men in on this so Matranga and Macheca don't give it to the papers that I'm playing favorites. Charlie will never let his men break the code and identify you. Look what he did in my case. Made the bartender go back to Sicily rather than testify. That's why I kinda respect him."

"He did that for me, Dave." "And what was the trade-off? I never did find that out. It had nothing to do with Mike, did it?" Hennessy's eyes searched the small man's face; it betrayed nothing but hurt indignation. "Dave. What are you saying? I loved Mike. You are implying that I…?"

"Don't mind me, Joe. It's just that Mike was like a brother to me. I know you didn't have anything to do with it." He smiled. "Like you say, though, you're not gonna let me forget, it was your favor."

CRIMINAL COURT NEW ORLEANS
MAY 7, 1890, 9:00 A.M.

Joe Provenzano and eight of his men had turned themselves in to police and a squadron of reporters. In the courthouse hallway, flanked by Chief Dave Hennessy, Provenzano bellowed, "This is what happens to honest labor leaders for peacefully objecting to scab workers trying to come into this city and take the jobs of honest citizens!"

A young reporter asked Provenzano, "Did you shoot Tony Matranga, Joe?" Provenzano looked at him in annoyance, "What shoot? I don't even believe he was shot. It's a publicity stunt." The Provenzanos were released on their own recognizance for a hearing the following day. Provenzano swaggered from the courthouse amid a throng of inquiring reporters and got into a waiting carriage.

MAY 8, 1890 10:30
A.M.

The first witness at the hearing for the Provenzanos was Vito Davonzo, a dockworker who had been in the wagon of Matranga men on the morning of the shooting. Provenzano was surprised not to see Charlie Matranga or even Joe Macheca in the courtroom. District Attorney Lionel Adams approached the witness with a spring in his step that made the Provenzanos snicker.

"Mr. Davonzo, would you please relate for the court the events of the morning of May 6th?"

Davonzo looked at Joe Provenzano and said, "We—the crew I was with --- finished our work at the dock unloading the *Foxhall* and started for home in a wagon. When we reached the corner of Esplanade Avenue and Claiborne, we were fired upon from a group of men hiding in the weeds on the corner."

"Can you identify any of the men in this courtroom as your attackers?" Provenzano looked at his men and smiled imperceptibly; he barely heard the witness answer, "I can".

The district attorney stepped to the side. "Would you please point them out?" The first person the dockworker pointed to was Joe Provenzano. Provenzano's jaw dropped. When he recovered, he shot a red-faced Hennessy an icy look.

The witness proceeded to identify all the other defendants. He was unshakable on cross-examination. The other dockers from the attacked wagon all followed suit, including Tony Matranga. Judge Joshua Baker bound the defendants over for criminal court and Provenzano and his men were released on bail.

Two days later in the Red Light Club a grim Provenzano faced Dave Hennessy. "Wouldn't identify us, huh? The rat bastard sent me a message that if I wanted to cooperate with cops, then the rulebook goes out the window." "I never would have believed it, Joe." "Well, it's true. And you're in with me, sink or swim, so you'd better figure a way to straighten it out."

Hennessy looked at Provenzano appraisingly; 'sink or swim'? this was a worm he couldn't afford to have turn. "Joe, you won't be convicted. Even if I have to alibi you myself. That's a promise." "It had better be." Provenzano's usual façade of cordiality was gone.

"And listen, Joe. Better we don't be seen together between now and the trial. Stop coming in here and we'll meet at pre-arranged places whenever necessary. Places where I'm not so well known."

"Oh, I got poison ivy now, Davey Boy?"

"It's for your own good, Joe, you're the one charged with the crime."
"Yeah, I guess so. Okay, Dave. You're the one calling the shots."

NEW ORLEANS CRIMINAL COURT
JUDGE BAKER'S COURTROOM
AUGUST 17, 1890

The prosecution portion of the trial had just finished. All of the Local Number 22 members involved in the ambush again testified, identifying Provenzano and his men as their attackers. The District Attorney looked dramatically at the jury. "The prosecution rests," he said with an air of triumph.

Provenzano's lawyer stepped forward. "Ladies and gentlemen of the jury, the defense in this case will show you that Joseph Provenzano and his co-defendants couldn't possibly have ambushed these victims. We intend to produce irrefutable evidence of that in the form of sworn testimony…"

His speech went on to describe the perfidies that befall well-meaning and altruistic union leaders like his client in the pursuit of better working conditions for the downtrodden workers. After a speech of forty-five minutes, he stepped back to the defense table and sat down.

"The defense calls Detective Thomas Duffy to the stand." Duffy arose and, swinging the doweled gate from the spectator section, ascended the witness stand and was sworn on. The defense attorney put his hand on Provenzano's shoulder. "Now, Officer Duffy, you are acquainted with my client, Mr. Provenzano?"

"By sight I am; I don't know him personally, though." "And on the evening of May 6th last, did you have occasion to see my client?" "I did," answered Duffy. "For what period of time, sir?" "From midnight until five o'clock in the morning."

"Could you tell us where you saw him, Officer Duffy?" "In the Bayou Club at St. Charles and Carrollton." Provenzano's lawyer looked smugly at the prosecutor. "And is that near Esplanade and Claiborne, Mr. Duffy?"

"No. It's on the other side of town."

"And can you identify any of the other defendants as having been with Mr. Provenzano?" "Yes, I can." "How many, sir?" "All of them."

There was a murmur through the courtroom. The prosecutor reserved the right to cross-examine Duffy at a later time. Nineteen other police officers swore on the witness stand to the exact same set of facts as Duffy.

On cross-examination and in his closing address, the prosecutor struck home one point: "How and why would *all* these police officers *just happen* to be watching *at five o'clock in the morning* the *same* defendants who *just happened* to be charged with this crime?" It was too much for the jury; a verdict of guilty was quickly reached despite the fact that the attorney for the policemen had demanded a grand jury investigation into the allegations of perjury. (They were later exonerated). The stunned Provenzanos were led back to their cells.

That evening, Hennessy visited Provenzano in jail as he had been doing since the trial started. Hennessy started the conversation. "Joe, I had twenty cops commit perjury for you. What more than that could I have done?" I even had you put in the *Star Chamber* dorm in the jail so you'd get special treatment."

Provenzano bared his teeth. "You have, Dave, and you're going to do more. Remember, I said you were in, sink or swim. And don't look at me like that. If you get any ideas of doing anything to me, there are ledgers that will get sent to the newspapers.

"No, Dave, I'll tell you what you are going to do. You are going to your pal, Mayor Shakspeare's house and he's going to make Judge Baker reverse the verdict. And I mean reverse it tomorrow. Tell Shakspeare that his job's on the line. He appointed you. Not to mention the casinos, whorehouses, and his interest in the Louisiana Lottery. He's taking graft from all of them and I got the evidence to prove it."

"Joe, you're talking crazy." "Am I? If that verdict's not reversed in the morning, you and Shakspeare'll wish I was crazy." Hennessy bit his lip.

"Okay, I'll see him. But I can't picture the Mayor doing anything for you." Provenzano looked back coldly. Hennessy arose. "Well, Joe, this makes it quits for us. I'll do what I can. Goodbye." Provenzano shrugged in answer and eyed Hennessy icily as he left. Neither man had offered the other his hand.

RESIDENCE OF MAYOR JOSEPH A. SHAKSPEARE
1616 CARONDELET STREET
NEW ORLEANS, LOUISIANA
8:00 P.M. THE SAME DAY

Chief David Hennessy pulled on the Mayor's doorbell. A heavy brass ball hydraulically returned to the door and Hennessy could hear the sound of feet clacking down the marble corridor inside. The massive oak door slowly swung open and Hennessy was confronted by Shakspeare's butler, an old Scot named Taggart. "Hello, Chief. Does the Mayor expect you?" "No, Taggart, but I have to see him on urgent business." "I'll tell him you're here, sir."

Hennessy was shown into the study. Presently, Joseph Shakspeare entered through oak pocket doors. A tall, fastidious man in his mid-Fifties, Shakspeare wore a silk smoking jacket over his pajamas. He eyed Hennessy over small, wire-rimmed glasses. "Hello, Dave. Antoinette and I were just doing a little reading in bed. What's the problem?"

"Well, sir, I just came from seeing Provenzano after his conviction and..." As he related the events of the meeting, he could see Shakspeare become more livid with each word. "That guinea bastard! Threatening me, is he?" "I told him he couldn't expect any help from you, Sir. But I thought I'd better relay the message."

Shakspeare was in deep thought. He looked pensively at Hennessy. "Dave, I want you to tell me just what he has on you and I want the truth. All of it." Uncomfortably, Hennessy related his whole association with

Shakspeare. Looking at Shakspeare, he could see his reflection flickering in the lenses of the tall man's spectacles.

"So he started out by informing on Randazzo. And it was he who provided you with most of the documentation that you furnished me against my opponent in the election?" "Yes, sir."

"Well, you can bet he's got all he says he's got on you. And what he says he's got on me, not that it's true, mind you. But it wouldn't look good. Especially after my association with you."

The Mayor rested his chin atop his bony fingertips and Hennessy could see small beads of perspiration forming on the top of his upper lip. It was a full minute before the Mayor spoke. "It's nine o'clock. Get your ass over to Judge Baker's house; it's only five minutes from here. Tell him to stop here at seven o'clock tomorrow morning, that I'll be waiting for him. I'm going to do this thing. And when it's over, I'm going to cut that Dago a new asshole.

"Before court tomorrow, you tell Provenzano that I want his records by five o'clock tomorrow afternoon. And there had better not be any copies. Now get moving." "Yes, sir," Hennessy said, starting for the door. As Shakspeare watched Hennessy leave, he thought to himself. *And as soon as I'm done with Provenzano, you'd better look for a job sweeping streets, Dave.*

At ten o'clock the next morning, court was called to order for the entrance of Judge Joshua G. Baker. The judge called the courtroom ton order. He looked coldly at Provenzano, then continued, "In the case of State of Louisiana vs. Provenzano, et al., I am rejecting the jury's verdict as inconsistent with the evidence. A new trial is ordered. The defendants are remanded without bail. There will be a memorandum opinion available for counsel in case anyone wants to take an appeal. We'll adjourn until one o' clock." He banged the gavel and strode from the courtroom.

Pandemonium broke out. Provenzano's men were slapping him on the back. There was a collective groan from the Matranga supporters.

Reporters were fighting to interview the defendants; Chief Hennessy was interviewed as well.

"I think the judge did the only thing he could do. The dockworkers were not believable. They are controlled by Joseph Macheca, head of the Mafia in New Orleans. When I took office, I told you I'd destroy the Mafia. Since then, I've amassed dossiers on ninety-four murders committed in New Orleans since 1868.

"In the weeks to follow, I will reveal much more of the criminal activities of Joseph Macheca." *Why mention Matranga and confuse the issue?* Dave thought. *Macheca's the one I want.* Provenzano, led by a sheriff, came up alongside Hennessy and smiled at the reporters, "you boys heard what the Chief said, it was all a hoax." Hennessy turned his back on Provenzano and left the courtroom.

The reporters hurried right down to Louisiana Steamship Lines. Informed of the retrial and of Hennessy's statements, a fuming Joe Macheca said, "Hennessy is investigating the Provenzano case the wrong way and he will pay for it." Later that afternoon, Charlie Matranga was interrupted while cavorting on the lawn with his children. It was Joe Macheca. Charlie sent the kids inside and the two men sat down on the porch. "Charlie, something's got to be done about Hennessy," Macheca said. "We sent him a message to keep his nose out of Italian affairs and he has his men commit perjury for Provenzano."

The grey eyes looked hard at Macheca. "Peppino, for nine years you've been telling me that and for nine years I've been telling you that the time will come." "But…" Charlie cut him off. "It is family business that you took an oath not to reveal.

"Where do you come off giving interviews to newspapers?" "I was angry and I…" Charlie's face was hard. "That's no excuse. A man must control his emotions. Tomorrow, meet me at the Stopp Inn and have Charlie Patorno with you." Macheca's face brightened. "Are we going to have our revenge at last, Don Carlo?"

Charlie gently placed his thumb and forefinger together over the portly man's upper and lower lip. "Keep this closed to anyone but me, Peppino."

As the Macheca carriage rumbled down the drive, though, Charlie said to himself, "You are right, Peppino. This time he has gone too far."

The next day, at a meeting attended by Macheca, Patorno, and his brother, Tony, Charlie laid out his feelings on the Hennessy/ Provenzano alliance. "Now that Provenzano's in with the cops, it is playing right into their hands to start shooting. That's why I gave the order to go into court and testify. I figured we'd try it their way. Well, we did and look what they did to us. I guess I should've known better, although the jury did convict them.

"But you can bet the retrial will be in the bag. In fact, I hear Hennessy's going to get on the stand himself next time and try to shift the blame over to us. Another thing is that Hennessy has Provenzano and his men in the Star Chamber of the prison, the ward they keep for all the grafted-up prisoners. They're getting special food, booze, women---anything they want." Tony Matranga rubbed the leg where he was shot.

Joe Macheca repeated, "They've got to be stopped." Charlie replied, "I'm going to have one last meeting with this dog, Hennessy, and see if I can get him to stop this business. I doubt that it will do any good, but at least I'll try. You fellows go on home. Charlie," he said to Patorno, "you stay here. I want to talk to you about something."

ABBIE REED'S RED LIGHT CLUB 257
DELORD STREET
NEW ORLEANS, LOUISIANA
SEPTEMBER 17, 1890
7:00 P.M.

Dave Hennessy was feeling good. He had spent the afternoon with Abbie's prettiest whore and had had a leisurely bath afterward. All was right with the world. He was seated in his usual booth playing casino with Abbie until Charlie arrived. "Charlie, nice to see you," Hennessy smiled.

Charlie sat down without a word and Abbie disappeared. Hennessy put the cards down. "So, Charlie, get it off your chest."

Charlie looked straight into the younger man's eyes. "Hennessy, I never wanted this. Why you did it, I don't know, but these thugs almost killed my brother, Tony, among other things. Then you sent all your cops into court and lied to get them off, and when that didn't work, you had the judge give them a new trial. In the meanwhile, you've been paying their board at the jail…"

"What's that supposed to mean?" said Hennessy, face reddening.

"It means you've got them installed in the Star Chamber like visiting dignitaries, with Abbie's girls having private visits with them and bringing them two-inch thick steaks and anything else they want."

Hennessy was completely fuming at this point. "Now you listen to me, Dago. Who in Hell do you think you are, coming in here and dictating to the Chief of Police? If there was any perjuring done, it wasn't by my officers. Furthermore, I had nothing to do with the judge's decision in the case. You think I could tell the judge what to do? And as far as what the prisoners get at the jail, if you want to squeal to somebody, try the Commissioners. And mark you well one more thing. At the next trial on October 22nd, I'm going to personally run that fat-ass Macheca out of town afterwards.

"Now, up until now, I never had anything personal against you, but this had to come in the end because you and Macheca are tarred with the same stick. So I'll give you a word of advice while I'm at it, Charlie. Get out of town while you can." Hennessy's face was beet red. Perspiration had formed a ring around the tight, black curls above his forehead.

The grey eyes that looked back at him were impassive and as inscrutable as an Oriental's. They faced each other across the table for ten seconds and a chill ran down Hennessy's spine. For the first time in his life, he felt the cold touch of fear. A small, forlorn smile formed at the corners of Charlie's mouth. "No, Chief. I won't be moving. I'll be seeing you in court on October 22nd. Good evening".

CENTRAL POLICE STATION
SOUTH BASIN & COMMON STREETS
NEW ORLEANS, LOUISIANA
OCTOBER 15, 1890 9:30
P.M.

A satisfied David C. Hennessy, attired in his blue uniform, waistcoat with gold braid, trousers with gold stripe down the leg, and police hard hat. The badges on his hat and over his heart said "Chief of Police of the City of New Orleans", briskly walked through the cool night from City Hall to Central Station.

A light rain had begun to fall earlier and the Chief shivered in his tunic. The meeting with the Board of Police Commissioners had gone well. Not only had his proposed budget for the fiscal year been approved, he also picked up some more business for his old outfit, the Boylan Detective Force. Since Tom Boylan had retired, Hennessy had appointed a friend of his, Bill O'Connor, Captain William J. O'Connor, to head the agency. Dave Hennessy had also retained one-half of the agency 'under the table'.

The Boylan Force, with its Hennessy-procured city contracts, labor contracts, and various other work, rivaled the New Orleans police force itself in manpower. Bill would be glad to hear about the new contract, thought Dave. A man approached with his coat collar turned up and Dave grabbed the handle of his truncheon and felt for the butt of his pistol, but the man passed, unseeing and uncaring. *Getting jumpy, Dave,* he thought to himself and turned to climb the six huge marble steps of the station.

ROYAL RESTAURANT
ROYAL & CUSTOMHOUSE STREETS
NEW ORLEANS, LOUISIANA OCTOBER
15,1890, 9:30 P.M.

As Dave Hennessy entered his office at police headquarters, the headwaiter at the posh Royal Restaurant across town was officiously seating a party of seven men for a late dinner. Charlie Matranga, Joe Macheca, John and Joseph Caruso, Charlie Patorno, Rocco Geraci, and

Salvatore Sinceri were seated around a large round table, and Charlie Matranga gave the headwaiter a ten dollar tip.

Busboys filled heavy, stemmed tumblers with cold water from large pitchers and put fresh butter and French bread on small china plates for each of the men. Wine was ordered and Joe Macheca proposed a toast, standing to his five feet, nine inches.

"To the success of Local Number 22 next week in defeating the Provenzanos, and to our boss, Don Carlo." Each man, in turn, made a similar toast: one to Tony Matranga for braving an assassin's bullet; one to the downfall of the Provenzano union. Finally, Charlie's turn came.

"My toast," said Charlie, "is to the Randazzo family, the ones that are still with us, and to Vincenzo. And to this being a most enjoyable dinner."

CENTRAL POLICE STATION
SOUTH BASIN & COMMON STREETS
OCTOBER 15, 1890, 11:10 P.M.

Dave Hennessy's size 11's swung down from atop his desk. "Let's call it a night, Billy Boy," he said to Bill O'Connor. O'Connor smiled, a florid-faced young man in his early thirties, with the beginnings of a beer belly marring his otherwise beefy six feet. "I've had worse nights, Dave," he said, smiling. "C'mon, I'm on duty anyway. I'll walk you home." It had rained all night, and the brisk autumn night was punctuated by a dewy chill and a slight fog. "Let's walk down South Rampart Street, Billy. This damned Basin Street's flooded again." The two friends walked over to South Rampart and turned south, walking on the lake side. They passed Gravier and Perdido Streets, and were approaching Poydras Street when the Chief said, "You know I had an ulterior motive in taking Rampart, don't you, Billy?"

O'Connor eyed the sign fifty feet in front of them. *DOMINIC VIRGETS' OYSTER SALOON.* "Not oysters at midnight again!" O'Connor grinned in mock humor, "I should've known." Small-time politician, Nick Virgets, was an ice dealer and former Criminal Court Clerk, who lived across the street from the Hennessys. He greeted the Chief effusively and brought the two policemen two dozen oysters to share, with a glass of milk for the Chief.

Hennessy eyed O'Connor mischievously. "See, Billy. This is the secret. You have to drink the milk." O'Connor turned his nose up. "I hate milk. I'd rather be sick." Hennessy and O'Connor were offered no check by Virgets; as Mrs. Virgets began to clean up, Hennessy slipped her a dollar.

The two policemen stepped out into the chilly night and crossed Poydras Street, then Lafayette, the next street being Hennessy's --- Girod. Dave Senior had settled at 275 Girod before his death and Mrs. Hennessy never could bring herself to move from the house they had shared.

When they reached the corner, O'Connor said, "Want me to walk you up to the house, Dave? You really shouldn't have let your bodyguard go, you know." Hennessy waved him off. "Don't be worrying, Billy. I'm all right." He gave O'Connor a slap on the back.

"Good night then, Dave." "'Night, Billy." Hennessy walked up Girod Street and crossed over at Basin Street toward Franklin; his home was in this block. Gasparo Marchese was fourteen years old. He had huge brown eyes and a pouty expression, which, along with his tousled chestnut hair, gave him the look of a lovable waif.

On this night, the dampness had put a shine to his olive skin. For the last hour he had walked the block between Rampart and Basin Street, looking for the man his father, Antonio, had pointed out to him outside police headquarters three days previous.

As Gasparo walked toward Rampart, he spotted Hennessy, but because he was so young, Dave Hennessy thought nothing of it when he turned and ran in the other direction, whistling. Just some kid out later than he should be, doesn't want to come near a cop.

As Hennessy put his foot on the sidewalk near Basin, four men emerged from the alley alongside the corner building across the street.

Hennessy saw them and tried to make it to his house. The roar of a shotgun blast shattered the stillness of the night. Then another. A half dozen more.

Dave Hennessy had made it to the front door of his house, his head spinning. He had been hit six times. With the heavy coat he was wearing, four of the hits had been minor. But he knew he had been mortally wounded by the other two. *"No. If I go inside, I'll die before I get help, and Mom's in there. Don't want her to see this."* He drew his revolver from its holster and threw a half dozen shots in the direction of his pursuers.

Hennessy turned and started to retrace his steps. One of the men approached him by coming half way across the street, kneeling and firing. The blast tore away the top of the Hennessy front door as Hennessy ducked for cover and, in a crouch, started back down Girod Street. The men pursued him from across the street, firing as they ran.

A Boylan cop, stationed at the top of Hennessy's block by Bill O'Connor without Hennessy's knowledge, ran toward them and was fired upon. He retreated back up Girod Street. Dave Hennessy laboriously reached Basin Street, running in a crouch, and turned. He stopped at 189, the home of Mrs. Gillis, a friend of his mothers'. He knocked on the door and collapsed on her front porch.

Mrs. Gillis answered the door to find Hennessy, gun in hand, seated on her front steps. "Sweet Jesus, Davey! What have they done to you?" "I'll be all right, Mrs. Gillis. Send for an ambulance. I'll wait here." "You will not!! Into my house with you. Can you stand, boy?" Dave tried but collapsed back onto the steps. "Afraid not, ma'am." Mrs. Gillis threw a knitted shawl over his shoulders. "Help'll be here soon, Davey. Not to worry."

Bill O'Connor had heard the gunshots and was hurrying up Girod Street as fast as his legs would carry him a revolver in his hand. Two of his patrolmen, who had been on South Rampart, were running behind him. When they reached the corner of Basin, a policeman neighbor, Thomas C. Anderson, joined them, and Dave Hennessy said, "Billy, they have given it to me and I gave them back the best I could."

Hennessy was weakening. O'Connor replied, "Who did it, Dave. Who gave it to you?" Hennessy grimaced in pain. He crooked his finger at Bill O'Connor and whispered, "Put you ear down here." When O'Connor complied, Hennessy whispered, "The Dagoes did it." Then, in a louder voice, "I am all right. My poor mother, that is all I care about. For myself, I do not care. It is only for her that I am troubled."

The two policemen who had accompanied O'Connor produced four sawed-off shotguns and one long-barrel which were retrieved from a nearby gutter. The men lifted Hennessy into the Gillis residence and laid him on a couch to await the arrival of an ambulance for Charity Hospital.

"Mrs. Montague, across the street, has a telephone, Captain O'Connor, so we've already phoned for the ambulance," said Mrs. Gillis. "well, I'd like to use it again to tell them to be sure to summon the house surgeons," O'Connor replied. "Of course," said Mrs. Gillis, "Mrs. Montague's just in there with the Chief. You go right over to her house."

When Bill O'Connor walked through the living room, Dave Hennessy spotted him through the crowds of neighbors. "Billy, if you're going over to use the phone, be sure to call Mayor Shakspeare and Police Commissioner Beanham."

CHARITY HOSPITAL NEW
ORLEANS, LOUISIANA
OCTOBER 16,1890, 2:00 A.M.

Crowds were gathered at the hospital by the time the ambulance arrived bearing Dave Hennessy. After his wounds were dressed in Emergency and he was taken to his room, the doctors permitted a short visit from Shakspeare, Beanham, Boylan, and O'Connor.

During that visit, Hennessy's mother burst into the room. "Davey! Davey! Are you all right, son!?" she screamed. "Yes, mother, don't get excited." Boylan broke in, "A fine specialist, Dr. Logan, was brought in and he's in conference with the other doctors, Mrs. Hennessy, so don't you worry." Shakspeare gently helped her to a seat, and said, "Dave will be fine, Mrs. Hennessy, and the cowards who did this will face justice. That I promise you." "I want to personally help hang them," said the feisty little woman.

Hennessy managed a painful grin, "Don't get her started, Mr. Mayor; what a temper! Now I want you all to go home and I'll be with you soon. You, too, Mom. That's an order."

Once they had escorted his mother out, Hennessy and the men had a fast confab. "In all honesty, I can't tell you I recognized the faces in the darkness and commotion. But there's no doubt who was behind it, Matranga and Macheca. They want me out of the way before the trial next week. What a surprise they're going to get when I mount that witness stand!" he smiled painfully.

"Sure, Dave," said Shakspeare gravely, "but rest now and we'll be back to see you tomorrow." "I'm all right, I tell you."

The Mayor immediately told his driver to take him to the home of young attorney William J. Parkerson. A sleepy Parkerson confronted the Mayor. "Mr. Mayor! What is it? Is something wrong?" Shakpeare marched past him into the sitting room. "Dave Hennessy's been shot by the Mafia. I don't think he's going to pull through."

"My God!" said Parkerson. "Now, listen, Bill. This is a perfect opportunity to get rid of these Dagoes once and for all --- Matranga, Macheca, and Provenzano. All of them. Didn't we just last week discuss the damage it could do if Provenzano was to start blabbing about the Louisiana Lottery? And you just having been appointed attorney to the Lottery? I.ve got big plans for you. And these greenhorns have been flies in the ointment for too long.

Now, here's what I want you to do. At 7:30 this morning, call the Times-Democrat and arrange for them to print a notice for mass meetings against the Mafia…"

CHARITY HOSPITAL NEW
ORLEANS, LOUISIANA
9:15 A.M.

Dr. Bloom softly closed the door behind him as he left Dave Hennessy's room. He looked at Tom Boylan, who was standing outside, and shook his head. "He's gone. We did everything we could, Chief Boylan." Boylan was aghast. "Oh, no! I can't believe it! He looked so alert." "His wounds were just too grave. He was awake and alert right up to the very end." "Well, at least I talked his mother into staying home with Bill O'Connor until noon. I'll go over and tell her." "Tell her the last thing he did was to ask about her," the doctor said sympathetically.

CITY HALL
NEW ORLEANS, LOUISIANA
OCTOBER 16,1890, 10:00 A.M.

The more Joe Shakspeare thought about it, the better he liked it. He had just been informed by Tom Boylan of Hennessy's death and it presented a perfect opportunity to get rid of Provenzano, Macheca, and Matranga at the same time; indeed, to get rid of the whole bloody Mafia before they cause so much heat on the city so as to disrupt the Mayor's own rackets, or, perish the thought, they get strong enough to muscle in themselves. He gritted his teeth. *That'll never happen,* he thought.

Shakspeare had always complemented the advantage of his impressive appearance by having extremely sharp instincts and an unerring sense of timing. In fact, he smiled to himself, his stage actor looks are what throw people off--- and he only needed them to go off balance for a second. That was the difference between winning and losing in this life --- when your shot came, you had to have the ability to be totally ruthless --- and no one had ever accused Joseph Ansoetegui Shakspeare of being lacking in that quality.

He put his feet up on the pool table-sized mahogany desk, and tilted back the massive red leather desk chair. The *Times-Democrat* early edition was in his hands. On the front page was an article signed by several Shakspeare lackeys, calling for mass meetings… "to assist the officers of the law in driving the murderous Mafia from our midst."

Shakspeare smiled. This was Parkerson's specialty. The young attorney had been Shakspeare's campaign manager and was a whiz with publicity. The Mayor's pleasant reverie was interrupted by his secretary.

"There are a couple of Councilmen to see you, Your Honor."

Shakspeare didn't have to ask who they were On his way to work that morning, he had stopped at the home of his chief councilmanic stooge, Councilman Duvall, with more instructions. The stern, long face of Councilman Duvall popped in the door. They had played this scenario with many different scripts many times before and both knew their parts by heart.

"If you're not too busy to see us, Your Honor, there's a matter of grave importance that we wish to discuss with you." "Matter of fact, I am busy, Duvall. The Mafia has just murdered the best damned Chief of Police this city's ever had." "Exactly why we're here, Your Honor." Shakspeare feigned surprise. "Well, why didn't you say so? Come right in." There ended the performance.

However, during this meeting, it was arranged that the Mayor would address City Council the following afternoon after the interment of Chief Hennessy.

CITY HALL
FRIDAY, OCTOBER 17, 1890
10:00 A.M.

Joe Shakspeare watched from the window of the Mayor's office as a cortége of black armbanded police carried the body to City Hall where It would lay in state all day. A huge crowd followed the cortége and shortly thereafter, began filing past the coffin. At noon, the Mayor's wife joined him, suitably veiled and attired in black right down to her silk stockings. Accompanying her was Bill Parkerson.

The Mayor stood next to Police Commissioner Beanham in the receiving line and shook hands with the mourners, one by one, sadly shaking his head, and vowing to anyone who asked that the assassination wouldn't go unavenged.

Shakspeare had ordered Beanham to see to the execution of a wholesale roundup of all Italians in the city; as a result, Charlie Matranga and his bodyguard, Tony Scafidi, had turned themselves in to the jail. Parkerson whispered to the Mayor, "There are more people here than when we laid old Jeff Davis out here last December." Shakspeare, appearing to brush a tear from his eye, gave Parkerson a sly wink.

Following a Requiem Mass at St. Joseph's, a huge crowd attended the interment at Metairie Cemetery, including every policeman, fire volunteer, and politician in the city. At the gravesite, Tom Boylan said to Bill O'Connor, "There's already a drive on to erect a fine large tombstone for Dave, Billy." "That's good, Tom, but what gets me is that poor Davey's grave is so close to the home of that swine, Macheca. I'll bet Macheca's cackling up his sleeve."

Boylan lowered his head and raised his eyebrows at O'Connor. "If he is, he's a lot crazier than I think he is. There is no more vicious gangster in this city than that lean and lanky bastard standing over there next to Mrs. Hennessy," He looked across the open grave towards Shakspeare.

"And believe you me, Macheca and his gang will find that out. Just thank God we're on the right side, Billy, because I'd hate to be an Italian in New Orleans tonight."

Thomas Duffy, one of the detectives who had alibied he Provenzanos at Hennessy's behest, stood nearby with tearstained face. "Is it true, Chief, that they've arrested Tony Bagnetto as one of the killers?" "From what I've heard, Tom, Scafidi turned himself in with Charlie Matranga to prevent being seized in the roundup. Why?"

"Because he's a low-down killer and a sneak, that's why. You know Messina, the artichoke king? Well, Scafidi tried to blackmail him and when Messina hollered cop, Scafidi tried to kill him. Also, Scafidi's got a fruit stand in Poydras Market. Another greenhorn opened a stand near his and was found with his throat cut. Scum like that shouldn't be allowed to live among decent people."

"Well, like I said, Tom, I'd hate to be an Italian in New Orleans tonight." Duffy, who had consumed flask of whiskey watching the funeral, started to cry. "That murderin' bastard thinks he's safe in prison; that's why he turned himself in."

PARISH PRISON
FOUR HOURS LATER

"Antonio Scafidi!" the jailer yelled, as he clanked his way down the prison corridor. "Si!" Scafidi answered. A squat, hairy, baldheaded, bull-necked man, Tony Scafidi had served Charlie Matranga as bodyguard for the last few years. He looked inquiringly at Charlie, who shrugged, "It must be your lawyer."

"But why are they not calling you as well, Padrone?" "It could be the cops. If so, answer nothing, Antonio." The jailer opened up the gate of the holding cell and Scafidi followed him in the direction of the visiting room.

Entering, Scafidi saw a man he did not recognize, facing him at a distance of about twenty-five feet. Thomas Duffy, after two or three stops at his favorite saloons, gave Scafidi a red-faced glare. "Do I know you, Signore?" Scafidi asked, approaching closer.

He could now smell the whiskey on Duffy's breath, and that, along with the crazed look of hatred on Duffy's face, spelled danger. As Duffy reached in his pocket, Scafidi made a move to duck behind the jailer, who was unarmed and wasn't having any of it. The jailer shoved him away just as Duffy fired his revolver. The shot hit Scafidi square in the neck.

The administration of the prison went into immediate pandemonium. Six guards rushed in from outside and wrestled Duffy to the ground; he put up no resistance. "I evened the score for Hennessy," he screamed. Duffy was handcuffed and taken to a cell. Scafidi, blood pouring from his neck, was rushed to the prison infirmary, where a team of doctors ultimately saved his life.

275 GIROD STREET
SAME AFTERNOON

During the funeral services while the house would be unoccupied, Bill Parkerson, at the Mayor's direction, and armed with a signed search warrant empowering him to search for evidence "material to the murder of Chief Hennessy" approached the two officers standing guard. One of them deferentially unlocked the door of the small house.

Parkerson refused an offer of help and sent him back to his post. Within the hour, he had found what he was looking for. He had removed the two bottom drawers of an old wardrobe in Hennessy's bedroom and behind one of them had found a small, locked metal box.

In it were documents relating to the Red Light Club, one a love letter from Shakspeare to Abbie Reed, dated six months earlier which Hennessy had filched during a sexual foray in Abbie's boudoir one night after they both had one brandy too many; proof of Shakspeare's substantial interest in the Louisiana Lottery Company; and, among other things, documents proving the Mayor's complicity, through straw men and kickbacks in numerous land zoning deals.

Parkerson considered having the documents copied but discarded the idea. The Mayor was nobody to fool with in New Orleans if you wanted to stay healthy. Parkerson stuffed the contents of the box into his valise and hid the jimmied box in a basement coal bin. *If it's found later, so what?* he thought.

CITY HALL
FRIDAY, OCTOBER 17, 1890 8:30 P.M.

The Honorable Joseph Ansoetegui Shakspeare, Mayor of the City of New Orleans, alighted from his brougham to face a bevy of newsmen blocking the entrance to City Hall. Gravely, he cleared his throat and addressed the crowd. "My own life…" he paused mid-sentence to see Bill Parkerson standing on the City Hall steps. Parkerson gave him a nod and a thumbs-up sign. Shakspeare nodded back imperceptibly.

Joe Shakspeare was such a master of oratory that the pause appeared as if he was just too overcome with emotion to speak. "…My own life has been threatened. I am convening a special meeting of City Council and asking for authorization to convoke a committee of fifty of our leading citizens to find the ways and the means to bring these assassins to justice. John Journee is acting chief and I ordered him to arrest every Italian he comes across."

Shakspeare brushed aside the reporters, who were in a state of high excitement, and grabbed Parkerson by the arm on the way by, and pulling him along. They went immediately to the Mayor's office where, upon examination of the incriminating documents, Shakspeare incinerated them in the fireplace.

"Í figured old Dave was smart enough to make a copy of Provenzano's stuff. He didn't disappoint me," said Shakspeare, warming his hands over the fire. As the Mayor prepared his mind to address City Council, he turned to Parkerson and said, "Bill, I knew I had picked a rising star when I chose you as my campaign manager. You're going to play a big role in this and when it's over, not only are you going to be a hero --- I am going to make you a very rich man as well."

The firelight threw shadows over Bill Parkerson's sandy hair and the way it illuminated his high cheekbones, while darkening his face directly below his glimmering blue eyes, gave him the look of a madman. "It's my honor to serve you, sir," he responded.

CITY COUNCIL CHAMBERS
CITY HALL, NEW ORLEANS
FRIDAY, OCTOBER 17, 1890
9:15 P.M.

The Mayor entered Council chambers with a phalanx of aides. Councilman Duvall caught his eye and hesitatingly began to clap his hands. He was joined by the rest of the members, but Shakspeare quickly took the podium and held up his hands for silence. He gazed solemnly around the oval dais and then to the rear of the sanctum to make sure that the Sergeant at Arms had let in a few, favored journalists and no one else.

"Gentlemen," he began, "tonight is a night that we all share in the deepest grief a man can suffer: the loss of a dear and devoted brother. Not only was David Hennessy a courageous and devoted champion of justice in New Orleans, he wasn't afraid to go up against the forces of evil in a forthright manner. Well, it cost him his life. And it cost us our brother. And it cost this city the best damned Chief of Police it's ever had."

An undercurrent of righteous indignation began throughout the Chamber. Shakspeare let it build until he had the atmosphere he was looking for. Then he raised his hand again. "I share your feelings to the fullest, gentlemen. But we must channel those feelings into the force of law against the cowardly assassins of Chief Hennessy. Else, who will be next? ...me?...you?...your families?"

The Council's mood was uglier than the favored reporters had ever seen it. Shakspeare continued. "With your permission, I'll read an open letter which I have written from me to you." You could hear a pin drop. The Mayor began.

'To The City Council:
It is with the profoundest grief and indignation that I make to you the official announcement of the death of David C. Hennessy, Superintendent of Police of this city. Grief at the loss of a true friend and efficient officer; indignation that he should have died by the hands of despicable assassins. He was waylaid and riddled with bullets almost at his doorstep on last Wednesday night, and he died on Thursday morning at 9:06 o'clock. The circumstances of this cowardly deed, the arrests made; and the evidence collected by the Police department show beyond doubt that he was the victim of Sicilian vengeance, wreaked upon him as chief representative of law and order in this community, because he was seeking the power of our American law to break up the fierce vendettas that so often have stained our streets with blood'.

Shakspeare wiped his brow and took a drink of water. His long, angular face had reddened, a curly, grey-flecked black lock drooped over one eyebrow; he was warming to the task. He hoped the new chief, John

Journee, was doing as well as he was. He had no cause for alarm there. By midnight, Chief Journee had rounded up 100 Italians, including Charlie Matranga, who had turned himself in.

Shakspeare, in total control of his audience, carried on:

'Heretofore, these scoundrels have confined their murderings among themselves. None of them have ever been convicted because of the secrecy with which the crimes have been committed and the impossibility of getting evidence from people of their own race to convict. Bold, indeed, was the stroke aimed at their first American victim. A shining mark have they selected with which to write with the assassin's hand their contempt for the civilization of the new world.

'We owe it to ourselves and to everything we hold sacred in this life to see to it that this blow is the last. We must teach these people a lesson they will not forget for all time. What the means are to reach this end I leave to the wisdom of the Council to devise'.

In case of backfires, the Council and Parkerson would be on the griddle, not Joe Shakspeare. On cue, Councilman Duvall volunteered, "Keep talking, Mr. Mayor, we're with you one hundred percent." The Mayor acknowledged his appreciation for their support.

'For years, the existence of stiletto societies among the Sicilians in this city has been asserted. Appeal was made, one by a prominent Italian during my former administration, to protect him from blackmail and murder, but he was afraid to give any names. I could do nothing for him. It is believed that these horrid associations are patronized by some of the wealthy and powerful members of their own race in this city, and that they can point out who the leaders of these associations are. No community can exist with murder societies in its midst. The Sicilian who comes here must become an American citizen and subject his wrongs to the law of the land, or else there must be no place for him on the American continent. This sentiment we must see realized at any cost, at any hazard. The people look to you to take the initiative in this matter. Act promptly, without fear or favor. Joseph A. Shakspeare, Mayor'

The tall man bowed deferentially and stepped down from the podium. The applause was a continuing thunderclap for the next minute and a half, as the Mayor took his honorary seat next to Council President and waited to hear the next speaker, the Honorable Councilman Duvall.

"Gentlemen," began Duvall, "in accordance with the Mayor's courageous request, I hereby move that we adopt a resolution to empower the Mayor to appoint a committee to deal with this crisis." The resolution passed by acclamation.

The Mayor returned to the podium. "Thank you for your confidence and support, Honorable Council Members. By virtue of the authority of your resolution, I hereby appoint a Citizen's Committee, made up of what I consider to be pillars of our society, whose duty it shall be to thoroughly investigate the matter of the existence of secret societies or bands of oathbound assassins, which, it is openly charged, have life in our midst and have culminated in the assassination of the highest executive officer of the police department, and to devise necessary means and the most effective and speedy measures for the uprooting and total annihilation of such hell-born associations and also to suggest needful remedies to prevent the introduction here of criminals or paupers from Europe.

"I appoint Edgar H. Farrar, Esquire, to serve as Chairman of said committee, as of tomorrow, October 18, 1890, on which date the committee will begin its existence, to serve ad hoc until its purposes and ends are accomplished. Since I have in mind to appoint eighty-seven names to the Committee, I'll not burden you by reading each and every name right now.

"However, my office will see to it that each and every one of youis provided with a copy of the members' names first thing in the morning. Thank you, gentlemen, and good evening. It's been a long day for us all. I suggest you follow my example and get some sleep."

There was thunderous applause as the Mayor and his entourage left the chamber. Fifteen minutes later, Joe Shakspeare entered the Red Light

Club and Abbie Reed disappointed a wealthy railroad man and escorted Joe upstairs.

In the privacy of Abbie's bedroom, the Mayor related some, not all, of the day's events. Abbie kissed him on the neck and stroked his hair. "Dave was a wonderful guy and a damned good customer of the club," she said wistfully. "Hang those bastards, if you catch them. I never liked that Provenzano anyway."

"How was he in bed?" Joe asked sarcastically. "Who? Joe Provenzano? Don't be silly," Abbie replied indignantly. "No. Dave." Abbie, despite herself, blushed a little, and giggled, "Oh, Joey! You know I never screw your friends."

She knew it was time to change the subject, and climbed aboard the tall man. As she mounted him, Joe Shakspeare smiled languorously and replied, "Then I must have a million enemies."

MACHECA ESTATE
METAIRIE, LOUISIANA SATURDAY,
OCTOBER 18, 1890 10:00 A.M.

Tony Bagnetto stood, hat in hand, before Joe Macheca. His huge face had a troubled look and he crumpled the hat nervously in his large, leathery hands. "I told the boss not to turn himself in but he wouldn't listen. Now, there's a hundred of them pinched." Joe Macheca looked only mildly concerned.

"Did Charlie say what he wanted me to do?" "Yeah. He says use your own judgment," replied Bagnetto. Bridget Macheca appeared. Joe, don't go in there! They'll kill you," she said, with an extremely distraught look on her face. "Don't worry, *cara mia*. It will blow over. Already, they've released 81of the hundred people they picked up last night. I'm going in.

"What should I do? Hide like a coward until they come to my own house for me? That would be playing right into their hands and showing evidence of guilt of a crime in which I had no involvement," said Macheca.

COURTHOUSE
NEW ORLEANS, LOUISIANA SATURDAY,
OCTOBER 18, 1890
12:30 P.M.

Upon entering the courthouse, Joe Macheca and Tony Baagnetto were unceremoniously taken to the Sheriff's cell room and detained. As they were being searched, a gun was taken from the big man, Bagnetto. Bagnetto shrugged. "I need it to protect Mr. Macheca."

The old deputy, a member of the White League of Reconstruction, said wryly, "Fraid y'all gonna need mo'n that, boy." Macheca glared at him. "What do you mean by that? We have done nothing wrong". The deputy just shrugged and took them to a holding cell which contained Charlie Matranga and the others.

Charlie smiled, "So you came, Peppino?" "Of course. Why are we being locked up with no charges?" As if in answer to his question, the old deputy appeared with a squadron of assorted sheriffs, police officers, and detectives, and they were hustled to a courtroom where Recorder M.S. Bringier sat as acting magistrate, for a preliminary hearing.

Lionel Adams, former district attorney of New Orleans, and now Louisiana's premier defense attorney, entered his appearance for the defense and was faced by District Attorney C.H. Luzenberg, who spoke first. "Your Honor, I move that this matter, with all its attendant publicity, and which is of the gravest concern to the citizens of this city, be heard directly by the Grand Jury rather than at this preliminary proceeding. That would also be more fair to the accused."

Luzenberg, a mild-appearing man with a reputation of one who will do anything to win, looked innocently at an enraged Adams.

"The best interests of the accused?!!" yelled Adams. "That's ridiculous. We don't even know who the accused are supposed to be! We demand a preliminary hearing to which we are entitled under the laws of this state and also of our constitutional right to be informed of the nature of the charges against us and to confront our accuser!"

Recorder Bringier, a Shakspeare appointee, shuffled his feet under the bench and said, "The District Attorney's motion is granted." Lionel Adams sprang forward, his agility belying his fifty-three years and 235 pounds. At six feet, four inches, he was almost eyeball-toeyeball with the little Recorder. Adams' blue eyes flashed below his close-cropped curly grey hair.

"The defendants will immediately file for a writ of mandamus to the Supreme Court, in which you, sir, shall be commanded to obey the law." The Recorder peered down his nose at the renowned attorney. "That, sir, is your privilege. However, you'd do well to remember that it is not I who am charged with breaking the law, it is your clients. Court adjourned!"

At the defense table, Charlie Matranga huddled with Adams, Macheca, and Dominick O'Malley, the ex-chief of police, now the head of a private detective agency, who served as Adams' investigator and was to serve in the investigation of the facts concerning the charges against the accused.

"You mean they can deny us a preliminary hearing and hold us without bail?" Charlie asked. Adams glared over Charlie's shoulder toward Luzenberg, then looked back at Charlie and said, "Charlie, until we undo it, they can do anything they damn well please. But if I know Luzenberg, he'll try to shove an indictment through the grand jury before we get a ruling on our mandamus petition; if he does, then, no, we don't get a hearing."

He looked at O'Malley "Dominick, you get right over to that restaurant where Charlie and most of these boys were having dinner when Hennessy got shot. Get statements from the owner, waiters, whoever can testify that they were there." O'Malley got up, "I'm on my way, boss. Don't worry, Mr. Matranga, it'll all get straightened out."

COURTHOUSE,
SAME DAY
2:00 P.M.

Despite their claim of alibi, Charlie Matranga and Joe Macheca, along with Tony Bagnetto, Bastiano Incardona, Antonio Scafidi, the Caruso brothers, and Sal Sinceri were held without bail and remanded to the Parish jail. As the eight men (the remaining eleven had not yet been charged) entered the receiving room, Joe Provenzano was in the midst of giving an interview in another part of the same prison.

"My boys and I were locked in jail when Chief Hennessy was killed so you can't blame us. In fact, Hennessy was to be the star witness in our trial next week and that's why he was killed. We were convicted by a pack of perjurers on orders from Charlie Matranga, and that's who ordered the murder of Chief Hennessy: Charlie Matranga. He's the head of the Stoppaglieri division of the Mafia in New Orleans. It's out of Monreale, Sicily".

A young reporter was scribbling furiously. He stopped and asked, "You're openly admitting that the Mafia exists in America?" "You kidding? They've got Mafia societies everywhere: in San Francisco, St. Louis, Chicago, New York, and here." An older reporter observed cynically, "It is rumored that you, yourself are a member of the Mafia, even a boss."

Provenzano drew back in mock horror. "Me? A boss!? I'm not even a member. I'm an American. Listen, we had a laborer's association when we had the stevedore business and we never let any greenhorns in it. All our men were Italians who were raised here. They were Americans. I'll show you what the Mafia thinks of the Provenzanos". He reached in his back pocket and pulled out a letter.

"Print this in your paper so the people will know the Provenzanos are Americans." The value of publicity and public opinion wasn't lost on Joe Provenzano.

PARISH PRISON
SATURDAY, OCTOBER 18, 1890

2:30 P.M.

The Parish Prison took up the entire block bounded by Orleans, Tremé, St. Anne, and Marais Streets, with the corner portion, at Orleans and Marais Streets, also housing the Fourth Precinct Police Station. In the middle of the block, on Orleans Street, there was an opening in the grim stone wall that enclosed the block. The opening was sealed by a pair of massive wooden gates, flanked by a watchtower manned by two armed guards. The watchtower also held a heavy iron winch from which the guards could raise or lower the barred, iron gate at the opening.

Inside the opening, was a foreboding cobblestone courtyard. The doors to the prison's administrative offices lay to each side of the courtyard, secured by yet another heavy iron gate.

The Hennessy prisoners would now total 19, and included Manuel Polizzi, Loreto Conitez, Carlo Traina, Rocco Geraci, Charlie Patorno, Frank Romero, and the two men who had accompanied Esposito from Sicily, Pietro Natali and Charles Poitza. Only little Gasparo Marchese,14, and his father, Antonio, along with Pietro Monastero, remained to be arrested. Gasparo as the boy whose alleged whistle signaled Hennessy's arrival, Antonio for nothing more than being Gasparo's father, and Monastero as the tenant of the building which allegedly housed the killers.

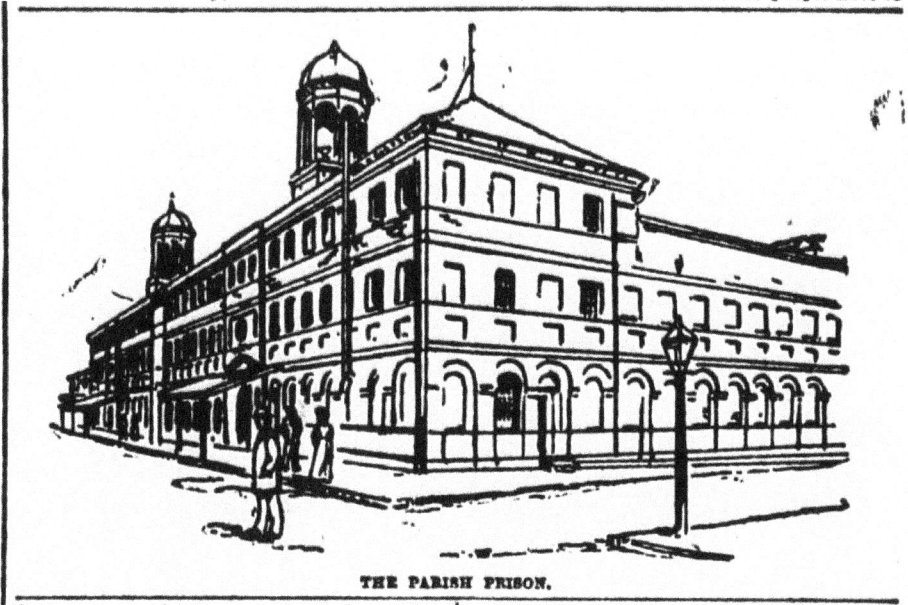

THE PARISH PRISON.

From the 15-March-1891 New York Sun.

The men in custody were now moved from the holding cell into the prison population. Captain Lemuel B. Davis, a tobacco-chewing, pot-bellied six-footer with a ubiquitous chaw in his mouth, housed them in cells along the first-floor corridor. He winked at Charlie Matranga. "Sorry Ah cain't put y'all up in the Star Chamber, but yo' freeunds, the Provenzanos, got it all booked up fo' now." Charlie smiled thinly at him. "Maybe you could find room for us anyway, Captain. As you said, they're friends of ours."

Davis guffawed. "Charlie, Ah lahk to go uppin mah apartment at naght n' know Ah kin walk out the front gate iffin Ah want. Y'all'd git tuh fahtin' n' kill one anothuh' afo' Ah cud stop yuh n'theeun *Ah'd* be in one a these here cells mahself." He spit a heroic spurt of tobacco juice against the stone wall of the corridor.

"How about some exercise, Captain? We've been cooped up in that holding cell for three days," Charlie asked. "Jist's soon's y'all git settled in heah, Ah'll give yuh two hours iffin yuh theeink yuh kin take it." "Take it? Why couldn't we take it?" "Wal, we got some pretty tough customers in heah. Summa y'all's pretty smawl, looks t'me". "We can take care of ourselves, Captain." "If you say so," drawled Davis.

As soon as the Captain and his guards had left, a voice rang out from up above, "Hey, Charlie. They're gonna hang ya! Ya hear me, Charlie? They're gonna hang ya, Charlie. That is, if you make it outta here." Joe Macheca yelled, *"Vafungu, Provenzano!"*

"Oh, you got Joe with you? They're gonna hang you, too, pigface! And after they do, I'm gonna fuck your wife!" Macheca's face went white, then purple, but Charlie restrained him. "Peppino, he's trying to look big to these scum in here. Don't answer." He held a frim arm on Macheca, who was trembling with rage. Charlie Patorno, who was known for having a cool head, said, "Come on. Let's go out in the yard and get some exercise."

This met with general agreement and in a half-hour the men were walking in groups in the exercise area, a pie-shaped yard between the corridors.

As they walked in groups of three and four, they were approached by a particular group of prisoners, all of whom had arms covered with tattoos. Their leader was a youth of about 23, with long, greasy blonde hair. His sleeves were rolled up despite the chill October day, displaying 16-inch biceps from weightlifting.

"Hey, there. Y'all the mayfia, huh? Well, y'gotta have permission tuh use this heah yard." "And who grants such permission?" Charlie said coolly. "Wayul, Ah giss y'came tuh th' right place. Me'n mah freeunds'r whut's called Captains of the Yard 'n we're the only ones who kin give that sort of permission. It'll cost you, but Mr. Provenzano says y'all'r meelyunaires."

Tony Bagnetto stepped forward. "Get lost, punk, before I break your head." Two inmates moved in behind Bagnetto. The first had an old lock inside a stocking which he used as a blackjack and gave Bagnetto a sharp blow behind the ear. Bagnetto crumpled to the ground.

The leader put a shank to Charlie's throat. "Make another move 'n yore daid, Dago." Inmates began to swarm toward them from along the walls of the yard. Instinctively, Charlie looked to the guard tower that overlooked the yard. The guard, who had been standing with his Winchester at port arms, took it and stood it against the rail. Then he cocked back his cap, folded his arms, and looked down with a malicious smile.

The Sicilians tried to group together as defensively as they could, but they were outnumbered ten to one. The Captains of the Yard and their minions beat the Sicilians with fists, rocks, and clubs, until they were all on the ground.

The leader looked down at Charlie balefully. "All that Mafia shit don't mean diddly-squat in here. Yore gonna pay jist lahk evvy othuh chump that comes in heah. Search 'em, boys, n' take evvything they got: watches, money, evvything." He looked down at the fallen men. "Mah name's Buck. This here's mah lootinent, Jethro." A tall, dirty-looking youth smiling through rotten teeth stepped forward. He kicked Joe Macheca in the stomach. "Like Buck says, yore gonna pay n' no one's gonna help yuh in heah. N' iffin ya don't come out, we'll be in tuh git yuh!"

Charlie had never been in a situation like this before. The worse thing he felt was the embarrassment of having let this happen to his men. Then helplessness. Then rage. His men looked to him for leadership. Charlie Patorno helped him to his feet. Tony Bags was still out cold. "Let's go inside," Charlie said.

Once inside the cellblock, there were catcalls from up above in the Star Chamber. "How's the weather, Charlie? Great day for taking some sun, eh?" Provenzano exulted. "Try to make it out every day, Charlie. I told all the guys what a nice guy you are and how much money you got. Haw, haw, haw!"

MAYOR SHAKSPEARE'S RESIDENCE
SUNDAY, OCTOBER 19, 1890
9:30 A.M.

A cynical smile pursed Joe Shakspeare's lips as he read the Sunday papers. He looked over his wire-rimmed spectacles at his attractive German-born wife across the glass topped wrought iron table on the patio of his mansion. "Get this, Antoinette. The *TimesDemocrat* has published a letter that weasel Provenzano has given them. And I quote. First of all, it says on the top, "A Letter From The Mafia." Pretty original, huh? Then, below that, there's a large cross which says on one side, "Honored Sirs", and on the other side, "Provenzano Brothers". The it begins.

"To Mssrs. Provenzano. You had better wake up and think of your outrage against justice, if you don't want to be done up by the Mafia. Hurry up and do this if you don't want to expose your life for your infamita. Wake up from your sleep and remember --- or you won't sleep the second time. You are adding to your infamita. In time. In time, your life."

"What hokum! Provenzano must have started writing the minute he heard of the murder. Well, it won't do the other gang any good and that's not a bad thing. But Provenzano's not going to walk away from this, either. He was on a sleigh ride with Dave. That's going to stop for these Dagoes in this city once and for all."

Antoinette smiled at him warmly. "I wonder if the people of this city appreciate what a fine mayor they have?" "As long as you appreciate me, dear, that's all that matters." "And is the Provenzano trial still coming up next week?" "No. I talked to Judge Baker last night. He's going to postpone it until January 12th." "Well, that's nice, dear. At least we won't have to be bothered with this nasty Italian business between now and the Christmas holidays." "My sentiments exactly, my love. Now let's enjoy our Sunday. We must hurry or we'll be late for church."

That night, an important message arrived from the Italian consul, Pasquale Corte.

ITALIAN CONSULATE
NEW ORLEANS, LOUISIANA
SAME DAY, SUNDAY, OCTOBER 19,1890

Pasquale Corte had been Italian Consul in New Orleans for fifteen years. It had been he who had dealt with Marshal Candelorio concerning Giuseppe Esposito in 1882. And he had no compunction in giving up one of his countrymen if there was a clear-cut violation of the law.

He was Roman by birth and had been brought up to respect the orderliness of things. In fact, if he had one failing, it was that he sometimes put form over substance. However, this was not to say that he was without compassion for his fellow Italians trying to exist in a foreign land amid alien rules.

Moreover, he had noticed the contempt with which many of those who called themselves Americans held his brethren, and this was especially true when it concerned Sicilians. At home, the Sicilians were held to be a strange, wild, inscrutable lot, but Italians nevertheless, and as such Consul Corte, would afford them the best services of the Italian government. However, protocol had to be followed.

The Consul was a short, squat, serious-looking man of forty-eight. His hair was as black as an Indian's. His liquid brown eyes intense and serious. A dark stubble had formed across his face due to the fact that he hadn't had time to shave before hurrying to his office on behest of Lionel Adams. But this was a serious matter indeed.

Consul Corte read back the letter to Mayor Shakspeare that he and Adams had composed. In it, he had voiced a strongly-worded complaint against the brutal treatment encountered by the Italian prisoners at the hands of the other inmates. "Signore Adams, that's all we can do right now. As soon as I receive the Mayor's reply, I'll contact Baron Fava, the Italian Minister in Washington. I'll have this hand-delivered to the Mayor's house right now. So, if you will be so kind as to return to my office at nine tomorrow morning, I expect we shall have the Mayor's reply considering the urgency of the situation."

"You're most gracious, Consul. I will go to the parish prisom and transmit to the prisoners your concern for their welfare and your diligence. I'm so sorry to have troubled you on a Sunday and would have never done so except that I consider the men's lives to be in danger." "They are lucky to have so conscientious an attorney as yourself, sir. Good day," replied the Consul.

After the attorney had left and the letter had been sent, the Consul stood at the large bay window, a troubled look on his face. He could sense trouble coming. And in large portions. Why, he wondered, do these people who consider themselves Americans refuse to accept us? Have we not come here in search of the same things that they have? He gazed out the window a long time.

ITALIAN CONSULATE
NEW ORLEANS, LOUISIANA MONDAY,
OCTOBER 20, 1890
9:00 A.M.

Mayor Shakspeare, after reading the consul's letter, had bid the messenger wait, and after some time had sent back a handwritten reply. When the Consul received it, he felt much better that the Mayor had given it priority and had recognized the seriousness of the situation. However, after opening it, the heaviness returned to the Consul's heart.

"…the rumor of maltreatment of the suspects is, I am satisfied, without foundation. On the contrary, I greatly fear that consideration for their personal comfort and the wishes of their friends has been carried beyond the limits of prudence."

Corte was dumbstruck. "Rumor?! Limits of prudence?! "Has this man gone mad?" he thought.

Corte ordinarily was a mild man, but Lionel Adams walked into his office to find him beside himself with anger. Corte shoved the Mayor's letter across his desk at Adams. "Mr. Adams, I am going to send a copy of my letter, and the Mayor's reply, not only to Baron Fava, but also to the Foreign Office in Rome.

"I am additionally sending a copy of the Mayor's address to the Committee of Fifty wherein he made the statement that, quote: "The Sicilian who comes here must become an American citizen and subject his wrongs to the law of the land, or there must be no place for him on the American continent."

"He said that?" marveled Adams. "It wasn't part of the speech that he released to the press, but, yes, he definitely said it and I have two witnesses who would swear to it. They would rather not have their identities known for fear of reprisals."

"Then, I would make you a further suggestion, sir, with your permission," said Adams."Not being an American lawyer such as yourself, any guidance from you would be greatly appreciated if it would help my people, Mr. Adams". "Then, I would also transmit my thoughts to the Grand Jury and ask for a full-scale investigation of the whole matter insofar as the assaults at the prison."

"An excellent suggestion, Mr. Adams. I will do it immediately," Corte replied, ringing for his secretary.

UNITED STATES STATE DEPARTMENT
TUESDAY, OCTOBER 21, 1890
2:00 P.M.

Secretary of State James Gillespie Blaine was a ringwise politician and perennial Presidential aspirant. His coziness with big business, railroads in particular, had won him Democratic reprobation (and a few hundred thousand dollars), and earned him the jingle, "Blaine, Blaine, James G. Blaine, that continental liar from the state of Maine."

Blaine instinctively blanched at the announcement that Baron Fava was waiting to see him. The last problem he had over Italians was the 1882 extradition of the bandit Esposito. Since then, he had resigned as Secretary in 1884 in a losing Presidential bid, then was re-appointed in 1888. He intended another Presidential run in '92, and he was very concerned that nothing would further blemish his reputation in the meanwhile.

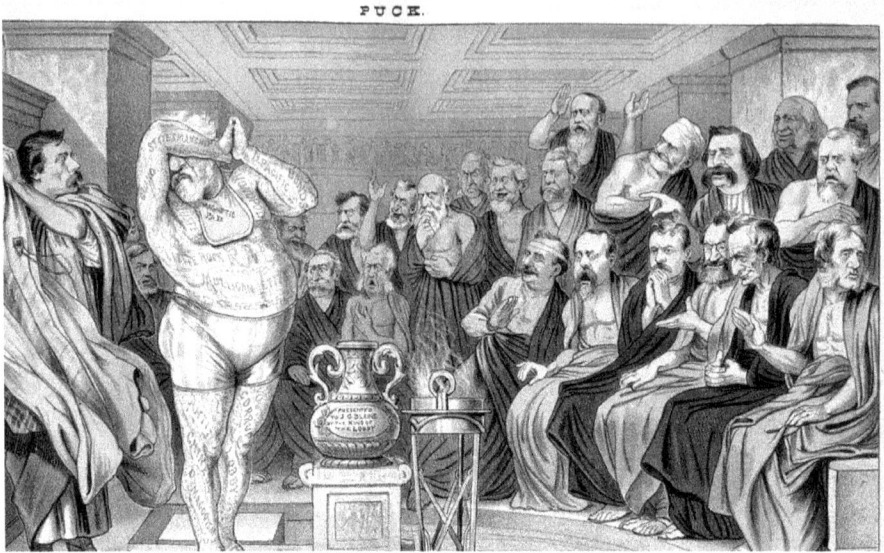

1884 Political Cartoon depicts Blaine as tattooed man indelibly inked with scandals.

He determined to concentrate on foreign policy and to continue the lucrative aiding of big business. "Show Baron Fava in," Blaine ordered.

The Baron, an Italian aristocrat from an old patrician family, walked with the erect bearing of a Prussian officer, his long nose emerging from between pale blue eyes, giving forth a graveness that was only lightened by an ironic lift to the corners of his thin lips, sending the impression that he was aware of the ridiculousness of life in general and diplomacy in particular.

He nodded gravely at Blaine before sitting and gave the proper greeting. Blaine beamed at him. "Baron Fava! Always a pleasure. What can we do for you?"

"I wish to convey to you, Secretary Blaine, a wire I just now received from the Marquis di Rudini, through the Secretary of Foreign Affairs from my country, concerning an incident which took place three days ago at the Parish Prison in New Orleans, Louisiana, in which Italians, both citizens and naturalized, were brutally assaulted and robbed. Moreover, the Marquis wishes me to protest the arrests, which were effected on a wholesale basis, with, from the best we can ascertain, no evidence.

"We further understand that there has been formed by the Mayor of New Orleans a vigilante committee, called the Committee of Fifty. We request that your office step in and see that it is disbanded and that our citizens and our naturalized Italian-Americans receive the 'due process of law' called for under the United States Constitution." The Baron sat in his chair, totally erect.

Blaine couldn't miss the intensity of the Baron's speech and decided against trying to finesse his way out of this one. However, Blaine had just made a speech wherein he had characterized future inter-American relations as having as their basis, 'just law and not the violence of the mob.' Maybe this could be turned to good use after all.

"Baron Fava, I'm shocked by what you have told me and therefore am going to send an immediate wire to the Governor of Louisiana to look into it."

****

Adams's detective, the fiery redhead, Dominick O'Malley, received a letter from the Citizen's Committee telling him to drop all investigations concerning the Matranga/Provenzano cases, which were upcoming, and also anything concerning Hennessy. Also, the Committee forbade him from interviewing witnesses concerning the cases, and ordered him to stay away from the Parish Prison and the Courthouse.

O'Malley's secretary had read the contents of the letter before handing it to her boss, and the shapely brunette stood by for a reply from O'Malley. She smiled to herself as she saw the blood rise in her boss's face. O'Malley chomped so hard on his cigar that he bit it in two. "Do you wish to dictate a reply, sir?" "Yeah!" he yelled. "Tell them I said 'fuck you' to all demands!" The secretary blinked her eyes. "Do you mind if I re-word that slightly, sir?"

The letter which did go out to the Committee Chairman, said, *inter alia*: "in response (to the Committee's letter), I can but say that I propose to conduct the business of my office without instruction from you or the committee you pretend to represent. Being unable to discern whence you derive any authority to "demand" that I should obey your behests with respect to the character of my employment I shall continue to reserve to myself the right to think and act without regard to your wishes. Later, I shall have occasion to "demand" at your hands the evidence upon which you have ventured to write of my "known criminal record and unscrupulous methods.""

MAYOR'S OFFICE, CITY HALL
NEW ORLEANS, LOUISIANA
WEDNESDAY, OCTOBER 22, 1890
NOON

Joe Shakspeare faced Bill Parkerson across his huge desk. "Well, Bill, Josh Baker has postponed the Provenzano trial until January 21st. By that time, I want to build a momentum against these Dagoes that will carry right through to their execution. And I don't want that weasel Provenzano to escape, either.

"Now what has the Committee been up to?" Parkerson pulled a copy of the Picayune from his jacket pocket. "Well, sir, we've requested through the newspapers that anyone with information to aid the prosecution should forward it to us anonymously. Along with that, we've requested the publishers to stop their reporters from interviewing witnesses to the case, and especially from publishing the interview. We want to keep the defense in the dark as much as possible."

Shakspeare: "How is Farrar taking all this?" Parkerson's brow wrinkled. "I'm afraid he's going to be a problem. The Times-Democrat has been giving us some flak over our secrecy and Farrar thinks it reflects badly on the Committee. He is also starting to bridle at the idea that the Committee is in keeping, as I said the other night, with the White League of Reconstruction.

"When I mentioned that, he blew up at me." "Don't worry about Farrar; we needed his good reputation to lend credibility to the Committee. But I can replace him now. In fact, I predict that he'll ask to be replaced before long."

"We've made pretty good inroads at the Daily States against O'Malley. They blasted him to pieces for helping the Mafia. I guess you saw it, sir." "Yes. It's important that we get rid of O'Malley. He's a damned good cop. I'd have had him working for me if he wasn't so damned honest," Shakspeare chuckled.

"He's hopping mad at George Dupre and Henry Hearsey, from the Daily States. The same day the article was printed, he sued for $10,000 for libel." The Mayor slapped his thigh and laughed heartily.

"That's Dominick, all right. A real hothead."

The Mayor looked seriously at Parkerson, and continued. "You know, Bill, the only thing we have to overcome is the alibi of all the main defendants having been in that restaurant, what's it's name?" "The Royal," Parkerson replied. "Yes. The Royal. I'm going to send the Health inspectors around to check for violations, but I imagine the alibi will still stand.

"However, if we stir up enough feeling against these people it wouldn't help them if they were at the Last Supper. And that's what I'm depending on you for, boy." "You picked the right man, Mr. Mayor. And I consider it a privilege to serve both you and my city." Parkerson's eyes had the mad gleam of a deranged zealot as he left the room.

As the door closed behind Parkerson, Joe Shakspeare let out a belly laugh. "I wonder if he really believes that crap, 'A privilege'. That's a hot one." He rose, put on his derby and was off for a late lunch with Abbie Reed.

Abbie greeted him with a wink as he entered the Red Light Club. "I've got something for you, Joey," she whispered, with a conspiratorial smile. "I'll bet you do," the Mayor smiled, patting her bustled posterior.

ITALIAN CONSULATE
NEW ORLEANS, LOUISIANA
WEDNESDAY, OCTOBER 22, 1890
NOON

Consul Corte put down the wire from Baron Fava with concern, then picked it up and read it again. "MET PERSONALLY WITH SECRETARY BLAINE YESTERDAY --- STOP --- EXPRESSED OUR COUNTRY'S CONCERN---STOP---BLAINE WIRED LA GOVERNOR NICHOLLS---STOP---NICHOLLS REPLIED THAT HE DID "NOT APPREHEND ANY TROUBLE"---STOP---TAKE ANY FURTHER STEPS YOU DEEM PRUDENT---STOP---FAVA."

Corte had spent all night drafting a complaint to the grand jury against the inmates involved in the beatings. He sent it by dispatch that afternoon along with copies to Baron Fava, Secretary Blaine, and Lionel Adams.

MAYOR'S OFFICE
NEW ORLEANS, LOUISIANA
THURSDAY, OCTOBER 23, 1890

A pretty, dark-haired secretary knocked before entering the Mayor's office. "Excuse me, sir. The Governor's on the line," she said. Shakspeare picked up the phone. "Governor?" A voice on the other end replied in a modulated tone, "Joe. How are you? How's Antoinette? Give her my best. The reason I called is this Italian business at the prison. Our State Department's giving me Hell about it. What's going on?"

"A bunch of crybabies, Frank. Some of the American prisoners roughed them up a little. The Italians probably threatened them." "Well, if it happened, I want the perpetrators indicted *pronto*, Joe. You know who they are?" "No, but I can easily find out from Lem Davis, the captain over there." "Good. You'll take care of it then and get these diplomats off my ass?"

"Sure thing, Frank. Let's get together over Christmas when you come to town." "It's a date, Joe. And, Joe, let me know when the indictments are handed down on those prisoners, will you?" Shakspeare hung up the phone and mumbled to himself, "He's not kidding."

Summoning the secretary, he said, "Call Lem Davis over at the Parish Prison and tell him to get over here as fast as he can."

That Saturday, the Committee of Fifty had an open letter published in the Daily States and the "Delta". In it, they appealed to Italians to come forward anonymously with information about their countrymen, supplying a Lock Box number and reminding them that "…vendettas must cease and assassinations must stop. To this, we must put an end, peaceably and lawfully if we can, violently and summarily if we must."

Edgar H. Farrar, Chairman of the Committee, read the letter for the first time in the newspapers and was incensed at its lawless undertones which he recognized immediately as authored by Parkerson. He decided to call a committee meeting for the following evening.

COTTON EXCHANGE BUILDING
FRIDAY, OCTOBER 24, 1890
7:00 P.M.

A disheartened Edgar H. Farrar stood at the podium and addressed the group of six dozen men assembled before him. "Gentlemen," he said, looking at Bill Parkerson, "the newspapers have made some troubling accusations against us.

Supposedly, they have received threats from this committee not to interview witnesses or print reports of testimony. Also, the Sheriff, Gabe Villere, was warned not to permit normal visits to the Italians. And, finally, the private detective, Dominick O'Malley, was supposedly ordered to drop the investigation of the case.

Now, there is this so-called "open letter" released to the press yesterday without my authorization, much less knowledge. "Now, does anyone here know anything about this?" There was no answer. Farrar pulled from his inside pocket a packet of letters. "I have here the letters that bore the threats; they are signed by William S. Parkerson and Walter C.

Flower." Farrar looked at both men. "Would either of you gentlemen care to comment?"

Parkerson arose. "They are our signatures, all right. There has been too much information being leaked out of this committee which will aid those murderers in the defense of their case." Parkerson looked at Flower, a local merchant whom Parkerson immediately had selected as a good foil to share ant potential blame for any extrajudicial measures which may become necessary later. Flower arose, "Edgar, I believe Bill's right. The tighter we keep the facts muzzled, the less those gangsters will have a chance to defend against."

Farrar's voice boomed through the room. "Gentlemen, we have banded together for one reason in this matter, to see that justice is not subverted. That doesn't mean we are going to subvert it ourselves.

"The accused are entitled to a fair trial under our laws. Those of you who are lawyers," he glowered at Parkerson, "should be the more so aware that these kinds of tactics are only feeding fuel for appellate reversals in the likely event that there is a conviction in this case."

Parkerson's eyes glowed like blue flames from an oil lamp. "If there are convictions, Mr. Chairman, you can rest assured that the accused *shall* be punished," There was a murmur of assent in the room. Farrar assessed the mood of the group and had second thoughts about having agreed to chair this assembly of --- bigots --- that was what it was all about, he suddenly realized, the Chief's murder was secondary.

It was who had murdered him. He had to admit he felt the same way, and he didn't really blame himself for the revulsion he felt against a secret society that enforced its code with murder. But he was yet to be 100% convinced that they had, in fact, committed this one, and he intended the committee's focus to be on evidence, witness, or jury tampering, not on manufacturing convictions.

Farrar looked at the faces before him, one by one, most were at worst, hostile, and at best, defiant. He sighed, "Gentlemen, I think it is time we went before the people and secured their mandate. I am calling a mass meeting at the Clay Statue for Monday night". That announcement was met with a cheer from the committee. They knew the people would be behind them. So did Farrar. But he didn't have to like it.

HENRY CLAY STATUE
ST. CHARLES, ROYAL, & CANAL STS.
NEW ORLEANS, LOUISIANA MONDAY,
OCTOBER 27, 1890
6:00 P.M.

Edgar Farrar was surprised at the turnout. What was to be a rally turned out to be a Monster Meeting. Thousands of residents of the Crescent City jammed around the old scene of the meetings of the white League of Reconstruction of bygone days. Farrar and three exconfederate officers addressed the crowd, which reacted favorably. Pleas were made to underwrite legal talent the equal of that of the defendants.

The Committee was awarded the right to raise $30,000 to further its work. One of the speakers, Colonel Eshelman, exorted the crowd against accepting any more Italian immigrants. "Why, if we don't band together, we'll be overrun by greenhorns. Right now, we have information that there's two steamers due to dock tomorrow morning, carrying 2,000 more of them. How many of those 2,000 are wanted fugitives in their own country and looking for a soft touch here? Are we just gonna take it?"

"Like Hell we are," shouted a voice in the crowd and 1,000 others yelled likewise.

Bill Parkerson noted with satisfaction the mood of the crowd and the faces, contorted with rage at the thought of the foreign invaders. He raised his fist in the air and faced them from the podium. "No!' he shouted. "No! No! No! No!" They followed his lead as one voice, "No! No! No! No!. Edgar Farrar viewed the sea of angry faces with regret; he vowed then to himself to resign from the Committee.

CANAL STREET DOCK TUESDAY,
OCTOBER 28, 1890
7:00 A.M.

Joe Shakspeare strode up the gangplank of the first of two ships which had docked there during the night, A cordon of police surrounded the ships. The Mayor was accompanied by virtually every member of City Council along with the Police Commissioner and a couple of drones from the Customs Department.

The mayor informed the captains of the ships that all passengers would undergo a rigid inspection to determine whether they were criminals, paupers, or had otherwise violated immigration laws, before anyone would be permitted to land in New Orleans The mayor strode back down the gangplank to the cheers of a large crowd of citizens from the previous night's rally who had made it their business to get to the dock early.

Shakspeare bowed graciously before entering his carriage for the trip back to City Hall. A hundred some families out of the eighteen hundred immigrants aboard were not permitted to land due to either poverty or one member of the family having been guilty of a real or imagined immigration violation.

COURTHOUSE
NEW ORLEANS, LOUISIANA
SUNDAY, NOVEMBER 9, 1890

District Attorney Luzenberg stood on the courthouse steps and held the press at bay, his thin blond hair whipping in the autumn breeze. "Gentlemen," he said, peering owl-like at them through his wire-rim spectacles, "during the course of the grand jury's deliberations, I have thought it prudent to order the courtroom closed from one o'clock every day in order to protect Grand Jury secrecy and prevent attempts at intimidation."

A young reporter spoke out from the crowd. "Sounds like a Star Chamber proceeding to me, and I don't mean the one over at the jail, either." The normally placid Luzenberg reddened visibly. "That's the way it is, gentlemen," he said, and entered the courthouse.

PARISH PRISON

MONDAY, NOVEMBER 17, 1890
3:00 P.M.

Charlie Matranga sat on a stool and faced Lionel Adams and Dominick O'Malley in the small cubicle reserved for attorney visits. A guard stood in the open doorway, forcing them to speak in low tones. Charlie's hair had been shorter than he normally wore it by the prison barber and Lionel Adams could see his cheerful exterior hid a haggard man. Dominick began the conversation. "Charlie, Lionel's got some news for you."

Lionel began, "The State Supreme Court earlier today ordered the recorder to give you a speedy preliminary hearing. They granted the Writ of Mandamus we filed on Monday, October 20th. Recorder Bringier again will be acting magistrate and he's set a hearing date for Saturday, November 22nd. If you remember, the last hearing was held on a Saturday. He's a Shakspeare man, as you know. Figures there won't be many people around on the weekend.

"However, I'm looking for the District Attorney to bring in an indictment before then, to be quite honest with you. Luzenberg doesn't want to give us a chance to examine the evidence before trial because for the most part it will be trumped up, and if there's no hearing he won't have to tip his hand."

Charlie's brow furrowed. "You mean if we get indicted before the date of the hearing, then we just don't get a hearing and have to go to trial cold?" he asked with disbelief. Adams ran his fingers through his wavy, iron-colored hair, and hunched his big frame forward. "That's the law, Charlie. Of course, we can file for a Bill of Particulars, but the information required to be given is subject to challenge by the prosecution. And you can't cross-examine a Bill of Particulars. But we'll have to cross that bridge when we come to it."

Charlie shrugged. "I guess there isn't much else we can do. How about this ruling by the Sheriff that I can't hold an interview with Dominick alone or with any reporters? And after letting Provenzano do whatever he wanted?" "Again, we have to go for a Writ of Mandamus. This time with Judge Marr.

"I've already talked to him about it and informally he's told me he will deny it, but will issue an order for you to have visits as long as it's during normal visiting hours. Listen, Charlie, Judge Marr, Sheriff Villere – they're all being given orders. Villere's ruling was as the result of an order from the Committee of Fifty. Marr's thinking is straight from Shakspeare. Shakspeare's at the root of our trouble, make no mistake about it, and he's a dangerous bastard."

Dominick O'Malley nodded his beefy red head. "That's where it's all coming from, Charlie. Every road I check leads to the Mayor. Why has he got such a hard-on for you guys?" Charlie spread his hands. "Who knows, Dominick? We've never done him anything but good." He looked at Adams. "So what's next, Lionel?"

"Once Marr rules, I'll appeal the Mandamus to the Supreme Court, but once they rule on it with the Christmas holidays coming up, the trial might be over. Meanwhile, I think Villere is trying to cooperate as much as his situation will permit. So arrange your visits during normal hours, preferably on the weekends, when not as many people will notice. Say Hello to Joe and the boys. Dominick and I have to go." The three men shook hands. Charlie, in his grey prison clothes, was taken back to the cell block.

****

After eleven days of deliberations, marked by legal skirmishes concerning the exclusion of defense attorneys and the press, the Grand Jury handed down two indictments against nineteen of the accused.

The indictments alleged "the existence of the secret organiza-tion styled 'Mafia'…'composed of Italians and Sicilians'…who 'in open defiance of the statutes of this state was responsible for the murder of David C. Hennessy, Chief of Police of the City of New Orleans.'".

The first count was for actual murder; the second for 'lying in wait'. Indicted on both were Natale, Scafidi, Traina, Bagnetto, Polizzi, Marchese, Monastero, Incardona, Sinceri, Comitez, and Poitza. Indicted only on the 'lying in wait' charge were Matranga, Macheca, James and John Caruso,

Patorno, Geraci. Romero, and the child Gasparo Marchese. The defendants preliminary hearing date of November 22nd was cancelled as moot.

COURTHOUSE
NEW ORLEANS, LOUISIANA
SATURDAY, NOVEMBER 29, 1890 10:00
A.M.

Recorder Bringier gaveled the arraignment proceedings to order. Lionel Adams declined to enter a plea on behalf of the defendants on the ground that grand jury secrecy had been breached via the presence of Court Stenographer John T. Michel during grand jury proceedings.

Adams also produced statements from grand jurors that Michel had attempted to influence their vote. Bringier gave Luzenberg an icy look, and said, "It's a constitutional rule, Mr. Luzenberg, which you well know, that *no one* is allowed to violate grand jury secrecy and that mean that *no one* is allowed present during the examination of the witnesses or deliberations. I will take this matter under advisement and postpone these proceedings until Tuesday, December 9th.Is that all, Mr. Adams and counsel?"

Adams stood to his full six foot four, "No, Your Honor. It isn't. I have here a motion to strike the entire findings of the grand jury for the grounds previously stated."

Adams approached the bench and handed the motion to Bringier. Bringier gave Luzenberg a contemptuous look, then another at William Parkerson and a few members of the Committee of Fifty, who were sitting in the rear of the courtroom. He yanked the motion out of Adams's hand. "This will also be taken under advisement until the 9th. Adjourned!" Bringier stalked out of the courtroom.

U.S. DEPARTMENT OF STATE
WASHINGTON, D.C. THURSDAY,
DECEMBER 4, 1890
1:00 P.M.

Secretary of State James Gillespie Blaine opened the wire from
Louisiana Governor Frank T. Nicholls:

"IN REGARD TO YOUR WIRE OF OCTOBER 21, 1890,
CONCERNING THE INCIDENCE OF BRUTALITY TO ITALIAN
PRISONERS BEING HELD IN THE JEFFERSON PARISH
PRISON IN NEW ORLEANS, PLEASE BE ADVISED THAT THE
LOCAL GRAND JURY HAS INDICTED TWO PERSONS
FORVARIOUS ACTS OF BRUTALITY AGAINST PRISONERS
PRISONERS IN THE PARISH PRISON. I HAVE BEEN ADVISED,
AND BELIEVE MYSELF THAT THE NATIONALITY OF THE
PRISONERS WAS NOT THE CAUSE OF THE
MALTREATMENT. DO NOT APPREHEND ANY FURTHER
TROUBLE REGARDING THE SAID PRISONERS."

Blaine put in a call to Baron Fava and shortly thereafter sent him a
copy of the Governor's wire.

COTTON EXCHANGE BUILDING
GRAVIER & CARONDELET STREETS
NEW ORLEANS, LOUISIANA MONDAY,
DECEMBER 8, 1890
7:00 P.M.

Cotton Exchange Building 1890

The meeting of the Committee of Fifty was well under way and fraught with controversy. Edgar H. Farrar called the men to order for the tenth time. "Simon," he said, looking at Simon Hernsheim, a committee member, "this is unbelievable. First of all, you come in here with information illegally leaked from someone in the Recorder's Office that Bringier is going to quash the original indictment on the grounds raised by the defense, then you and Sam Walmsley here say you're going to be appointed to the new grand jury by Luzenberg. He can't do that: it's illegal. And in any event, your presence on this Committee would preclude you from serving impartially."

William Parkerson arose, a look of scorn on his face. "Oh, come off it, Edgar. *Impartiality!* Who are we kidding here? There's no one in this room impartial. Those Dagoes are going to hang for killing Chief Hennessy and we all know it. Who better than some of us to help facilitate the event?! You say Luzenberg can't have them appointed to the grand jury? I say, 'who's going to stop him?'" Parkerson's eyes were bugging out in the familiar mad gleam. The Committee members growled their agreement with his views.

Farrar faced the group, his patrician face looking nobly haggard. He pushed back the strand of long, blue-grey hair that had fallen over his right ear. "Gentlemen, although my decision was made before the events of today, this reinforces it. I must confess, I intend to hand in my resignation. I agreed to head this Committee to make sure the law wasn't circumvented by the defendants. However, I will not be a party to anything that is unquestionably illegal. You have two weeks to find yourself another chairman."

Parkerson looked back at Farrar defiantly. "I nominate Jim Flower to serve as of December 22nd." He looked at Hernsheim. "Second," said Hernsheim. Parkerson looked about the room. Walmsley raised his hand. Slowly, every man in the room joined him. Parkerson faced Farrar with a snicker. "No problem, Edgar, you're replaced."

Farrar viewed the room for the last time. He wanted to call them fools. He wanted to say a lot of things. But these were men he had lived and socialized with for twenty years. And he realized he had never really known them at all. He was the outsider whereas he had always thought of himself as having commanded their respect. He shook his lionine head sadly and walked from the room. He did not return again although on Sunday, December 21st, he released a statement that the press of business and a prolonged absence from the city was the cause of his resignation. The day after Christmas, Edgar H. Farrar and his family left for New York to catch a steamer for the continent. He didn't return until Spring.

COURTHOUSE
TUESDAY, DECEMBER 16, 1890
10:00 A.M.

Recorder Bringier gaveled the second arraignment to order. Lionel Adams arose. "Your Honor, the defense wishes to object to the indictment returned two days ago by the newly empaneled grand jury which indictment is no more than a duplicate of the first indictment." Bringier, impatiently, "Is that your objection? That a true bill was found on the same charges?"

"No. That is not my objection, sir. My objection is that two of the members of the Grand Jury are not only members of the Committee of Fifty, but also have contributed money to a subscription raised by the committee, which is being used to aid the prosecution."

Bringier looked at Mayor Shakspeare, who was in the back of the courtroom, then back at Adams. "Your motion is denied, sir. The accused, however, will be arraigned on December 22nd in front of Judge Joshua Baker, who has been assigned to hear this case."

"What!? screamed Adams. "By what means did this case get taken from Judge Marr? It was Judge Marr's case!" He glowered at Luzenberg, who looked back smugly.

Luzenberg stood up. "If Mr. Adams will lower his voice, The case has been reassigned to Judge Baker because the State can't try it until after the Provenzano trial, which is scheduled for January 12th of next year, and Judge Marr won't be available during the month of February. If the defense hadn't made us go through the whole grand jury proceedings twice, perhaps we could have tried the case this month before Judge Marr. That's impossible at this late date. So, if there's any blame, it lies with the defense, not the State."

Adams stalked to the prosecution table and faced Luzenberg, placing both his huge hands on the table. "What did you have to do to get Judge Marr out of this case, you slimy bastard?" Bringier rapped the gavel. "I'm going to adjourn this hearing before I have to hold you in contempt, Mr. Adams, and I'm sure you don't want to spend Christmas in jail with your clients. Adjourned!"

SECTION "A" CRIMINAL DISTRICT COURT COURTHOUSE
ST. PATRICK HALL, CAMP & LAFAYETTE STREETS

NEW ORLEANS, LOUISIANA
MONDAY, DECEMBER 22, 1890, 10:00 A.M.

      Judge Joshua D. Baker entered the courtroom from chambers. All arose. The judge ascended the bench and proceeded to arraign the case of State of Louisiana vs. Charlie Matranga, et al. Lionel Admas stepped forward and was greeted warmly by Judge Baker. Adams looked over at the defense table and said, "I'd like to introduce to the court, Your Honor, the Honorable Thomas J. Semmes, who will be assisting me in the defense portion of this case." A tall, courtly, bearded man stood up and bowed slightly toward the bench, "Your Honor."

      "Senator Semmes needs no introduction, Mr. Adams, we served together in the Confederate Senate before Senator Semmes became Attorney General of Louisiana. It is certainly an honor to have you in my courtroom, Senator Semmes." Semmes bowed again.

      Adams spoke first. "Your Honor, there is nothing personal in this. As you know, I have the highest respect for you. However, I believe it is my duty to my clients to object to the way the District Attorney has allotted this case, having taken it from the judge originally assigned, Judge Marr". Baker's face reddened slightly. Luzenberg was on his feet to object but Baker waved him down.

      "Motion denied."

      Then, cooling off some, he looked back at Adams and said, "Lionel, we've known each other a long time. I'm sure you'll find I'll give your case a fair hearing. If not, then you have the right to take an appeal." Adams, knowing the game was up, replied, "Very well, Your Honor."

      Baker, mollified, said, "However, your objection is noted on the record. Now, how do the defendants plead to the charges before them which are murder and accessory thereto, and lying in wait and accessory thereto, so I understand that all defendants plead not guilty to all charges?"

"That's correct, Your Honor," answered Adams. "Very well, we'll take each defendant and each charge. Will the attorneys for the various defendants now enter their pleas?" When this was accomplished, Baker concluded, "As you know, I'll be hearing the Provenzano case, which is scheduled to begin on January 12th. Let's see, that's three weeks from today. I expect it to take about two to three weeks.

Baker smiled. "I suppose I'll be seeing you all there in one capacity or another." He nodded at Charlie Matranga, Joe Macheca, and the rest of the defense team and the prosecution. "Well, gentlemen, have a Merry Christmas," again looking at the defendants, "or as merry as it can be under the circumstances. And we'll set the trial date in this case for Friday, February 27th, 1891. Court's adjourned."

PARISH PRISON
WEDNESDAY, DECEMBER 24, 1890 CHRISTMAS
EVE, 2:00 P.M.

All of the defendants were brought to a bullpen holding room for a mass conference with their attorneys and their investigator, Dominick O'Malley. The murder case was discussed as well as the upcoming Provenzano trial. Mostly, it was a show of support on the part of the defense team, who were being hounded by members of the defendants' families. The family members were to be allowed to visit upon the departure of the attorneys and the investigator.

As the attorneys prepared to leave, Lionel Adams and Senator Semmes stayed behind with Charlie Matranga. When they were alone, Adams said, "There's more news, Charlie, and it's not bad. I've known Josh Baker for a long time, you know, and he thinks the world of Tom Semmes here. If Shakspeare wasn't involved in this, I'd have been glad to get him. The Mayor's the whole problem here. He's determined to get rid of you Italians because he sees you as a threat to his own rackets.

"Well, Senator Semmes and I ran into Josh Baker at a Christmas party last night. The wife of one of Senator Semmes' old Confederate buddies whipped up the party in honor of the Senator being in town. Tom and I buttonholed Judge Baker in a corner. He knows the charges are trumped-up on most of you fellows, but his hands are tied. However, we did commit him to one thing, and his word is his bond, he'd especially never embarrass himself in front of Tom Semmes as a southern gentleman.

"Anyway, we committed him, if a strong prima facie case isn't presented against you, he'll throw out the charges against you before the case goes to the jury. But just against you, nobody else. We had to take what we could get."

Charlie said with concern, "But how about Charlie Patorno and Joe Macheca? They don't deserve this." Senator Semmes looked at Charlie and spoke with command. "Son, be glad *you're* out of it. And having seen the evidence against you, I can virtually guarantee that. The others will have to win it on the square." "I didn't mean to sound ungrateful, sir," Charlie replied.

"It's just that I feel a responsibility to these men; they look up to me". "I know a little about responsibility, son.," the old warrior said, "but every little bit helps, and this is more than a little bit. When the charges against you are dismissed, it will take the wind out of the prosecution's sails." Charlie remembered his adventures of thirty years prior in Cuba with Captain Raphael Semmes, Senator Semmes' cousin. Charlie smiled.

"Sure. Thanks to both of you for everything, including coming out here on Christmas Eve." He waved over to Dominick O'Malley, who had been sitting across the room. The red-faced Irishman came over and sat among them. "Dominick," Charlie said, "I---all of us--we can't thank you enough for all the effort you have put forth for us. That grand jury information let them know they can't pull these kind of tricks without us knowing about it. Also, I know you caught a lot of Hell from the non-Italian people in this town. Thanks."

Dominick smiled. "All it ever takes to put me hard to work is for someone totell me that I *can't* or that I'm *forbidden.* They made a big mistake there." The men laughed. Lionel said, "Dominick's so stubborn that once he started to believe in Santa Claus, he refused to stop even when he grew up."

The lawyers and O'Malley left and Charlie was taken to the visiting room where his wife and brother, Tony, awaited him. It was the first time he had permitted his wife to visit and at the sight of him in the grey prison clothes with a day's growth of stubble, she broke down. Charlie looked at Tony uncomfortably and held his wife for the permitted short opening embrace. "How are the children, cara mia?" Through her sobs, Rita Matranga choked out, "They want to see you, Charlie. They can't understand where you are. Its Christmas. I haven't been letting them out of the house for fear one of their friends will say something."

"I told you I don't want them to see me like this, cara. It's no good. Soon I will be home." She looked at him as he was told to move to a seat across the table. "Are you sure, Charlie?" "I'm sure," he said, thinking of the words of Lionel and Senator Semmes.

"Oh, my beloved, make it soon. Please God, make it soon." When the visit was drawing to a close, Charlie had Tony stay behind for a minute so they could talk alone. "How has the fund-raising gone?" he asked his brother. Tony looked back soberly – he could always depend on Tony. "Good, Charlie, I've gotten word back from Paul Kelly in New York, and from Chicago, St. Louis, and San Francisco. Almost seventy-five thousand has been raised. It's on its way."

"That's good, Tony, we're gonna need it. Adams and Semmes get ten grand apiece. They're worth every cent of it. Dominick gets five. And the other lawyers at least a thousand apiece. Plus, we need some maneuvering money if we get a shot with the jury. They're trying to destroy us, you know." "I know, frati", Tony said. He could have said more because he could feel the mood building on the streets of New Orleans. It was so ugly, he didn't even want to contemplate where it would lead. No need to try and describe it to his brother. He had enough t worry about.

When Charlie returned to the cell block, Captain Davis was just returning Joe Provenzano to his cell from a visit of his own. The Star Chamber prisoners were permitted special, unsupervised visits in a special room provided for that purpose. As he passed Charlie's cell, which was near the stairs to the second tier, Provenzano yelled, "Merry Christmas, Charlie. It's the last one you greaseballs will see, so me and my boys hope you enjoy it. Har, Har, Har!" He was feeling no pain from the half flask of brandy his hooker visitor had brought with her.

Charlie made no reply. Charlie Patorno, Charlie's cellmate, peered through through the small wicket opening in the door. "Go on, you rat bastard! Get your drunken ass upstairs!" "Fuck you, Patorno, you'll swing, too, *novente passante.* big shot underboss. Rat? Who's testifying against who in my trial next month? Merry Christmas to all! *Bon natali, Christiani!"* Lem Davis hustled him up the stairs.

In a few minutes, Captain Davis returned to Charlie's cell. "Charlie, I gotta do what I'm told but that little loudmouth'll be outta here in a couple of weeks when his trial's over. Theein Ah'll move Y'all up tuh the Star Chamber and the dispensary cells next to it. Y'all'll be much mo'comfitible up there.

"Ah'll be glad tuh see that little loudmouth go; he's a pain in the ass!" "Thanks, Captain, we'll appreciate it." Lem Davis licked his chops. "Ahm sho y'all weeil," he replied.

****

Just before midnight, Manuel Polizzi got a cell-partner. Manuel Polizzi had always been obsessed with a burning desire to be a man of respect, a member of the Honored Society of his father's homeland, Sicily. In fact, his father had been a member of the Stoppaglieris, along with Charlie Matranga, before his death two years ago.

Manuel had been a puny child and the American kids had always picked on him and called him a wetback in the mistaken idea that, because of his name, Manuel, he was a Mexican. Indeed, he could have passed for one, with his olive skin, almond-shaped black eyes, and Indian-like black hair. Manuel was a hard worker and was a successful fruit merchant in the Poydras (French) Market. He dutifully offered Charlie Matranga, as the head of his sect (even if he wasn't a member –yet) a percentage of his earnings in hopes that the boss would someday call on him for a "service" --- anything to prove his mafiusu ---that he, too, was a man of respect like his father had been. But the call never came.

Many times when he was in a group of Sicilians, Manuel had to hold his tongue for fear of speaking against Charlie. He knew that if it ever got back, that not only would he never get initiated, but that he'd also likely get a visit from the feared Scafidi or Bagnetto, both of whom controlled the Italians and most of the other merchants in the market. Those sorts of visits could prove terminal.

Still, he wondered, why doesn't Charlie appreciate me? Why doesn't he see that I am a natural to become an *omu qualificanto* like my old man? He decided the thing to do was to volunteer for such a piece of work and therefore prove once and for all that he was a 'capable man', one who could kill and hold his silence as well.

Manuel waited for the right moment. Finally, when he heard on good authority that there was a 'piece of work' to be done, he went to Charlie and volunteered. Again he was rebuffed. Charlie told him that the man he had volunteered to kill was a good friend of Charlie's and that Charlie wouldn't think of harming the man.

Two weeks later, the body of Vincenzo Ottumvo was found floating in the Sixteenth Street Canal. It was the same Ottumvo that Manuel had volunteered to kill. When Manuel later hinted to Tony Bagnetto about it, he got a visit from Charlie Patorno and Tony Scafidi. They told him the value of one minding one's business.

Since then, although he still sent the boss a percentage of his earnings, Manuel lived in fear. He knew now that he would never be made a member, and that his own life might be in danger as well. He stayed away from them after that. And now, just because of his past associations, here he was charged with a murder he knew nothing about.

He was terrified. He hated the jail. And he was beginning to hate his co-defendants. He could hear Christmas carolers from Beauregard Square, across the street from the prison, as the door to his cell was unlocked.

MAYOR'S MANSION
11:45 P.M.

Joe and Antoinette Shakspeare had entertained all night. In the parlor, there was a fifteen foot spruce festooned with brightly-colored decorations of angels, the Magi, Virgin Mary, Joseph, and baby Jesus, along with candy canes and garlands. As the Mayor and his wife escorted their guests to the door, Joe Shakspeare put his arms around the shoulders of Bill Parkerson and Jim Flower.

"Boys, I know you'll make the difference this town needs as unofficial leaders of the Committee. Next month we'll get this Provenzano matter out of the way; then we'll settle with Chief Hennessy's killers once and for all." The huge oak door was open wide, showing a large holly wreath on the outside.

As Shakspeare stood with his back to the doorway, Abbie Reed, who had been brought by a beard, the ever-useful bachelor, Councilman Duvall, passed by. Abbie was dressed in a high-necked long black velvet dress with a small, red Christmas decoration on the breast, her hair coiffed in a demure upsweet; she looked very prim indeed.

In passing, she surreptitiously goosed the Mayor, and whispered sweetly, "Goodnight, Mr. Mayor." And turning to Antoinette Shakspeare, she said, "Wonderful party, Mrs. Shakspeare." As the party of guests descended the front steps, the Shakspeares called out, "Merry Christmas, everyone!"

Joe Shakspeare gave his wife an affectionate squeeze and Antoinette said, "That Miss Reed is so nice. I don't know why the wives avoid her. Just because she runs a club. It can't be too disreputable, dear. You go there." Shakspeare did a double-take and gulped before answering, "That's right, dear." *I wonder does she suspect,* he thought. Antoinette blinked innocently up at him, "Come on, Joe. We've got to hurry to midnight services or we'll be late."

PARISH PRISON
THURSDAY, DECEMBER 25,1890
CHRISTMAS DAY
2:00 P.M.

As Charlie Matranga, Charlie Patorno, Sal Scafidi, and Joe Macheca walked the exercise yard, Manuel Polizzi approached them accompanied by his new cell partner. "Charlie, this is Frank DiMaio. Just came over from Sicily; got pinched pushing the queer." Charlie nodded sternly at DiMaio, then said, "Excuse us, we're talking."

DiMaio separated from the group. Charlie said to Polizzi, who he had nicknamed, 'Joe', "Walk with us a minute, Joe, I want to tell you something." Polizzi gave Charlie a terrified look and fell in beside him.

"Joe, don't bring in any outsiders into our company. This is a bad time. Cell partner or no cell partner. Say as little as possible to him and try to get moved to another cell. Understand? *Sensa dic?*" "I don't tell him nothing, Charlie, but I'll do as you say." "Good. Merry Christmas, Joe." The other men said, *"Bon Natali"*. *"Bon Natali,* fellows," Polizzi stuttered and tripped backing away. He went back and joined DiMaio.

Scafidi said, "It's a good thing that little weasel don't know anything or he'd be spilling his guts out."

SECTION "A" CRIMINAL DISTRICT COURT COURTHOUSE
ST. PATRICK HALL, CAMP & LAFAYETTE STREETS
NEW ORLEANS, LOUISIANA MONDAY,
JANUARY12, 1891
10:00 A.M.

The trip from the Parish Prison to the Courthouse was about a mile. In the Provenzano case, the prisoners were transported by mule-drawn 'Black Maria' in two loads, one carrying the Provenzanos, the other, the Matrangas. All arose at Judge Joshua D. Baker's entrance. For the prosecution were district attorney Luzenberg, assistant district attorney John J. Finney, a stenographer, and a clerk. The defense table was manned by lawyers James C. Walker and Arthur Dunn. All of the defense attorneys on the Matranga team were on hand since this, the upholding of the charges against the Provenzanos, would enhance the defense's position. Also on hand sporadically were Mayor Shakspeare and many of the members of the Committee of Fifty.

After calling the Matranga Local 22 members who were shot at, Walker took over on cross, asking, "Did you have anything to do with the murder of Chief Hennessy?" When Finney went to object, Luzenberg kicked him under the table and he sat down. Lionel Adams and Senator Semmes were on their feet, "Objection, Your Honor!"

Judge Baker peered patiently at them through his wire-rimmed glasses,"\ "You gentlemen have no standing to object," he said, looking at Luzenberg, "but *you* do, Mr. District Attorney. Or does the Court have to do it for you?"

Luzenberg got to his feet reluctantly. "I was about to register an objection, Your Honor, before that outburst." "He was like Hell," said Dominick O'Malley, sitting next to Charlie Matranga on the prosecution witness bench. "No way he wants to make martyrs out of the Matrangas; he wants Provenzano to get off and he's throwing the case."

In short order, the defense portion of the case began. First to testify was Joe Provenzano. The wiry little Sicilian mounted the witness stand and smirked imperceptibly at Charlie Matranga. Dandydressed Jimmy Walker asked him the first question, "Why are you here, sir?"

Provenzano faced the jury and said loudly, "Because me and my men, as Americans, had the courage to face the Mafia on the docks." Again, no objection from Luzenberg; Judge Baker gave him a sour look. Provenzano continued, "the same Mafia that killed my friend, Chief Dave Hennessy!"

"Objection," Luzenberg said listlessly after the damage had been done with the jury. "Sustained," said Judge Baker.

Tom Duffy was brought in from the Parish Prison where he was serving six months in a separate wing for the shooting of Sal Scafidi. Duffy again placed the Provenzanos at the Bayou Club at St. Charles and Carrolton, on the other side of town at the time of the shooting. This time the district attorney did cross-examine. "Officer Duffy --- or should I say, former officer --- you are in the parish prison for shooting Salvatore

Scafidi, are you not?" Duffy answered defiantly, "That's right. He's a Mafia member and he killed Chief Hennessy!" Jimmy Walker hid a smile, as did Provenzano.

Adams again was on his feet. "Your Honor!" "Sit down, Mr. Adams," warned Judge Baker. Then, turning to the witness, "And you, sir, confine your answers to a 'yes' or 'no' or your sentence will be extended for contempt. The jury will disregard the remark of the witness."

Twenty police officers corroborated Duffy's identification of the Provenzanos, but this time the prosecution didn't point out that it would have been inexplicable that all these officers would be watching the exact men charged in the shooting at five o'clock in the morning.

The trial lasted ten days. On Friday, January 23rd, 1891, the jury acquitted all defendants on all charges after only an hour's deliberations. Joe Provenzano clasped his hands over his head in a salute of victory, and thumbed his nose at Charlie and Tony Matranga.

Provenzano was swarmed by reporters on his way out of the courthouse and made an eloquent speech, "---this America is a great country and the jury was quick to know me and my men were just poor working men being shook down by Mafia thugs!"

The only casualty in the trial had been the new police chief, John Journee, who had refused to appear with his men as a perjured witness. Mayor Shakspeare had the Police Board replace him with a new, more compliant chief, Dan Gaster, two days before the trial ended.

****

Back at the Parish Prison, Captain Lem Davis strode into Charlie's cell. "Wayil now, Charlie, that them boys is gone, Ah kin move y'all up to the Star Chamber 'n the Dispensary cell beside it. Be mo' comfitible, 'fyuh know whut Ah mean?" Charlie looked up at him from the bunk. "Fine, Captain, as long as you've got it fumigated from that pack of rats who were just living there." The prisoners climbed the iron stairway to the second floor. On the left, the first door led to the dormitory.

Tony Bagnetto said, "We'll go in here, Don Carlo, and you take the Star Chamber. It's a better room." Charlie looked at him patiently, a good man, this Tony Bags, "No, Bags, I don't want to sleep in the same room as that snake, Provenzano. Joe Macheca, Charlie Patorno, the Carusos, Romero, Sal Sinceri, and Rocco Geraci will bunk in here. Let the Marcheses, Incardona, yourself, the greenhorns, Monastero, Traina, Comitez, and Polizzi bunk in the Star Chamber".

Polizzi looked warily at Charlie. His cell partner, DiMaio, had been mysteriously released in the middle of the night and Polizzi had a horrible feeling that Charlie was plotting to kill him.

SECTION "A" CRIMINAL DISTRICT COURT COURTHOUSE
ST. PATRICK HALL, CAMP & LAFAYETTE STREETS
NEW ORLEANS, LOUISIANA MONDAY,
FEBRUARY 16, 1891 10:00 A.M.

The big day had come. The courtroom was mobbed with members of the press, politicians, relatives of the accused, Hennessy's mother and friends, Joe Shakspeare, Tom Boylan, and various and sundry others. Judge Baker called the court to order and began voir dire selection of the venire of prospective jurors. The full array of defendants, recently arrived via Black Maria from the Parish Prison, sat around the defense table.

Luzenberg stepped before the bench. Your Honor, the State requests a severance at this time. We desire to charge solely the defendants whom we believe were directly involved in the murder of Chief Hennessy." Judge Baker looked toward the defense table. "And what does the defense say?" Lionel Adams rose to his feet. "The defense has no objection, Your Honor."

Charlie Matranga nudged him as he sat down. "What's going on?" Adams leaned across and whispered to him, "This just shows that they have absolutely no evidence on the other defendants. Their presence here would only confuse things. The only disadvantage to us is that we could have had twelve peremptory challenges for each of the defendants. But on balance, it's to our advantage." Charlie relaxed and conveyed the information to the other defendants.

Judge Baker continued, "Then who do we have left as defendants in this part of the case?" "Macheca, Matranga, Scafidi, Bagnetto, Polizzi, Monastero, Incardona, and the two Marcheses," replied Luzenberg. "Very well. Trial on the remaining charges will commence at the close of this trial."

Appearing for the prosecution were Luzenberg and Finney, with Luzenberg this time as lead counsel. They were assisted by three attorneys provided by the Committee: Judge William L. Evans, a former district court judge known as "Hangin' Billy"; and two of Provenzano's defense counsel, Jimmy Walker and Arthur Dunn, both of whom had been friends of Hennessy's. The Sheriff, Gabe Villere, who had two brothers on the Committee of Fifty, sat at the prosecution table as well.

Lionel Adams and Senator Semmes were assisted by A.D. Henriquez, Arthur Gastinel, and Charles A. Butler, representing the whole array of defendants jointly except for Charlie Patorno, who had retained John Ferguson and Ferdinand Armant. Also at the defense table was Dominick O'Malley.

Judge Baker voir dired about 100 prospective jurors every day for eleven days. Finally, twelve jurors and two alternates were selected from a total of 1,375. The foreman was a Jew, Jacob M. Seligman, a respected jeweler. Number Two, also Jewish, was a real estate broker, Solomon J. Mayer. There was also a drummer, four clerks, two grocers, a bookkeeper, an iron molder, and a machinist. Testimony began on Friday, February 27, 1891.

MONDAY MORNING
MARCH 2, 1891

For his opening witness, Luzenberg called the name Peter Rossi. A darkly handsome young man of medium height strode forward and got on the witness stand to be sworn. Luzenberg gave a sidelong glance to Adans, who was sitting next to Charlie Patorno. "Your name, sir?" "Peter Rossi."

"And by whom are you employed?" "The William J. Burns Detective Agency of Chicago, on loan to the Boylan Detective Agency in New Orleans." "And what is the nature of the work for which you were loaned to the Boylan Agency, Mr. Rossi?"

"An undercover assignment. I was given a cell with one of the defendants in this case in hopes he would make incriminating statements to me." "Which defendant?" asked Luzenberg. Rossi looked at the defense table and zeroed in on Manuel Polizzi. "Manuel Polizzi."

"Could you point him out, please?" "Right over there, sitting to the right of Mr. O'Malley." "And for how long did you share a cell with Mr. Polizzi?" "Two months, sir." "And, during that time, did he, in fact, make incriminating statements?" "Yes, sir, he did. On numerous occasions."

"Liar!" screamed Polizzi. The defendants and their relatives started to boo. The judge called the courtroom to order and the District Attorney asked the next question, "And could you tell us the substance of these admissions as you remember them?"

"He told me that he was ordered by Charlie Matranga and Joe Macheca to kill Police Chief David Hennessy and that he carried out the killing with Antonion Scafidi, Antonio Marchese, Antonio Bagnetto, abd Pietro Monastero."

Slowly, Manuels Polizzi's eyes approached those of Charlie Matranga. When he saw the grey eyes staring at him, Polizzi was gripped with cold, sheer terror. He thought he would pass out and collapse on the table. Judge Baker called a recess. During the recess, Polizzi had his attorney ask for a conference with Luzenberg.

Luzenberg and Finney came into the side chamber of the courtroom and at seeing them, Polizzi blurted out, "I want to confess!" His attorney, Charles Butler, arose abruptly and said to Luzenberg, "This man is obviously distraught He doesn't know what he is saying." Luzenberg looked down coldly at the miserable little Sicilian. Polizzi's English was so bad that Luzenberg called, not only for a stenographer, but also for an interpreter.

Butler, a young attorney who was also assisting in the joint defense of the prisoners *en mass,* said to Luzenberg, "I had no idea this is what he wanted you for and I refuse to be a party to this. Moreover, I am faced with a conflict here in that I am defending the other prisoners as well. Therefore, I refuse to defend this man further, nor do I want ot hear any of his ravings." With that, Butler left the room.

When the stenographer and the interpreter were present, Luzenberg looked at the miserable little man and said coldly, "Tell him to make it fast. I have no intention of interrupting this trial and losing momentum."

He faced Polizzi, "Out with it!" Polizzi stammered, "On the night before they shoota da Chief we meeta at Macheca's house and we draw straws to see who does-a the shooting. Me, Scafidi, Marchese, Bagnetto, and Monastero get picked. I testify. Please no hang-a me!" Luzenberg looked back in disgust. He leaned over to Finney.

"Macheca was in the Royal Restaurant all night". Looking back at Polizzi, Luzenberg said, "Now, this was the night of the shooting, right? It couldn't have been the night before or any other night?" Polizzi was trembling. "That's-a right, boss. The same night. I sure. No mistake. About three hours before it happen."

Luzenberg turned to the Sheriff's officers. "Get him out of here." Polizzi screamed, "No! No! They'll kill me!" "I'll get you a new attorney and a segregated cell at the prison. That's the best I can do, Manny. Now, let's get on with this trial." Turning to Finney, he said, "Make sure what he said doesn't get to the press or Rossi's testimony will be nullified."

The trial resumed over vigorous defense objection. After hearing argument, Judge Baker said, "The court appoints Charles J. Theard to defend Mr. Polizzi." Polizzi jumped to his feet. "At's-a no good! He's a partner of Henriquez. I'm-a no trust him!" Exasperation was creeping into Judge Baker's normally placid courtroom demeanor.

"Well, I'll give you one more choice, Mr. Polizzi. Will John Q. Flynn, Esquire, approach the bench?" A young lawyer in the spectator side of the courtroom got up. "John, I hereby appoint you to defend this man. Is there any compelling reason why you cannot do so?" Flynn answered respectfully, "No, Your Honor. I'd be happy to defend him."

The next witness was a real estate agent named Kline. Luzenberg approached the witness dramatically. "Mr. Kline, did you ever see any of the defendants before?" Kline nodded his head. "Yes, sir. I did." Luzenberg stepped back. "Would you please point them out?" "Well, sir. There was only one. The heavy-set gentleman sitting over there." He pointed directly at Joe Macheca.

Luzenberg faced the jury. "Let the record reflect that the witness has just identified Joseph Macheca. And under what circumstances did you meet Mr. Macheca, sir?' "Well, I was a rental agent for the property on the corner of Basin and Girod Streets last August and he rented the building from me."

Luzenberg gave a satisfied look to the jury. "Under the name Joseph Macheca?" Kline shuffled his feet under the witness chair. "No, sir. He used the name Peter Johnson." Three employees of Kline corroborated the identification.

Luzenberg called a Boylan detective to the stand. "Did you, sir, see Mr. Macheca on the night of October 15, 1890?" "Yes, sir. I had him under surveillance. He had dinner with a party of people at the Royal Restaurant at Royal and Customhouse Streets. About one o'clock in the morning a newsboy came in with the news of Chief Hennessy's shooting and I heard Mr. Macheca remark that he was very happy to hear it and that he was sorry to hear the wound had not been fatal."

A newspaper delivery man placed Scafidi, Polizzi, and the elder Marchese at the corner of Hennessy's house shortly before the shooting: a black man identified the same three as the shooters; Monastero was identified as the tenant of the shop; an uncle of Scafidi's testified that Scafidi had an oilcloth coat similar to one found at the scene; others implicated Polizzi to shotguns similar to those used in the crime.

The by-now deranged Polizzi screamed and fainted and when he awoke, was so incoherent that he had to be placed in a straitjacket for the duration of the trial. Committee members attempted to show that O'Malley was trying to influence the jury. All in all, Luzenberg produced 67 witnesses in four days, using a rapid-fire approach which averaged two witnesses per hour including cross examination.

The Adams/Semmes team kept the cross down to a minimum, contending that their client's innocence was beyond doubt. Conversely, Luzenberg took the same tack with the defense witnesses, who numbered 84 in a whirlwind three days.

The main thrust of the defense was to establish that of the nine defendants, Charlie Matranga and Joe Macheca were across town in the Royal Restaurant and couldn't possibly have been at the scene if the crime. Next, that Bastiano Incardona was merely seen in the vicinity of the shooting on the night of the murder, without more. As to the other defendants, members of their families identified them as having been at home on the night of the shooting and not even having known Chief Hennessy.

As the defense closed, Luzenberg stood up and said, "Your Honor, the State moves to dismiss charges against Bastiano Incardona for lack of evidence." Judge Baker replied, "Motion granted," as he looked at Adams and Semmes. They both stood up and Adams said, "The defense moves to dismiss charges against Charles Matranga on the same grounds." "Motion granted."

Senator Semmes said, "The defense moves to dismiss charges against Joseph Macheca on the same grounds." Judge Baker looked toward the back of the courtroom at the bristling Shakspeare and replied, "Motion denied." "But, Your Honor, the evidence against my client and Mr. Matranga was identical. They were both having dinner in the same restaurant. How could you dismiss one without the other?" questioned Senator Semmes.

"Senator Semmes, I respect your concern for your client, but you seem to forget that he has been identified as having rented the shoemaker shop under an assumed name for the accused murderers. It's for the jury to decide if there was complicity."

So far, the trial had taken nine days with a total of 151 witnesses having testified. The prosecution and defense each took a day making their summations. Finally, Judge Baker charged the jury and they were released to deliberate on March 12th, 1891, at 6:15 P.M.

NEXT DAY, FRIDAY, MARCH 13, 1891
2:53 P.M.

The jury filed grim-faced into the courtroom. The atmosphere crackled with apprehension. The strain was on the defendants' faces as they and their relatives and supporters anxiously searched the jurors' faces for a sign of their fate. The jurors' faces betrayed nothing. Polizzi let out a sob and buried his head on the table. Luzenberg and Finney looked confident. The court clerk handed the verdict to Judge Baker, who read it and handed it back. The clerk, in turn, handed it back to the jury foreman.

Judge Baker looked at Mr. Seligman, the jury foreman. "Have you reached a verdict, gentlemen?" Seligman answered in a monotone, "Yes, Your Honor, we have."

"And would you read that verdict, please?" "We find the defendants Macheca, Bagnetto, Gasparo Machese, and Antonio Marchese not guilty." Reporters from all over the country scrambled for the door. Joe Macheca beamed at Charlie Matranga, who had been permitted to attend the proceedings even after the dismissal of the charges against him, at the request of Lionel Adams. "Whoever said that Friday, the 13th was unlucky, eh, Don Carlo?"

Seligman continued, "As to the remaining defendants, Polizzi, Monastero, and Scafidi, we are hopelessly deadlocked and cannot reach a verdict."

Bill Parkerson, seated in the back of the courtroom next to the Mayor, let out a lusty, "BOO!" He was joined by Tom Boylan, Bill O'Connor, many of the members of the Committee of Fifty, and even

Mrs. Hennessy, the Chief's mother. "Fix1 Fix!" Parkerson continued.

Judge Baker gaveled the courtroom to order. "Mr. Parkerson, as a member of the bar of this court --- for the present, at least --- you know better than that! Any more and you'll be arrested for contempt." The courtroom degenerated into pandemonium. Before the defendants and even the jurors could be released, special security arrangements had to be made for their protection. The prisoners had to be returned to the Parish Prison to await trial on the lesser charge that wasn't disposed of at the first trial.

****

VOL. XXIX.—No. 733.   NEW YORK, MARCH 25, 1891.   PRICE, TEN CENTS.

AT THE BOTTOM OF IT ALL.
COWARDLY JURIES ARE THE FIRST CAUSE OF MOB RULE.

MANY IN THE PRESS EXCUSED MOB RULE BY ACCUSING THE JURORS OF COWARDICE OR BEING 'FIXED'. HERE THE SATIRICAL MAGAZINE'PUCK' ON MARCH 25, 1891, SAYS, 'COWARDLY JURIES ARE THE FIRST CAUSE OF MOB VIOLENCE'

COMMERCIAL ALLEY
NEW ORLEANS, LOUISIANA
FRIDAY, MARCH 13, 1891, 5:00 P.M.

Bill Parkerson looked out the large, bay-front window of his second-floor office over Commercial Alley and saw what he had been waiting for--- a group of about two dozen men were approaching, walking on both sides of the narrow street and in the street as well. The large man who led them, Lloyd Ross, a sugar planter, had arms like tree trunks and shoulders to match.

Parkerson smiled to himself, "Now maybe we'll get some justice done around here." The men trudged up the steps to Parkerson's office. Ross spoke for the rest of the men, "Well, Bill, you said they'd buy the jury and they have. Now we're here to make sure they get what's comin' to 'em. "Will you lead us?"

Parkerson's eyes gleamed wildly. He could feel an erection beginning inside his plaid wool trousers and stuck his hand in his pocket to keep it down. "Of course, boys, but this isn't the place to disclose it. Let's all meet tonight at Frank Hayne's house." Ross looked back dully, "What time, Bill?" "I'll see you all there at 7 o'clock," said Parkerson, escorting them to the door. As soon as they had gone, Parkerson headed for the Mayor's office.

PARISH PRISON
SAME DAY, SAME TIME

Since the day that the Burns detective, Peter Rossi, alias DiMaio, testified and Manuel Polizzi had tried to make a confession, but was rebuffed, the little Sicilian was kept in isolation in the prison on the third floor in what was known as the "White Manchak" gallery. After the verdict, Polizzi was brought back to the prison in a separate van, incoherent. As he was being led up to his cell, he asked to see Captain Davis.

When Lem Davis had to climb the three flights of steel stairs leading to the isolation wing, he didn't like it. His size thirteen feet weren't in the best of shape anyway, and the climb seemed to make them worse. He appeared in front of Polizzi's cell.

"Whut is it, Manny? "N it better be guhd cawse Ah ain't partial tuh this climbin'". Polizzi looked at him desperately. "Captain, I don't wanna hang. Please save me!"

"Eeus that whut ya brought me allaway up heah fo'? Damn, Manny, a jury jist acquitted most a y'all, n'it's unlikely they'll even retry the rest a yuh." Hope gleamed in Polizzi's beady eyes. "You mean it's over? They're not going to hang me?"

"Hell, no, Manny. Now, don't go cawlin' me up heah agin, or *Ah'l* hang yo missibul li'l ass." "But why can I not go home?" "Cawse yore steeil bein' held on t'othuh charge. Leastways 'til they drop it. But that charge don't carry hangin', so don't worry about it."

Polizzi clutched the bars. Oh, Captain, *mille grazie! Mille grazie!"* With that, he collapsed onto his bunk.

Davis spit a burst of tobacco into the nearest corner. *Weird l'il cuss,* he thought, but he couldn't help but feel sorry for the tortured little guy. As he descended onto the second tier, he stopped by the dispensary, which was filled with all the Italian prisoners from the Star Chamber as well. "Wail, boys, corngratulations are in order."

Scafidi poured him a glass of Kentucky whiskey, which he took in his big paw. He looked at Charlie Matranga. "Waill, Charlie, corngratulations. Guess y'all'l be outtahere tamawra iffin yuh kin git a judge tuh set bail on a weekend on t'othuh charge." Charlie smiled at him.

"Not that we don't like your hospitality, Captain, but I hope you're right." Joe Macheca walked up. "What did that malad' upstairs want?" he asked. "Oh, ol' Manny's steeul worried about gittin' his neck stretched," Davis drawled. Macheca spit on the floor.

Davis downed the Kentucky in one gulp. "Waill, boys, Ah'll arrange a visit fo yuh tamawra iffin yer not spring by then/" Charlie took his hand and walked him to the door. "Thanks for everything, Captain. And tomorrow, whether we're released or not, a friend of mine will be in to see you with a token of my appreciation." Davis looked down at him.

"Shucks, Charlie, you've awriddy took keer of me jist fine," he shook Charlie's hand, "but Ah appreciate it n' Ah'll make shore that innyuh y'allthat don't git sprung'll at least have their --- needs --- taken keer of." He winked at Charlie and went down to his apartment. Charlie returned to the jubilant group. Joe Macheca and Tony Bagnetto sat side by side, Bagnetto's huge arm draped over young Gasparo Marchese's neck. "Salute, Don Carlo!" Bagnetto said, "we won." The boy, Gasparo, said, "I knew they couldn't beat us, Uncle Charlie." Macheca said happily, "You've led us through another one, boss." The other men cheered and Charlie smiled back.

"When do you think we'll get out of this pigsty, Charlie?" Macheca asked. "Soon, Peppino. Maybe tomorrow morning. Monday at the latest," Charlie answered. A large cheer went up from the men. Scafidi began to sing and all the men followed in, facing him. Charlie moved to his bunk and sat down, deep in thought.

The voice of Charlie Patorno brought him out of his reverie. "What's wrong, Charlie?" Charlie looked around to see Patorno's face registering concern. Patorno took a seat next to him on the bunk. "I don't know, Charlie, just a feeling. Something's not right."

FRANK HAYNE'S HOUSE
CORNER OF ROYAL & BIENVILLE STREETS SAME
DAY, 8:00 P.M.

Bill Parkerson faced a group of approximately sixty men who had jammed into Frank Hayne's house for the meeting. "Gentlemen," he said, "we're here tonight to do our duty to the people of New Orleans just like our fathers before us have since well before the days when we ran "Spoons" Butler out of town".

In the gaslight, the faces were contorted with excitement. The shadows gave their expressions a surreal look which Parkerson relished. He knew they would do what they were told. Gratefully. The feeling of power was sexually exciting to him. Parkerson ran a hand through his sandy hair and pointed to the two Villere brothers, siblings of the sheriff, which were sent with him by the Mayor to add a stamp of legitimacy to the proceedings.

"I'm sure you've noticed that Omer and Septime Villere are here to help right this terrible wrong that was done upon the people of New Orleans today by the bought-and-paid-for jury of Jews." "We're with you, Bill," yelled Ross to an echo of supporting applause.

Parkerson's eyes began to roll as he almost experienced a climax, but he held himself back and continued, eyes blazing. "Men, I know you're with me. Now, what I suggest is this. We sign a petition to be published in tomorrow morning's papers, calling for a mass meeting at the Henry Clay statue in Canal Street at ten o'clock in the morning. I've got the petition right here and in it each signer agrees that he is willing to carry out the will of tomorrow's meeting"

Parkerson produced the document and smiled to himself. It had been a blank piece of paper signed by Edgar H. Farrar and left behind to be filled in and serve as his resignation. Now Farrar was going to be the lead signer calling for the meeting at the Clay Statue. What irony! Parkerson loved it.

The petition was passed around and signed by most of the men present, including eight Committee members, and over fifty others. It read as follows:

"MASS MEETING: ALL GOOD CITIZENS ARE INVITED TO ATTEND A MASS MEETING ON SATURDAY, MARCH 14, AT 10:00 A.M. AT THE CLAY STATUE, TO TAKE STEPS TO REMEDY THE FAILURE OF JUSTICE IN THE HENNESSY CASE. **COME PREPARED FOR ACTION!"**

Parkerson took the signed petition and handed it to an underling to rush down to the various newspaper offices. He once more faced the crowded room. "All right, men. I'll need a committee to bring the arms." A dozen men raised their hands. "Fine. We keep the arms above Amos Baldwin's hardware store. Amos is waiting there now. Go and get the arms and bring them here."

He paused and said, "The Vigilannce Committee is adjourned until tomorrow at ten A.M."

1890

NEW ORLEANS POLICE CHIEF DAVID HENNESSY WAS AMBUSHED BY GUNMEN outside his home on Oct. 15, 1890. As he lay dying, Hennessy reportedly blamed "the dagoes," and the killing was widely believed to be a Mafia hit. Dozens of Italians were arrested, but a jury trial in 1891 ended without convictions. The next day, an angry mob stormed Orleans Parish Prison and killed 11 Italians, touching off an international crisis. No one was ever tried for the lynchings.

NONE GUILTY!

The Jury in the Hennessy Case Declares Their Verdict.

MASS MEETING!

ASSASSINATED

Superintendent of Police David C. Hennessy Victim of the Vendetta.

Ambushed at His Doorstep and Six Bullets Shot Into His Body, One of Which is Pronounced Fatal.

The Murderers Declared to be Italians of the Criminal Class

VIGILANTE MOB: The criminal case of the suspects in Hennessy's death resulted in mistrials and acquittals. Outraged residents called for a meeting on Canal Street the next day "to take steps to remedy the failure of justice." A crowd gathered at the parish prison, near the site of Municipal Auditorium, forced its way in and lynched 11 Italian men. Several of the victims had not even faced trial; three were Italian nationals. The local press and even the mayor defended the mob action as justifiable, but the federal government paid reparations to the families of the men.

COMING TOMORROW Allard Plantation becomes City Park

MORE PHOTOS, STORIES Expanded photo galleries on nola.com/175years

In other news | What was reportedly the first football game in New Orleans was played on Jan. 1, 1890, with the teams battling to a scoreless tie. The game ended when the ball landed in the New Basin Canal and sank.

SATURDAY, MARCH 14, 1891

The morning editions of the newspapers all carried the notice of the meeting with editorials concerning it. The Picayune said the meeting was "in the interest of peace…and justice"; The TimesDemocrat decried "the failure of justice" and said it was "entirely meet and proper" to discuss "the steps necessary to remedy the wrong complained of."

The Daily States, managed by a Committee member whose brother was on the Vigilance Committee, went further, castigating O'Malley and screaming for retribution.

MAYOR'S MANSION
9:30 A.M.

Antoinette Shakspeare bounced out onto the sunlit terrace behind her home through two tall French doors to find her husband standing with his face up to the warm morning sun. "Did I just hear you talking on the phone, dear?" she asked.

The Mayor stood with his hands behind his back and took a large breath of the crisp, chilly air. "Yes, dear. Just Bill Parkerson. Nothing important. You know, the Governor's in town today, and I just had a wonderful idea. As soon asI hung up the phone with Parkerson, I called the Governor and he and Mrs. Nicholls are going to meet us for lunch and drinks at the Pickwick Club, how does that sound, dear?"

"Oh, how romantic, Joe. It's so private there. I'll have you all to myself." Joe Shakspeare gave her a wink. "Just what I had in mind, my love. Where no one can find us."

COMMERCIAL ALLEY
9:45 A.M.

Parkerson and most of the signers from the previous night's meeting marched from his office toward Canal Street. Some were armed.

HENRY CLAY STATUE
ST. CHARLES, ROYAL, & CANAL STREETS
10:00 A.M.

A crowd of about five thousand milled around the statue in confusion as Parkerson's group approached. They made way as the vigilance Committee members filed through their ranks and, reaching the statue, marched three times in a circle around it. Some of the members of the crowd joined the ranks of the Vigilantes.

When this was done, Parkerson, Wickliffe, Walter Denegre, and James Houston mounted the granite pedestal at the base of the statue. The scene, ironically, was the same site which had seen crowds gather for the attacks on the Metropolitan Police Force in 1874, by the same White Magnolia and White League of Reconstruction which had killed Dave Hennessy's father for being a Metropolitan and for which Dave, in turn, killed White Magnolia Arthur Guerin. And now the White Magnolias and the White League were going to avenge that same Dave Hennessy, Jr.

Parkerson felt the rush of power as he looked down at the anxious faces awaiting his orders. He raised his hands and there was complete and utter silence. He spread his hands outward, palms down, took a deep breath, and began to speak.

"People of New Orleans, once before, I stood before you for public duty. I now appear before you again actuated by no desire for fame or prominence. Affairs have reached such a crisis that when men living in an orgabized and civilized community, finding their laws fruitless and ineffective, are forced to protect themselves, when courts fail, the people must act! What protection, or assurance of protection, is there left if, when the very head of our police department --- our chief of police --- is assassinated in our very midst, by the Mafia society, and his assassins again turned loose on the community?

"The time has come for the people of New Orleans to say whether they are going to stand for these outrages by organized bands of assassins, for the people to say whether they will permit it to continue?"

There was a rumble in the crowd which rose to a swell of, "No! No! Bring on the Dagoes!!" Two detectives had been assigned to surveulle the meeting. The older one, a thin,middle-aged man in his late forties, said to hisyoung partner, "Buck. Looks like this is goin' to turn nasty.Keep yo' eye out fo' a cab. Ah think we're goin' to be hightailin' it to the prison afore this is over."

Parkerson continued, "Will every man here follow meandsee the murder of David C. Hennessy vindicated?" Ross, the huge planter, raised a club and shouted, "Yes! On to the Parish Prison!!" The chant was joined by thousands more.

"Are there men enough here to set aside the verdict of that infamous jury, every one of whom is a perjurer and a scoundrel?" "On to the Prison! Hang the murderin' Dagoes and then we'll find the Jury!!" "There is no more infamous thug in this city than Dominick C. O'Malley." "Hang him!! Shoot him!!" "I now pronounce him a suborner of witnesses, a briber of juries, and the most infamous thing in this community! I now, right here, publicly, openly, and fearlessly denounce him as a suborner and procurer of witnesses and briber of juries! Men and citizens of New Orleans, follow me. I will be your leader!!"

Parkerson's face was flushed, a purple vein throbbed down the center of his forehead. His crazed eyes gleamed in the morning sunlight.

The next speaker was Walter Denegre, brother of Committee of Fifty member George Denegre. Denegre was a part-time minister and no stranger to whipping up the emotions and passions of the crowd. His attack on the trial was even more blistering. "Ladies and gentlemen," he said, "the law has proven a farce and a mockery. It now reverts to us to take upon ourselves the right of self-preservation. And that self-preservation should not forget the corrupt and bought jurymen in the employ of the wretch, Dominick O'Malley." More cheers. The older detective turned to his partner. "That does it, Buck, get right over to Dominick O'Malley's office and tell him that Des Kelly says for him to get his Irish ass out of town, and quick! Before it's danglin' from a rope. And tell him this is not time for one of his witty remarks! Got it?"

He looked urgently into Buck's young face. Buck was abashed: he had never seen anything affect the jaded old detective before. "Sure, Des. I'm on my way."

The summation speaker was John Wickliffe, an experienced courtroom orator and editor, known for his way with words. A man of tall, sinewy grace with greying temples and a full beard, Wickliffe's words rang with sincerity. "If such actions as the acquittal of these assassins are to be further tolerated, if nothing is done to portray forcibly the disapproval of the public of this infamous verdict, no man can expect to carry his life safe in the face of organized assassination.

"Fall in and follow us! Bill Parkerson will be your captain, Jim Houston will be your first-lieutenant, and I will be your secondlieutenant. Will you come!?" "Yes! Yeah! Yeah" "Then let's go!" Every weapon in the crowd was raised above the head of the man holding it. "Yeah! Yeah! Yeah! Yeah! Yeah! Yeah!"

"We knew we could depend on you. And in closing, I ---we--want every Italian in the audience and in this city to know that, as Bill and John have just said previously, we carry no animosity to their race as a whole. It's only against those members who come here thinking they can flout our laws and get away with murder ---against those members of that miserable and cowardly society, the Mafia, we take this action. Do you agree?" "Yeah! Yeah! Yeah!"

Parkerson, Houston, and Wickliffe were hoisted down from the granite pedestal and the mob headed back toward the Hayne house, a large group fell in behind each of the three leaders. When the mob reached the

Hayne house, weapons were distributed to the now rabid members and groups of men began streaming toward the prison through Royal, Bourbon, Dauphine, and Rampart Streets, picking up more members from each street.

PARISH PRISON
10:40 A.M.

Des Kelly could see the ominous structure looming before him as the cab tore up Orleans Street. "Whip 'em, cabby! This is a matter of life and death! And I ain't kiddin'!" The horses raced up to the corner of Beauregard Square and Kelly leaped out and raced across the street to the Fourth Street Police Station at the corner of the prison on Orleans and Marais Streets. Kelly ran in.

"Sergeant, there's a mob on its way here to hang the Italians!" he yelled. The sergeant looked up from his edition of the Daily States. "Is that so?" he said unconcernedly. "I hear the governor's in town, too." He went back to his newspaper. Kelly grabbed the newspaper. "Didn't you hear me, man? There's a mob on the way here to lynch the Italians. Raise an alarm!!"

The white-haired sergeant grabbed the paper back with a beefy hand. "You raise an alarm, sonny. I'm not liftin' a finger to save the murderin' Dagoes. You got no respect for the Chief?" Kelly looked behind the sergeant and saw at least a dozen uniformed officers and detectives studiously ignoring their conversation. He glared at the sergeant. "Fuck you, fatso. I'll see you at the Review Board. He raced for the door. The sergeant looked at his back. "Likely you will, sonny; likely you will."

Kelly raced down Orleans Street to the main gate of the prison. The heavy iron gate blocked his way but the huge wooden doors that closed behind it were standing open. A jailer eyed him through another set of bars across the open cobblestone courtyard. "Open up!" Kelly screamed. "Sez who?" answered the jailer. Kelly flashed a badge. "Open up and get Lem Davis down here! Tell him it's Sergeant Des Kelly!"

"Evvything 'round here's an emergency", moaned the jailer, taking out his keys and opening the gate. He called to an unseen cohort, "Get the

Cap'n. Man says it's impawtint." He shuffled across the courtyard and opened the massive iron gate to the prison. Kelly ran past him. "You'll have some movement in that lazy ass of yours before this morning's over, me boy," he said.

In the Star Chamber and the dispensary, the men were sitting around discussing the hangovers they had from the victory party of the night before. Joe Macheca sat on a bunk across from Charlie Matranga and Charlie Patorno. "What's taking them so long with the bond, Charlie?" the portly man asked. Charlie shrugged. "Who knows, Peppino? Weekend ---this--that---who knows?"

He looked across at Patorno, who, by that time, could read his boss's thoughts almost as well as he could read his own, He knew something was bothering Charlie. Patorno chimed in to change the subject. "How's your head, Joe?" he asked Macheca. Joe Macheca smiled across at him and said, "Charlie, I never drink. But if a man didn't celebrate after the ordeal that ended yesterday, well, he wouldn't be human. The whole city had us hung before the trial even started. So I guess it's better to be hung over than to be hung, no?" He laughed at his own joke.

Tony Bagnetto, who had heard it, also let out a hearty laugh. "That's a good one, Mr. Joe." He nudged young Gasparo Marchese and rumpled his hair with a meaty hand. "Is funny, yes, little Marchese?" The boy smiled self-consciously and nodded his head. The other men were sitting around in various stages of undress, talking and smoking.

****

Young Gasparo was the first to hear it. At first he cocked his head. Then he said to his father, "Father, what is that noise?" Antonio Marchese was a stocky, balding man with thick, hairy arms and a short, thick frame. "What noise, Gasparo? You've been here too long. You are hearing things, *figghiu.*" The men laughed.

All but Charlie Matranga and Charlie Patorno. They exchanged a meaningful glance. Gasparo said to his father, "No, father. Don't you hear it?" Before his father could dismiss the boy's words again, Charlie Matranga held up his hand. "Silence!"

The men looked dumbstruck as Charlie Matranga cocked his head in the same manner as had Gasparo. The room fell silent. It was then that they all heard. A distant rumble. But there was no mistaking the hostility of it --- no mistaking the ominous discord. It grew louder. The mobs swarmed out of Royal, Bourbon, Dauphine, and Rampart Streets, and swelled into well over 5,000 that would converge into one screaming, bloodthirsty, armed rabble in the square opposite the prison.

Lem Davis appeared at the door of the dispensary and motioned Charlie into the hall. The normally unflappable Davis didn't conceal the expression on his face from the men in the room, though. It conveyed urgent concern and naked terror.

PICKWICK CLUB
CORNER CARONDELET & CANAL STREETS
NEW ORLEANS, LOUISIANA
NOON

PICKWICK CLUB

The governor of Louisiana, Frank Nicholls, and his wife were seated with Mayor and Mrs. Joseph Shakspeare at an elegantly set corner table at the Pickwick, New Orleans's most exclusive club. Nicholls, a popular governor, had lost an arm in the War.

Frank Nicholls, elegant of bearing and quick of mind, was a party man and tried to stay out of local problems. He and Shakspeare had been longtime political --- and business –allies: the Southern Pacific, the Louisiana Lottery, and others. But this time Nicholls was concerned, urgently concerned.

"Joe, that Italian consul Corte tracked me down at my lawyer's office. Wanted me to send troops to the prison to protect the Italians. I turned him down. He then asked for you and I told him I expected a call from you shortly. Finally, a call came and Corte ran out of the office saying a mob was at the prison".

Joe Shakspeare shrugged. "Governor, the so-called 'mob' is a vigilance committee comprised of the finest and most respectable citizens of this city. Off the record, if I wasn't Mayor, I'd be out there with them." Antoinette Shakspeare chimed in, "Oh, he would not! Joe's such a pussycat. He just acts tough."

"In any event," said the Mayor, "there's nobody better able to handle this than the Committee. If any Dago doesn't like it, they shouldn't have murdered our Chief od Police. I'm not going to intervene. In fact, until you just mentioned it, Frank, I didn't know there was anything to intervene about. And we still don't know, except for some second-hand hearsay phone call to Corte. Now, let's enjoy our lunch."

"I'll second that," smiled Marylou Nicholls, "Frank's so serious." She elbowed her husband. "All right, all right," Smiled Frank Nicholls as the soup arrived. But he didn't enjoy his lunch.

STAR CHAMBER
PARISH PRISON
LATE MORNING

The usually imperturbable Captain Lemuel B. Davis was in a high state of excitement. He tried to keep his voice to a whisper. "Charlie, a detective I know was just downstairs. That mob outside is a lynch mob They say after they're done here they're goin' tuh hang O'Malley and the jurors. The detective's on his way to the jurors' houses now tuh warn 'em. This guy don't lie, Charlie. Ah don't know what to do. Iff'n Ah wuz t'let y'all go, they'd lynch me shore. Probably too late for that innyway. They'll be in here inny minute."

Charlie eyed him intensely. "Does that mean you're going to give us up to them, Captain?" Davis ran a big hand across his nose in frustration. "'course Ah'm not gonna give Y'all up, Charlie, goddamit, but Ah'm not gonna git Mah neck stretched, either. Them Magnolias is plumb crazy. Owney thing Ah kin think of this quick is tuh turn y'all loose in the prison 'n it's evvy man fo' hisself. Maybe we kin rustle up some reinforcements afo' they find y'all. Ah'v got a call in to the Mayor."

"Forget the Mayor. He's probably the one who agitated all this." Lem Davis grabbed Charlie by both arms. "Lissen, Charlie, Ah'v got an idee. Ah think Ah know where Ah kin hide one'r two y'all. Now don't git lost on me. Stay right here at th' bottom of the steps. Iff'n Ah ain't back within fahve minits, tein at most, do the best y'kin fo' y'self. Ah'm leavin' th' door open; now tell'em tuh git goin' afo' they're caught."

Charlie nodded and the big man ran down the stairs at a gallop. Charlie re-entered the room. Every face looked to him anxiously. Joe Macheca spoke first. "Don Carlo, what is it?" Charlie raised both hands.

"The noise we heard is a mob. A lynch mob. They're coming here for us and they'll be here any minute. The Captain's left the door open and he's giving us the run of the jail to hide ourselves any place we can. Says it's the only thing he can do until help arrives. So every man hide yourselves the best you can. I hope we all come through this together. Hurry, there's no time to spare."

Bastiano Incardona looked back incredulously. "But, Don Carlo, the charges against me have been dismissed. I know nothing of the death of Hennessy. It was proven in court! Mother of God! Are they mad?" Charlie looked at him compassionately. "There's no time to discuss it, Bastiano. Hurry!" The men scrambled into their closthes and, like horses in a stable fire, began scrambling out the door. Antonio Marchese had a big, hairy arm around Gasparo's shoulder.

As they hurried toward the door, he stopped and cried to Charlie, "Padrone, no let-a them get my boy! Please! Padrone, I've lived my life. But Gasparo. He's-a never done-a anything in his life except what-a I'm-a tell him. Please, Padrone."

Charlie put his hand on the big shoulder. "Leave him with us, Antonio. There might be a way." Hope sprung into Bastiano's eyes. "I know you will save him, Padrone". He stopped and kissed Gasparo's cheek. "You stay with-a you uncle Charlie, Gasparo. I'm-a be all right."

Gasparo clung to his father with both arms. "Then let me come with you, father. I don't want you to leave me." The elder Marchese broke his son's grasp and handed the struggling youth to Charlie Patorno. Tears were in his eyes as he gasped, "Goodbye, *figghiu miu*" With that, he scurried down the iron stairs.

By this time, the noise outside was a thunderous roar. The crowds of people had converged into one mass on Orleans Street. Six thousand people lined the street and spilled into Beauregard Square. The group that had followed Parkerson and a man named Charles Ranlett was in the vanguard.

Parkerson strode up to the iron gate at the front entrance. The sleepy deputy who, a few minutes before had confronted Des Kelly, was now fully awake. Parkerson glared at him and said, "We want the Dagoes out here that murdered Chief Hennessy and we want them now!" The deputy looked back timorously and said, "I have no authority to do that, sir. You'll have to speak to the captain."

"Open the gate!" commanded Parkerson. "I can't do that, sir," was the deputy's reply. "I'm ordering you to let us into the prison!!" screamed Parkerson. The deputy just stood there, quaking in his boots. Parkerson eyed him for five seconds. "Boy, don't let me catch you when we get inside!"

Parkerson stepped back and surveyed the wall of the institution. The nearest opening was the heavy oak door leading to Lem Davis's apartment. "This way, men," screamed Parkerson, who headed for the door. A battering ram was set up but after four tries the weakened door still wouldn't give.

AN EPISODE OF THE LYNCHING OF THE ITALIANS IN NEW ORLEANS

    Parkerson spotted a Samson-like black man standing at the edge of the crowd. "Grab that man!" Parkerson yelled. "A couple of you men, take your pikes and pull me loose one of those paving stones out of the street." Four men wedged loose a massive stone, weighing about two hundred pounds.

"Lift it up and hand it to him!" Parkerson said, pointing to the black man, who looked back in terror.as Parkerson approached him. "Boy. You're going to take that stone, make a run at that door, and knock it down. And don't tell me you can't do it. If that door don't go down, we'll start by hanging you!"

The men dropped the stone into the black man's huge arms. He stood for a second, wild-eyed in terror, then rocked on his knees for a second and charged the door. As the two-hundred pound missive propelled by two hundred fifty pounds of desperation, hit it, the door smashed into toothpicks and the crowd looked in wonder.

Ranlett, standing beside Parkerson, yelled, "Now, we have the prison, we will bring those people downstairs, and the law will be vindicated in broad daylight. We will have a public execution." The mob surged in.

The door led to a vaulted hallway. The door to Davis's quarters was immediately on the left, then the hallway continued to run to the gate connecting it to the rest of the prison. Meanwhile, Lem Davis had returned to the foot of the stairs leading to the Star Chamber, where he encountered Charlie Matranga, Charlie Patorno, and young Gasparo Marchese. Davis's shirt was open and he was covered with sweat.

"Damn, Charlie, this is gonna be bad!" he yelled. "Ah've put guards all around the prison but there's a couple thousand people out there. We've gotta move fast. Ah've arranged something for the two of you --- Ah guess we might could fit the boy in too. But HURRY! Follow me!"

As Davis started off down the corridor, Gasparo put his arms around a pole and hung on for dear life. "I'm not going anywhere without my father!" he screamed. Charlie Patorno grasped him around the waist and pulled but the youth's grip held fast. Davis turned and yelled, "Leave him or Ah'm leavin'the three a y'all. COME OWNN!!"

Charlie Matranga turned and hollered to Gasparo, "Come on, boy. Your father wanted you with us." Tears streamed down Gasparo's cheeks. "NO! No, uncle Charlie. I want to stay with my father! I will not leave him!" He tightened his grip on the pole. Patorno looked at Charlie. Charlie bit his lip and said to Patorno, "Come on, Charlie. I don't think the crowd will harm him. Let's go!"

The two men raced behind Davis down the dimly-lit, disinfectant-smelling corridor toward the women's side. When they reached the heavy oak door connecting the two sides, Davis spoke to a stocky matron there. "Heah they are, Pinny. They're awl yores now!" He turned to the two Charlies. "Good luck, boys. It's the best Ah cud do fo yuh, but Ah think it'll work out. Ah gotta go see whut Ah cud do fo't'othas."

Charlie grasped Davis's meaty hand and attempted to kiss him on the cheek, a move which Davis deftly evaded. "Captain, we won't forget you." As Davis ran down the corridor, he yelled, "An Ah sho' won't fogit Y'ALL!"

Matron Penelope Dugent pulled them unceremoniously inside and slammed and locked the heavy door, "Follow me," she ordered. They were led down still another corridor to a flight of steps, which they ascended. At the top was Penny's office.

"Take that desk and slide it out of the way!" she commanded. As they did so, Penny went to a tool cabinet and removed two large claw hammers. "Now, take these and lift up a couple of those floorboards. Make sure you don't lift any but where the desk covers".

The two Charlies did as ordered. As the floor boards were removed, a space between the 12-inch joists was revealed; the joists were 18 inches apart. Penny looked down. "Good thing y'all'r little fellas. Ah'd nivir fit in there. Git on in." Charlie Patorno looked at Charlie Matranga, who shrugged hopelessly, and did as he was told. Patorno did the same. Penny hammered the boards shut over them and slid the desk back into place. She then took a seat behind the 4x7 foot desk, put her hightop-clad feet on it, and began reading a book.

The mob had battered down the gate leading from Davis's quarters to the rest of the prison, and was now roaming the corridors looking for victims. Davis, meanwhile, had locked all the non-Italian prisoners around the "white yard" where the white prisoners took segregated exercise.

Manuel Polizzi, in a state of frozen horror, had been released to find a hiding place, the same as the other Sicilians. As he descended from his thirdfloor condemned cell, he found the dispensary and the Star Chamber empty. Wild-eyed, he ran down the remaining flight of stairs to the first floor and raced down the first floor corridor away from the noise of the mob. He came upon Salvatore Sinceri racing in the same direction. "Sal, where can we hide? Help me!" he wailed. There was no time to argue and Sinceri merely said, "Follow me!"

The two men came to a rear staircase, where Davis kept his pet bull terrier in a packing-crate kennel. "In here," said Sinceri. They yanked the bulldog out by his chain and squeezed into the packing crate.

Pietro Natali, one of the Sicilians who had accompanied Esposito to America thirteen years prior, found himself alone and ran to a wash-house on the far side of the "white yard". He crawled under a bench in the far corner of the room which held mops and buckets, and pulled some of them in front of him until he was concealed.

John Caruso had been one of the first of the Sicilian prisoners to race from the dispensary area. A guard had advised him to head for the women's side, but Caruso had run the other way and come to the "white yard" just as the prisoners were being locked into holding cells. He jumped in with the rest, and, having the Scandinavian looks of his mother, wasn't noticed.

The group led by Parkerson had reached the dispensary area and raced up to it via the iron staircase, only to find no one but young Gasparo Marchese. "Where are the rest, boy?" Parkerson screamed at him. "Tell me or we'll hang you!" Tears streamed down Gasparo's face, "I don't know, sir. I don't know. Please don't hang me or my father. My father didn't do anything." Parkerson gave him a slap on the face. "Where are they, I say!" The boy wretched and said miserably, "I don't know! I don't know!"

One of the mob grabbed him and said, "Let's hang him first!" Parkerson grabbed him by the arm."Leave him! We got no time to waste on him while the others get away, and no time to carry him with us. Leave him!" With that, he started down the stairs. Gasparo called after him fearfully, "Please don't hang my miu Babbo!"

"Wait a minute!" called Ranlett. "The condemned wing is upstairs. A guard told me that that's where they're holding Polizzi; let's search it!" The men turned and ran up the stairs to the third tier, the "White Manchak" gallery. They found the iron gate to the gallery locked. Meanwhile, Wickliffe's "squad" had gone on to the "White Yard" and, peering into the cells, had noticed no Italians; they had not seen John Caruso.

However, one of them looked up from the yard which was covered with an open-grilled floor, and said, "There's some of them!" Joe Macheca, Antonio Marchese, and Antonio Scafidi had come to a rear stairway that led up to the rear of the "White Manchak" Gallery and had frantically ascended it, looking for refuge. At the top they found the "condemned" cells, even Polizzi's, locked and empty.

They tried to descend the stairs again only to see the mob enter the "white yard" below them. They were thus stranded onthe gallery, standing on an open grillwork floor, visible to the mob below, and to Parkerson's men on the other end. Rifle and shotgun fire from both directions was directed at the men.

Joe Macheca looked at Antonio Marchese and Antonio Scafidi. "Mother of God! We're trapped up here! There's no way out!" Macheca spotted an Indian club that the condemned men were permitted to work out with during exercise periods. He lunged overand grabbed it as a rifle bullet whizzed past his head.

He then ran to a locked cell and tried to batter the lock off the door. "If we can get inside these cells, they won't have an open shot at us." Scafidi curled up in a ball on the floor. "What's the difference? They'll only come up here and shoot us anyway. We're done for." As he said it, a shotgun blast tore through his rectum and as he turned over he was hit by two more rifle shots from the far end of the gallery. Simultaneouly, a volley of shots tore through the other two men. Joe Macheca fell dead with the Indian club still clutched tightly in his hand, broken in half by his desperate efforts to break the lock on a cell. Antonio Marchese died worrying about his son's safety.

Bastiano Incardona, who had the charges against him dismissed for lack of evidence, had spotted the Macheca group up the stairs and had started to follow them when he heard the mob below entering the yard. So he stopped at the second floor and hid in a cardboardbox in a closet while the execution of three on the third floor took place, escaping discovery.

Manuel Polizzi heard the shots from his position crunched up inside the dog kennel packing crate. He let out a frightened whimper. "They're killing them; they'll kill us all!" "Shut up!" snarled Sinceri, "you're moving the box and going to get us caught. If you don't like it here, get out!"

Polizzi crawled around him. "I will! I'm not going to get caught in here like a dog. They'll shoot right through this thing and never give us a chance to explain! If I could just explain to them, they'd know I had nothing to do with the Chief's murder. I'm going to explain!" He crawled around Sinceri and out the opening. "Fool!" whispered Sinceri after him.

Polizzi began hysterically running in the direction of the noise. He ran down a corridor and made a left turn right into the gargantuan arms of Ross, the sugar planter. "Signore, I am Manuel Polizzi. I am innocent of any crime. I want to tell you…" Ross grabbed him by the back of the neck and was about to shoot him point-blank with the sawed-off shotgun when Parkerson stopped him.

"Ross! No!" The command made Ross turn around. Polizzi slumped in his arms. "Oh, Signore. Thank you! I knew you would understand! I am innocent! Oh, thank you!"

Parkerson looked at Ross. "We can't kill them all in here, it's not fair to the rest of the people---take him outside!" Slowly, Ross nodded, a smile crossing his cruel lips. For his part, Parkerson was attorney enough to know that once the blame was shared by the mob, there was very little chance of being held personally responsible.

Polizzi was dragged out onto St. Anne Street to the cheers of the mob, and thereupon dragged to the corner of Treme Street, where stood a lamp post. A rope was thrown over it, and the screaming Polizzi was strung up by the neck. As he swung, a dozen men with Winchesters moved into an empty space made by the crowd and emptied their weapons into the lifeless form.

Meanwhile, Antonio Bagnetto had been discovered by Wickliffe's party in the "White Yard". He was shot and though in great pain succeeded in stifling his cries and attempted to simulate death. The party began to leave, when Wickliffe said, "Make sure he's dead. "Four men with Winchesters marched toward Tony's inert form. When he saw the men prepare to empty their weapons into him, Tony got up and pleaded for his life.

Wickliffe looked down coldly. "Put a noose around his neck and take him outside with his goombah! Search the cell he just came out of!"

The party entered the cell and found Loreto Comitez, Frank Romero, Rocco Geraci, Pietro Monastero, Carlo Traina, James Caruso, and Carlo Poitza, the other Sicilian who had come over with Esposito in 1878, cowering in a corner. As the prisoners saw the gunmen in the doorway, they put their hands up to their faces to shield themselves.

"There's a nest of 'em in here, Mr. Wickliffe," yelled one of the men. Wickliffe left Bagnetto for a minute and came to the open cell door. "Good! That's the rest of them.""What about Incardona?" shouted one of the men.

"He wasn't involved; the judge dismissed the charges. Forget him. Open fire!" Dozens of bullets and shotgun loads were fired into prostrate, screaming men.

Finally, Wickliffe said, "All right, men. Cease fire! Let's get this one outside! Bill Parkerson said to bring this one with us!" They dragged the wounded hulk of Tony Bagnetto along with them toward the entrance.

As the sound of their footsteps diminished a solitary figure moved among the mass of dead bodies. The diminutive little Sicilian, Carlo Poitza, a solitary figuramong the mass of dead bodies. The diminutive little Sicilian had jumped behind the portly Pietro Monastero just as Monastero was hit and going down. Poitza had stayed immobile under Monastero's crushing weight, but the bullets that had torn the others apart had spared him their deadly message. He was alive.

Tony Bags was dragged out the same door as had been Polizzi onto St.Anne Street with the noose already around his neck. Near the hanging body of Polizzi on the corner of Treme Street, a large tree grew in Beauregard (Congo) Square just off the street. "String him up on that oak!" the crowd yelled. A boy scampered up the tree trunk to clear the large branch near the bottom.

At the sight of Polizzi, Bagnetto screamed, "No hang-a me! Shoot-a me!" and he struggled with his captors in hopes that he would be shot. Ross was nearby and clubbed him over the head. Then, half-unconscious, the mob hoisted him by the neck up to the branch. The swinging of Bagnetto's huge body was too much for the rotten old branch to take. With a soft, crunching sound it broke and the swinging, still-alive Bagnetto slowly accompanied the rotten branch on its descent groundward.

"Stay up there, boy!" the mob yelled to the youth in the tree. "Find a bigger branch! That one was as rotten as he is! HAR! HAR!" The boy smiled and scurried for a higher branch. "This one'll do it," he yelled, and climbed down to catch the rope thrown up to him. He looped it around a higher limb and threw it down to the crowd. A dozen of them hoisted the more dead-than-alive Bagnetto back up until he was securely swinging.

The mob let out a triumphant cheer.

Across the street, the mob, at Parkerson's orders, boosted him up to stand on a window ledge of the prison. With his foot on the granite sill, and hanging onto the barred grillwork outside the window for support, Parkerson addressed the mob. "Citizens of New Orleans!" Parkerson yelled over the din of cheering voices---he paused for silence and Ross clubbed a noisy man next to him who had too much to drink. "Let the Captain speak!!"

Parkerson continued, "Citizens of New Orleans, of the men who stood trial and bribed a jury for their acquittals, we have taken care of Polizzi---there he swings---" The mob cheered. "Bagnetto— there he swings," Parkerson pointed and the mob let out another cheer. "And all the rest. Macheca, Scafidi, Antonio Marchese, and Incardona," he paused. "The three remaining defendants were the young Marchese who was only a boy and probably not involved, and the two defendants, Matranga and Incardona, who had their charges dropped by the judge for lack of evidence. So we got 'em all."

The mob let out another cheer. "In fact, we even got a few who were charged with the murder, but weren't in the first trial."

The mob yelled, "Let's get O'Malley and the jurors!" Parkerson held up his hand for silence. He assumed a courtroom air of piety as he continued. "I have performed the most painful duty of my life today. If you have confidence in me and in the gentlemen associated with me, I ask you to disperse and go quietly to your homes!"

The mob yelled, "We want O'Malley." "I pledge you that O'Malley shall be dealt with. Now take my word for it! Mob violence is the most terrible thing on the face of the earth! I called you together for a duty! Now go to your homes and if I need you I will call you! Now go home and God bless you!"

"God bless you, Mr. Parkerson!"yelled a woman member of the mob and Parkerson was hoisted onto the shoulders of some of his nearest supporters for a triumphal march down Marais Street to Canal and the Henry Clay Statue.

PENELOPE (PENNY) DUGENT'S OFFICE
WOMEN'S SIDE
PARISH PRISON
ORLEANS & ST. ANNE STREETS
AN HOUR LATER

The two Charlies heard Penny's heavy footsteps returning to her office. "It's all clear," she said in a throaty voice, and began sliding the desk back. She soon had pried the floorboards loose, and, giving a hand to each man, pulled them out of their makeshift entombment. They got up shakily and dusted themselves off.

Charlie Matranga looked gtrimly at Penny and said, "How bad is it?" although he could already tell by the look on her face.She averted his eyes and looked at the floor from where they had just come."It's not good,"she said solemnly, and began moving the desk back into place.

"Two uh y'all'r swingin' from a tree and lamppost out yonder," she pointed out the window, "and a bunch more downstairs."

Charlie grabbed her by the shoulders. "The boy---I promised his father --" "He's all right; he's downstairs---father warn't so lucky," she sighed. Both Charlies raced down to the "White Yard" to find Lem Davis supervising the removal of the bodies from the death cell.

The three other victims had already been brought down, Joe Macheca, Tony Scafidi, and Tony Marchese. Gasparo Marchese had lifted the dirty grey prison blanket that had been placed over his father's face, and was kneeling on the ground beside the stretcher on which Tony Marchese lay, with his arms wrapped around his dead father's neck. Charlie Matranga went over to him and placed his hand tenderly on the back of the boy's head, but Gasparo, inconsolable, didn't notice, sobbing, "My father, come back. Please come back," into the cold ear of the dead man.

Charlie looked across the yard at the visibly-shaken Charlie Patorno, and shook his head sadly.Then he pulled down the blanket from the face of the corpse next to Tony Marchese. It was Joe Macheca, his jowly face contorted in a death mask of rage and hatred.the broken Indian club still in his hand in a death grip.

Charlie knelt beside him. "Look what it has come to, Peppino," he whispered, "you were right. Hennessy was the devil incarnate. Look what it's all come to." He gently pried loose the Indian club, laid it beside his dead friend, and smiled sadly. "Well, old friend, you fought them to 'til the end, didn't you?" He reached over and kissed the ashen face and slowly replaced the blanket.

He then viewed Frank Romero's body and remembered the boy he had left Sicily with three decades ago. Charlie shook his head sadly.

John Caruso had emerged from his hiding place and was sobbing before the body of his brother. Carlo Poitza stood alone looking for his old partner, Natali. Just as he said it, Sal Sinceri emerged from a corridor accompanied by Natali, who had abandoned his washroom hideout as being too close to the action as soon as the mob had left, and had crawled into the dog kennel packing crate with Sinceri. They both smiled ruefully. "I am here, Carlo," was all Natali said. The two men wrapped their arms around each other.

Bastiano Incardona came up beside Charlie Matranga fearfully. "It was horrible, Don Carlo. I saw it all. They are animals, these people, animals!" His tone drifted off. Charlie looked up at him. "I noticed the informer, Polizzi, doesn't seem to be here,or is he under one of these blankets, too?" Incardona shook his head, "No, Don Carlo. He's one of the two they took out."

"Who was the other one, Bastiano?" Charlie asked softly. "It wasTony Bags—Bagnetto, Signore." "Ahhh," Charlie replied, "so it was the poor water buffalo!?"

Shot or hanged:
Joseph P. Macheca
Antonio Marchese
Antonio Scaffidi
Rocco Geraci
James Caruso
Loretto Comitez
Pietro Monastero
Louis Traina
Frank Romero
Manuel Polizzi
Antonio Bagnetto

****

Lem Davis left the men who were cleaning up and came over to Charlie. "Charlie, Ah know yuh got a lot on yore mind but Ah need some help. Ah caint fo'th' lahf of me figger out whut t'do with y'all now. It ain't safe tuh stay here but there's still a lot uh people outside 'n it prob'ly ain't safe tuh moveout, either."N whut could Ah move y'all in? The Black Maria'd be a dead giveaway. That's iff'n Ah had a place tuh puty'all in in the first place or the authority t'take y'all there."

The dilemma was solved with the arrival of Lionel Adams and Senator Semmes with a release order signed by Judge Baker. Upon hearing the news of the Clay Statue meeting, the two quick-thinking attorneys had watched it, and, seeing the ugly mood of the mob, had rushed to the residence, first, of Judge Marr, which was closer, and not finding him home, to Judge Baker's house.

By the time they arrived, Joshua Baker had heard the news.As he admitted them, he said, "I can't tell you gentlemen how sorry I am. There is never an excuse for anything like this. I'll sign an order for the release of the defendants on their own recognizance pending further action on your part to drop all further proceedings against the survivors." He bowed his head. "I'm afraid the order won't do some of them any good, though."

On the way to the prison, the two attorneys commissioned two extra carriages and picked up Charlie Patorno's attorneys, John Ferguson and Ferdinand Armant. The entourage first stopped at police headquarters and was greeted by a grave Tom Boylan.

Adams spoke first. "We're going to the prison. This is a release order for all prisoners.We demand a police cordon accompany us to prevent any further attempts at violence on the part of the remaining crowd." "Of course, Lionel," replied Boylan, adding, "This was nothing I wanted to happen. Dave Hennessy was a dear friend of mine and I wanted to see his killers punished. But not like this."

Adams shook his head. "And what did you think that *Committee of Fifty* that you served on had in mind?" Boylan looked away.

Adams and Semmes left the building and were soon joined by two dozen armed officers for the trip to the jail, where they cordoned off a pathway from the wagons to the front gate. As the four attorneys walked down the corridor toward the 'White Yard" a gray pall of death reigned over the morose interior of the prison.

Lionel Adams and Senator Tom Semmes, during the war, had seen death before, but never in such an eerie setting. They came upon Charlie and the others in the yard and showed them the release order. Only

Bastiano Incardona looked relieved. "You mean-a I can go home?" he asked. Senator Semmes nodded his head sympathetically.

"Let's go, Charlie," said Lionel Adams, viewing the grisly scene. Charlie balked. "We're taking our dead with us. Let them see what they have done. Can we put them in the *Maria*, Captain?" Lem Davis nodded his head. "Shore, Charlie, Ah'll have the boys carry 'em out."

"I want to stay with my father," screamed Gasparo Marchese. Charlie looked at John Caruso kneeling beside his dead brother, and said softly, "Giovann', you and the boy ride with your family in the Maria, eh?" Caruso looked up and said, "Si, Padrone, it's what we want."

The grim procession filed out of the prison through the cordon of police. Charlie looked up at the two swinging bodies by the corner, Polizzi and Tony Bagnetto. Through a lump in his throat, he said to Lionel Adams,

"Mr. Adams, have them cut down and brought with the rest." "They're going to need the bodies for autopsies, Charlie," Adams said. "Their families need them more right now," Charlie replied resolutely. "You want Polizzi, too?" Adams asked. "Him, too."

Senator Semmes looked concerned. "All right. For safety's sake, though, get your men in the carriages and let's not waste any time getting out of here. These people appear to just be gawkers but others might return".

At that moment, a frail little Italian woman clawed her way through the crowd to the lamppost, and, looking up in horror, let out the wail of a banshee. It was Manuel Polizzi's common-law wife.

The eight survivors and the attorneys slowly piled into the carriages and the Black Maria and the corpses were put in, including the two who were cut down from the tree and lamppost. The little Italian lady climbed in with them, still wailing, and the procession slowly pulled out into Orleans Street.

Inside the carriage, Charlie had regained some of his composure and was already thinking ahead. He said to Adams, "Let's go to my house first; I want to pick up my family. Then we'll go to Peppino's house. There's more room and seclusion there and I want to think what to do next." He turned to Charlie Patorno,

"Charlie, would you mind gathering up the members of the various families and bringing them out to Peppino's? And bring the priest. We'll have to make funeral arrangements." Patorno nodded. "Sure, Charlie, sure. If we can go by my house on the way to yours, I'll hop off and get to it."

When the procession reached the Matranga house, Charlie's driveway was blocked by armed members of his dock workers Union Number 22. Charlie had the wagons sit at the end of the drive so as not to alarm Rita, Dolores, and Carlo any more than necessary. He walked up the drive, climbed the three steps of his front porch and used his key to open the locked front door.

He found his brother, Tony, and his wife in the parlor consoling the sobbing Rita. The two children saw him first. "Papa! Papa! You're not dead!" they cried, racing across the room and throwing their arms around his neck. "No, I'm not dead," Charlie replied, putting an arm around Rita, who had come over to him in tears and collapsed.

Tony was the first to smile. "Ma frati! What a relief! I went to the jail when I heard of the meeting. By the time I got there, they had already…" he looked at the children. "…Bags and Polizzi. From the street, I could hear shooting from within, but there was no way to get near the place or get inside, so I thought the only thing to do is to come back here and watch out for the family."

Charlie embraced him. "You did right, frati," he said. "Come now, we must all go to Peppino's house. All the family members are going to be there soon." "Is uncle Joe there?" asked young Carlo, hopefully. Charlie avoided the boy's gaze, and looked first at Tony, then at Rita. He shook his head imperceptibly.

Rita began to cry. They got in their own carriage and soon four carriages of grim-faced people and a police van of corpses and their bereaved relatives set off for the Macheca estate

MACHECA ESTATE
METAIRIE, LOUISIANA

Joe Macheca's drive was also blocked by members of Local Number 22, carrying rifles and shotguns. After they were briefly permitted to view the bodies, the procession proceeded up to the house. Bridget Macheca, a large, matronly woman, her hair pulled back in a bun, stood anxiously on the wide, open porch, her arms around the two Macheca children, both boys.

She watched as the Matranga family got out, along with John Caruso, young Gasparo Marchese, Bastiano Incardona, Polizzi's wife, who was still sobbing, Sinceri, and the two greenhorns, Poitza and Natali. The union members who had followed them up the driveway, began unloading the bodies.

Bridget Macheca, her face a mask of anxiety and horror, looked at Charlie and smiled nervously in her apprehension. "Where's my Joe?" she asked, softly at first. Then she screamed it, "Where's my Joe!!??" Charlie put his arm around her. She lifted her large head and shrieked, "They've murdered my Joe! I told him they would!! I told him not to go! They've murdered my Joe! Oh, God! What are we going to do without him?!!"

****

EPILOGUE

AFTERMATH & FALLOUT
 ITALIAN CONSULATE\
NEW ORLEANS, LOUISIANA
SATURDAY, MARCH 14, 1891
AFTERNOON

Pasquale Corte's secretary rushed in the door. Maria Bonafiglia was a pretty girl of nineteen with long, lustrous black hair and deep brown eyes. She was the daughter of an old friend who had immigrated around the same time as Corte in 1876. Her usually sunny disposition was not in evidence. "You were right, Consul! I'venever seen anything like that. Now they've gone for O'Malley and the jurors, I think. Do you think they'll harm all Italians?"

She broke down, weeping on a sofa. Corte clenched his teeth and gripped the sides of his desk. He had seen the announcement in the morning papers calling the meeting and had noticed all the activity on the way to the Clay Statue. He had read it right.

"Mario!" he called to an aide. "get me that goddamned Mayor on the phone. And hurry!" A few minutes later, the young aide stuck his head back in the door and said, "The mayor's office told me to tell you that he was gone for the day and couldn't be reached. However, they did know of the doings at the jail; eleven have died."

Corte slammed his fist on the desk. "That bastard! He's behind all this! Maria, compose yourself! I need you to take this message and wire it immediately to the Marquis di Rudini." Within the hour, the following message was telegraphed to Italy:

NEW ORLEANS, MARCH 14, 1891
MOB LED BY COMMITTEE OF FIFTY TOOK POSSESSION OF JAIL--STOP---KILLED ELEVEN PRISONERS, THREE ITALIANS REST NATURALIZED ITALIANS ---STOP---I HOLD MAYOR RESPONSIBLE---STOP---FEAR FURTHER MURDERS---STOP---I ALSO AM IN GREAT DANGER---STOP---REPORTS FOLLOW. CORTE.

The following morning, Corte dispatched a comprehensive letter to Baron Fava, the Italian Ambassador to the United States, saying, in pertinent part,

"Mr. Minister: I have not time to describe the horrors of the slaughter which the populace, under the leadership of the principal members of the vigilance committee, has committed against unarmed prisoners, some of whom had been acquitted and some of whom had not yet been tried. (I went to see the Mayor who was unavailable. I saw the Governor and) (I)n view of the immediate danger to the prisoners and the colony, I requested him, in my official capacity as consul, to send troops or a guard of police to the place in order to prevent the massacre. He told me that he could do nothing until he was requested by the mayor…I went down (to the prison and) (W)hen I came near I saw a number of dead bodies hanged to trees; I saw the massacre was over…"

****

The Daily States newspaper, owned by the Dupres, members of both the Committee of Fifty and the Vigilance committee, ran the following editorial endorsement of the mob's actions: "Citizens of New Orleans, you have in one righteous upheaval, in one fateful gust of mighty wrath, vindicated your laws, heretofore, desecrated and trampled under foot by oath-bound aliens who had thought to substitute Murder for Justice and the suborner's gold for the freeman's honest verdict. Your vengeance is consecrated in the forfeited blood of the assassins. Stop there! Return to your homes and resume the peaceful pursuit of your avocations."

****

OFFICE OF THE PRIME MINISTER
ROME ITALY
SATURDAY, MARCH 14, 1891

The Italian Secretary of Foreign Affairs sent Corte's telegram to the newly-elected Prime Minister, the Marquis di Rudini, a Sicilian himself, and former Mayor of Palermo. A Conservative, di Rudini's love for Italy was only surpassed by his love for Sicily. A purple vein throbbed on his temples as he read Corte's wire.

The thought of these barbarians murdering Italian citizens, especially Sicilians, was so unthinkable to the Prime Minister that he viciously crumpled up the communiqué and jumped to his feet. "Wire this message to Baron Fava immediately in Washington. Tell him I am shocked and appalled by this barbaric action on the part of the butcherous mob. Tell him the American government must make the Louisiana authorities to realize their duty to protect Italian nationals on American soil, and that the government of Italy expects the mob leaders, who were so quick to take the law into their own hands themselves, to be suitably and quickly punished. And while you're about it, dig out that copy of the speech the Mayor of New Orleans made which says, "…the Sicilian who comes here must become an American citizen and subject his wrongs to the law of the land, or else there must be no place for him on the American continent,"

"I've been chafed over that ever since I read it. Is this the law of their land?! A bunch of bloody savages! Tell Blaine that we protest such singling out of Italians as in the Mayor's speech. And also tell him we protest the activities of the infernal *Committee of Fifty,* and the wholesale arrest of innocent Italians….and that we expect indemnity for the families of the victims. Now get that out immediately."

Secretary Blaine, although professing sympathy for the incident, initially told Baron Fava he could make none of the assurances demanded by di Rudini.

THE MAYOR'S OFFICE, CITY HALL NEW
ORLEANS, LOUISIANA
SUNDAY, MARCH 15, 1891, 9:00 A.M.

A triumphant Joe Shakspeare sat at the head of the conference table in the press room. In the corner behind him, two large uniformed officers held a haggard Joe Provenzano by each arm, his feet barely touching the floor.

Shakspeare greeted the reporters amiably and rose to his feet. "Gentlemen, I'll make this brief. I believe the good citizens of this fair city, ably led by the best and most prominent of their number, yesterday have proven, as in the past, that they will not tolerate some foreign-born assassins coming here to terrorize and murder."

He looked toward Provenzano, "Bring him forward!" The two policemen stood Provenzano in front of the Mayor. Provenzano's eyes were averted. The Mayor glared at him. "Joe Provenzano, I have sent for you to talk plain, straight English, and I mean every word I say to you. I and every other citizen am disgusted with the Dago disturbances and determined that they shall end immediately. Mr. Peters has told me that you threatened him and I ordered him to swear out an affidavit against you. You need not deny it as your people deny everything, for we all know that you are one of the leaders of a bloodthirsty gang.

"You are now using the longshoremen as a means of recapturing the fruit landing. You have shown your hands and I call you down…This is not the first time that the Provenzanos have made trouble but it must be and shall be the last You have not learned the lesson taught your race by the people of New Orleans, it seems, and I want you when you leave here to go home and tell your friends that if you make any more trouble, the police and Mayor of this city will not consider themselves for the lives of you and yours…I am not afraid to talk to you this way because I am not afraid of you or the Italians…I intend to put an end to these infernal Dago disturbances, even if it proves necessary to wipe every one of you from the face of the earth."

Provenzano was led from the room past the open and hostile spectators in the Mayor's office. Afterward, Shakspeare was congratulated warmly all around for his courage.

THE MAYOR'S OFFICE, CITY HALL
NEW ORLEANS, LOUISIANA
TUESDAY, MARCH 17, 1891
2:30 P.M.

Joe Shakspeare, shamrocks in his lapel, faced a smiling Bill Parkerson across the big mahogany desk of the Mayor of New Orleans, on which were stacked piles of newspapers, the last shipment of which had been delivered by train and then by messenger to the Mayor's office only moments ago.

"Well, Bill," said the Mayor, "I've been in close touch with the wire services---George Denegre gives me full access to the *States'* information. Most of the papers in the South and on the West Coast are with us 100%; but the Northeast and Midwest are giving us Hell, especially in the big cities like Boston, Chicago, New York and Philadelphia---although we do have some support, even there". He laughed, "There's even a rumor that Italy might declare war".

Parkerson said proudly, "Well, sir, I'm getting letters of congratulations from all over the country." The Mayor eyed him with calculation. He didn't like the proprietary way the young snip was eyeing his office.

"Well, here's one that's not so congratulatory, Bill. The *Buffalo Express* says that you in particular and the other ringleaders of the mob need to be brought to justice, '…preferably on the gallows.' So don't get so cocky. This whole thing could backfire. It's best if it just dies a natural death from here.

"You are to keep a low profile. Also, I've spoken to Luzenberg over the weekend. Lionel Adams and Senator Semmes had spoken to him about dropping all remaining charges against the survivors and I advised him to go ahead. In accordance, yesterday all charges were dropped". Parkerson was dumb-struck. "Against Matranga, too?" Shakspeare nodded. "But he was guilty!" "Not as guilty as you were, Bill. Remember one thing. It is illegal to take the law into your own hands. Especially if it results in somebody's death".

Parkerson started to speak, but the Mayor motioned him to be quiet. "I told you that I thought you were the right man to oversee that the killers of my dear friend, Chief Hennessy, were brought to justice. I never authorized you to lynch them. You took that upon yourself. It was successful and it had a lot of popular support. But that doesn't mean I approve of it. Don't overdo it, Bill. Go back to your office and don't ruffle any feathers for the time being." He took a long look at Parkerson.

"You understand me, Bill?" Recognition was dawning on Bill Parkerson. He had been useful and now that was over. And if he protested, it could mean a murder trial. He bowed his head, the fire gone from those burning eyes. "I think I understand you perfectly, sir.

I hope you'll remember that I served you well such as in retrieving the papers from the Chief's house."

Shakspeare looked at him pointedly. "Papers? I don't recall any papers, Bill. Good day, Bill. Keep in touch." As soon as Parkerson had left, the Mayor called in his secretary. "If Bill Parkerson calls, I'm out; if he comes here, tell him I'm in conference."

OFFICE OF THE SECRETARY OF STATE
OF THE UNITED STATES JAMES G. BLAINE TUESDAY,
MARCH 31, 1891, 10:30 A.M.

Jim Blaine's lips became thin, although they were invisible under his thick, wiry, salt-and-pepper beard, as he looked up from his desk at the aristocratice features of the Italian Ambassador Baron Saverio Fava. The bags under Blaine's eyes gave him a soulful look, the more so this morning because of the news he was hearing.

"Mr. Secretary", Baron Fava announced. "I am being withdrawn as Ambassador to the United States with all haste. The Marquis Imperiali, who is secretary to the Italian legation, shall remain here temporarily to finish the remaining business of the legation".

Blaine frowned. "Then I take it, that as far as Italy is concerned, diplomatic relations are severed." Fava stood to attention, but said not without sympathy, "I'm afraid so, Mr. Secretary."

L'ILLUSTRATION

SAMEDI 14 FEVRIER 1891

Baron SAVERIO FAVA.
(Fotografia Merritt, di Washington).

Italian PM, The Marquis Antonio di Starabba Rudini Italian Ambassadoe to the US, Baron Fava

U.S. Secretary of State James G. Blaine   *U.S. President Benjamin Harrison*

OFFICE OF THE PRIME MINISTER OF ITALY ROME,
ITALY
FRIDAY, APRIL 3, 1891,
10:00 A.M.

Marquis di Rudini faced the press at the conference he had called. "Both the London and German press highly approve of the withdrawal of our Ambassador to the United States in view of this deplorable incident." "Have you heard from the U.S. government since Monday?" an Italian reporter asked. DiRudini waved a communiqué. "But of course! Secretary Blaine sent a copy of this dispatch to Marquis Imperiali at the Italian legation on the same day as Baron Fava was withdrawn. Although the American government decries the incident, they claim not to be in control of the politicians of Louisiana. That would be like us saying that we had no control of –say—Palermo. A ridiculous proposition. It leaves a pained impression upon me." A wizened old newsman, a friend of di Rudini's, said, "You mean we now control Palermo?" di Rudini joined in the laughter. "While I lead this government, we do, anyway. Seriously, right now, I shall simply wait for further details of the New Orleans affair, of the characters of the slain men, of the actions of the Louisiana authorities, and of the intentions of the United States government, but, whatever these may be, I am quite sure that a settlement thoroughly satisfactory to both parties will be found and that the friendship which binds the two nations will remain unalterable and secure."

MAYOR'S OFFICE
NEW ORLEANS, LOUISIANA
FRIDAY, APRIL10, 1891,
5:00 P.M.

An extremely agitated Mayor Joseph Shakspeare jumped up from his desk and moved across the room at the entrance of the District Attorney. "Luzenberg, I've been trying to get you for two days. Don't you return messages?!" Luzenberg reddened. "I'm sorry, Your Honor, but I've been in with the Grand Jury since Wednesday." "That's what I wanted to know about; what's going on?"

"Well, we've got a friend chairing the panel. You know Bill Chaffe. I intend to present evidence to them for another five days or so, and I expect to have indictments against O'Malley and possibly one of the defense lawyers and a couple of the jurors by the beginning of May."

"The beginning of May is too long! Speed it up. And make sure you don't seek indictments against Senator Semmes: he's well loved throughout the South." "Don't worry, Mr. Mayor. It's just one of the minor attorneys who was O'Malley's liaison." "Good.These Washington politicians are giving the Governor Hell. And he, in turn, is giving me Hell. We've got to end this thing clean or it gives us all a black eye. Get on it and keep in close touch."

****

On April 27, 1891, the United States Attorney for New Orleans submitted to the U.S. Attorney in Washington a "thorough investigation as to the nativity and citizenship of the alleged Italian subjects who were killed in the parish prison on the 14th of March last," outlining the identities, arrests, indictments, and dispositions of the cases against the suspects, and the detailed results of the mob in taking the law into its own hands.

He found that of the victims, only two were U.S. citizens although six more had evidenced intention to become citizens, the remaining three were definitely aliens. He reminds the U.S. Attorney that according to Italian consul Corte that no applicant could be considered a citizen without 5 years U.S. residence and having been granted final papers "as provided by section 2165 of the Revised Statutes of the United States." But following the line his boss was looking for, ended by saying that "once these persons had renounced allegiance to their King…they ought to be held to have renounced all claim to the protection of the country of their nativity."

MAYOR'S OFFICE
CITY HALL
NEW ORLEANS, LOUISIANA
TUESDAY, MAY 5, 1891,
10:30 A.M.

District Attorney Luzenberg waved a sheaf of papers triumphantly as he approached the desk of the Mayor of New Orleans. "Here it is, Your Honor. Indictments against O'Malley and five others, including one of Patorno's lawyers, for attempted jury bribery. Signed and sealed by Bill Chaffe, Chairman."

Shakspeare took the indictment and read it aloud. "…We cannot be mistaken in the assertion that the verdict was a startling, amazing, a bitter disappointment, shocking to public opinion, and provoking the repeated accusation that some of the jury had been unfaithful to their high office. The meeting embraced several thousand of the first, best, and even the most lawabiding of this city…6,000 to 8,000…spontaneous uprising of the people. The magnitude of the affair makes it a difficult task to fix guilt upon any number of the participants…the thorough examination of the subject failed to disclose the necessary facts to justify this Grand Jury in presenting indictments." "and going back:" "…no harm or injury was done to either persons or property, beyond the one act, which seemed to be the object of the assemblage at the Parish prison." "In other words, we beat O'Malley six to nothing," the Mayor crowed.

A smile crossed his lips. "Spontaneous uprising"…I like that. How do you prosecute a 'spontaneous uprising'!?" He pulled from his desk drawer a copy of the *New Orleans Item* for Sunday, March 15th. "Luzenberg, I've saved this article as, in my opinion, having been the most favorable towards the mob's action. I'll read it to you.

'The military precision, skill, and rapidity with which the prison was stormed and taken, the care exercised to do no harm except to the guilty parties, the wonderful forebearance of the angered populace, except to the object of their vengeance, are all commended; while no complaint is uttered against the officials for their failure to interpose resistance to the avengers of outraged justice.'"

"Chaffe's indictment practically parrots that article word for word. I don't think we could have done better, Mr. District Attorney. A fine job!" Shakspeare shook his hand warmly. "See that the papers get a copy of that indictment right away. The Picayune first. Then go lock up that villain O'Malley---if you can find him. I haven't gotten a report on his return to town since the lynch---executions. Seligman's, either. They'll be back though. Like the proverbial bad penny."

WHITE HOUSE WASHINGTON, D.C.
LATER THAT DAY

President Benjamin "Little Ben" Harrison found it troubling that again he had to meet with his Secretary of State concerning the annoyance in Louisiana. "Well, Jimmy," he said, holding a copy of the wired indictment in his hand, "this takes some of the sting out of it for the United States, but what about that hothead, di Rudini? Why has he broken off all communications with us? What exactly did you say to him in that last dispatch? The one he said ---pained him--wasn't that his word?"

Blaine nodded wearily. "All I said, Mr. President, was this. I told him that we recognize in principle that a friendly power has a right to claim compensation for injuries suffered by one of its subjects. However, in this particular case, the United States of America does not admit that an indemnity is due because (a) we do not have all the facts in our possession; (b) the Federal government has no rights or responsibility for the actions of a sovereign state; and, (c) in any event, only two of the eleven victims were Italian citizens, the rest having been naturalized American citizens."

"Sounds good to me, Jimmy. But these Italians are temperamental. We have to get this thing settled in the near future for a couple of reasons. As I said before, there's an election year coming up and the Democrats are going to try again to put old Cleveland in Besides, and even more important, the Italians have been chosen to be one of the arbiting countries in the Bering Sea Controversy.

We've already stuck out our necks up there and seized six Canadian ships for violating our *mare clausum* policy, which is, in my humble opinion, of questionable legality.

"However, the pelagic sealers are going to totally deplete the seal herd if sea-sealing is not stopped, so we have to defend that stand. Not to mention, we've gotten some pretty good campaign contributions from the Alaska Commercial Company. The arbitration decision is going to cost the United States at least a half-million if we lose, Jim, and it's nothing to sneeze at. We need all the help we can get...and Italy's vote could be crucial.

"Then there is the Colombian Exposition coming up in Chicago next year. It's supposed to honor Christopher Columbus's discovery of America and be the biggest World's Fair in history. How will itlook if we're not on speaking terms with the Italians!!??"

Jim Blaine heaved a sigh and spread his arms. "You've foreseen everything, Mr. President. I just don't know what we could do that hasn't already been done. Hopefully, this indictment will break the ice."

ITALIAN CONSULATE
NEW ORLEANS, LOUISIANA
WEDNESDAY, MAY 6, 1891

Upon reading the text of the indictment in the morning papers, Consul Pasquale Corte was quick to rush off a letter to foreman Chaffe, challenging both the indictment and how its language squared with reality, but again addressing the fact that "…an extra judicial body appointed by the Mayor from the beginning premeditated, as it appeared in its appeal, the killing of the prisoners; that the same body assembled on the night of the 13th of March to take, in cold blood, the necessary steps to kill, for political purposes, defenseless but fearful adversaries; that about twenty parties, among thm some representing the law and order, executed said project, preventing before the commission of the deed the admittance in prison of the large crowd of children, women, and others, gathered through curiosity; that innocent Italian blood was shed; that not only nothing was done by the authorities to prevent it, but a few officials contributed directly or indirectly on order to accomplish the work, and finally, that the names of the participants in the killing, as well as the instigators, are of public notoriety."

****

Shakspeare was quick to seize upon Corte's letter as a means to hopefully get rid of this incessant thorn in his side:

"To His Excellency, Francis T. Nicholls, Governor of Louisiana Governor: Under date of May 6th, 1891, the Consul of Italy at this port, Mr. P.Corte, saw fit to address W.H. Chaffe, Foreman of the Grand Jury, then in session, a very remarkable letter. The evening of the day in which it was written, the Consul sent copies of the letter by the hands of his secretary to the daily papers for publication. I enclose a printed copy of that letter.

"Your Excellency, being resident in New Orleans, is fully aware of the fact that ever since the assassination of Superintendent of Police

Hennessy, on October 15, 1890, the papers have teemd with all manner of vaporings from Mr.P. Corte in the shape of interviews, etc. For these reported sayings he could not properly be held as an official responsible, and sincehe was scarcely credited with one statement before another was made either exactly the opposite of or largely qualifying the first, his vagaries and blusterings were regarded by all but his own people as either laughable or contemptible.

"The letter of May 6th, however, to the Foreman of the Grand Jury is over his official signature, "P. Corte, Consul of Italy", and must be noticed. It has been noticed by the Grand Jury and very properly returned by that body to the writer as being impertinent. Besides being impertinent, the letter contains ststements absolutely false and beyond question known to be false by Mr. Corte.

"If as Italian Consul, Mr. Corte has ever had any usefulness here, he has outlived it and has become through his own acts not only an unacceptable person, but an element of danger to this community, in that by his utterances, he incites his inflammable people to riot or sullen opposition to the laws and customs of a country they have sought as an asylum....

"For these reasons, I have the honor to request that you ask of the Honorable Secretary of State at Washington, the recall of Consul Corte's Exequartor by the President. This application would have been made to you sooner, but for the reason that I desired to place in your hands to accompany your note to the Secretary of State, a report made to the Mayor and Council by the "Committee of Fifty". I enclose a copy and beg to call your Excellency's attention to that part of it relating to Mr. Corte. I have the honor to be,

Your obedient servant, Joseph A. Shakspeare, Mayor of New Orleans".

UNITED STATES CAPITOL
HOUSE OFCONGRESS, SOUTH WING
WEDNESDAY, DECEMBER 9, 1891
10;15 A.M.

President Harrison was addressing his annual meaasge to Congress; he had been speaking for about an hour and now it had come time to cover "the Italian problem". Little Ben could see the Marquis Imperiali in the visitor's gallery.

"And now I wish to briefly address ourtroublesthis year with Italy. As you know, they stemmed from a most deplorable and discreditable incident which took place in New Orleans on Saturday, March 14th, which was indeed an offense against law and humanity: the lynching of eleven men of Italian background. I wish to stress thar the incident did not have its origin in any general animosity against the Italian people nor in any disrespect to tbe government of Italy, with which our relations were of the most friendly character.

"We have expressed our regrets to the Italian Prime Minister and although the temporary absence of a Minister Plenipotentiary of Italy at this capitol has retarded further correspondence, it is not doubted that a friendly conclusion is attainable."

Imperiali smiled down from the gallery. Mission accomplished.

ITALIAN CONSULATE
NEW ORLEANS, LOUISIANA
THE FOLLOWING DAY…

Having been alerted by Marquis Imperiali's office, Consul Corte read the President's address on the subject in the local papers. Still, the New Orleans press wouldn't accept censure for the incident.

The "*New Delta*," edited by John Wickliffe, lynch mob leader, opined: "President Harrison indulged in adjectives which are not warranted by the facts and made statements in which he will not be supported by the country."

Corte looked, dumbstruck, at his secretary, "These people still won't take the blame for the mob's actions. I can't believe it!! Are they blind or are we living in a land where lawlessness is a way of life and they only pay lip service to their vaunted notions of justice? I have been here too long. I stuck it out for di Rudini, but enough is enough. I am going to request to be brought home as soon as possible."

Maria Bonfiglia, full btreasts heaving in sobs, collapsed on a nearby sofa, throwing her dictation pad on the floor in the process. Corte's short, muscular body was instantly beside her. For the past year he had wondered how their relationship had progressed to a physical stage and, even more so, how this lovely creature could find him, Pasquale Corte, attractive? He was almost fifty, for God's sake.

Maria continued to sob. Corte's hands gently stroked her long, brown hair. "But you are going, too, my little pigeon. Do you think I would go without you?"

Maria tearfully looked up at him. "But I don't want to go to Italy. My home is here." "Nonsense," said Corte gently, "although you were only four when you came here, you are an Italian and you will love the country of your birth as no other; it's in your blood---believe me."

Maria looked doubtful. "You think so?" "Assolutamente, cara mia," Corte said reassuringly. "And you won't leave without me?" "Could I leave my heart?"

Corte (and Maria) did in fact leave for Italy on May 24th, to Shakspeare's great relief. But before he sailed, Corte gave the press a detailed personal account of the lynchings, chiefly blaming the Mayor. With the *Daily States* owned by the Dupres and the *New Delta* edited by John Wickliffe, both lynch mob and vigilante leaders themselves, Corte's account garnered only a lukewarm to cool response.

ITALIAN LEGATION
WASHINGTON, D.C.
MONDAY, APRIL 12, 1892
LATE MORNING

The Marquis Imperiali reread the note from the U.S. Secretary of State. "The government of the United States of America," said the note,"respectfully offers to the government of Italy, the sum of 125,000 francs ($25,000) as compensation for the families of the victims of a mob action in New Orleans, Louisiana, on March 14, 1891, said payment to be distributed by the Italian government.While the injury was not inflicted directly by the United States, the President nevertheless feels that it is the solemn duty, as well as the great pleasure of the National Government to pay a satisfactory indemnity."

The Marquis's face evidenced satisfaction. He had already received his orders on what to do in this event, which had been anticipated since Little Ben's speech of last December. The Marquis dictated a reply.

"The King's government accepts without prejudice to the steps which itmay be proper for the parties to take, Therefore, upon instruction from His Excellency, the PrimeMinister di Rudini, I am authorized to inform you that the diplomatic relations between Italy and the United States are from this moment fully re-established."

Democratic response to the payment was predictably political, decrying the payment of "a lump sum of the taxpayer's money unauthorized by Congress," attempting to reduce in Congrees the appropriation amount for emergencies arising in the diplomatic and consular service from $80,000 to $60,000. And on and on and on.

On December 6th,1892, Little Ben Harrison, covering the subject for the second time in an annual message to Congress as a lame duck, having lost the election to Grover Cleveland the previous month, finally laid the hot potato to rest by saying, "The friendly act of this government in expressing to the government of Italy its reprobation and abhorrence of the lynching of Italian subjects in New Orleans, by payment of 125,000 francs, or $24,330.90, was accepted by the King of Italy with every manifestation of gracious appreciation, and the incident has been highly promotive of mutual respect and good will on the part of the parties involved."

ELKS CLUB
121 S. BASIN STREET (formerly 40 Basin Street)
NEW ORLEANS, LA
FRIDAY, NOVEMBER 12, 1943
10:00 A.M

Buford Alley had unexpectedly spent the last two weeks listening to the life and times of the recently-deceased 97-year-old Charlie Matranga. "Wow," he said to Dr. Matranga. "What a story! But that part was fifty years ago. What happened next?" Doctor Matranga leaned forward and poured himself some hot tea, sipped it, and smiled at Alley.

"Well, the snake showed its true colors right after the lynching. As you might have detected, this was all about money, not Hennessy, who the leaders of this scheme, Shakspeare, Houston, Wickliffe, Denegre, and the rest cared nothing for. And immediately after the lynching, a bill was introduced in City Council, ordinance #5256, wherein all work and business on the New Orleans docks would be awarded to a newly-formed corporation, the Louisiana Construction & Improvement Company. Now, this was on April 25, 1891, barely a month after the lynchings, so you can see it was planned well in advance.

"The new corporation had eight men leading it, all Committee of Fifty members and/or vigilante lynch mob members. Its President was James D. Houston, a lynch mob leader who presented himself as a 'businessman/ politician' but was more a ruthless, violent, opportunistic thug.

"Following the Civil War, Houston had received political appointments, first as Sheriff, then as Tax Collector. Houston had already been in three gun battles going back 20 years, resulting in the death of four men, and conducted in daylight right on the streets of New Orleans.

"Due to his political connections, Houston was never convicted in these deaths. But anyway, this new corporation secured favorable leases to properties all along the waterfront, giving it a virtual monopoly to any work there.

"My father just kept his head down in the beginning and the following year, 1892, a reform ticket under an Irish-American, John Fitzpatrick, ran Shakspeare out of office. Two years later, Houston died, and two years after that, 1896, Shakspeare kicked the bucket. So any plans for revenge on my father's part were taken care of by the man upstairs, you could say.

"As to Provenzano, I couldn't really tell you. He and his family stayed in Barataria and he never returned to this city. In fact, he was never heard from again, that's all I can tell you. Whether or not my father got his revenge, I don't know. If he did, he never told me. Between you and me, I hope so, but that's all I can tell you on it". The doctor's smile was grimly ironic.

"My father and Charlie Patorno kept up their interests in the French Market and in the importing business. My father kept his interest in the steamship line and the dock union. It was impossible for the powers that be to completely freeze the Italians out of the docks although a competing union, the Louisiana Longshoremen's & Screwman's Association, composed of whites and blacks, but no Italians, under Houston's control, got a bigger share than they formerly had.

"But slowly things improved. My father wisely made alliances with the international union, Houston died, Shakspeare was no longer a faction, then he, too, died. And any remaining politicians with similar ideas, knew that any attempt at a future outrage against Italians would not be stood for by the Italian government, the federal government here, and the newly-formed national organization for Sicilians, Unione Siciliano, of which my father became an officer.

"Things leveled out, mainly due to my father keeping a cool head and a methodical plan for himself and our people. Immigration actually increased by the end of the century and a lot of our boys served and died right along with the rest in World War I, just as they are doing now. And many rest on the fields of Europe. The people here are well aware of that and for a while, where fresh kids and drunks would razz an Italian over Hennessy by saying, "Who killa da Chief?" slurs like that are rarely heard anymore.

"Actually, despite operating under the extreme handicap of what had happened, my father managed to live quietly and unobtrusively, for the next half-century, as a successful businessman. He was a wonderful father, husband, and all-round family man and we, his family, will always be very proud of him".

The doctor and Bewf raised their water tumblers in a silent toast to Charlie. "Doctor, your story was more than I ever expected and a monument to a great man. Only thing is, with this wartime patriotism, which is great, it might not be the best time to remind the people of their own failings. So, after giving it some thought and with your permission, I think to do the story justice, it shouldn't be told until after the war because I would want to hit the perpetrators of this outrage with full force. This story deserves a book. Meanwhile, I'll just do my normal column, extolling your father as a revered patriarch of the Crescent City and we'll put the book on the back burner for now, if it's all right with you.

Doctor Matranga looked candidly at Bewf. "If that is what you think, Mr. Alley, then I have faith in your judgment. Just keep in touch once in a while in the meantime."

The two new friends parted amicably.

Outside the Elks Club, Bewf got back into the '39 Plymouth business coupe, taking one last look at Kate Townsend's refurbished brothel and smiling to himself. His small suitcase was locked in the trunk. He tooled down Bourbon Street in the Autumn sunshine. It had gotten a bit chilly so he only cracked the vent window. The cigarette lighter popped out and Bewf pushed up an Old Gold with his right thumb, pulling it out of the pack with his lips. He put the lighter to it and watched the smoke rush for the cracked vent. He would drive straight through to Atlanta, get home Sunday, and be at his cubicle at the *Constitution* Monday morning typing his next "Back Alley" column. It would be titled, *"Mysterious Centenarian Dies In The Crescent City"*. As he typed, something made his fingers work a staccato five keys at a time. *"Who Killa da Chief?" "Who Killa daChief?" "Who Killa da Chief?"*

THE END

,

www.ingramcontent.com/pod-product-compliance
Lightning Source LLC
Chambersburg PA
CBHW052034090426
42739CB00010B/1908